Praise for *Last Rites*

"A treasure trove of morbid intrigue. Never has a work of nonfiction read more like a thriller novel. Leaving no gruesome detail unexplained, *Last Rites* is the way history books should always be written."

SOUTHERN CALLS
The Journal of the Funeral Profession

"For anyone who ever wonders why funerals are the way they are, this book weaves history and modern funeral rites in a way that compares historical norms with current funeral rituals. A must-read."

BRIAN WATERS
host of *Undertaking: The Podcast*

"To other histories of funeral customs in North America, we can add this richly researched and annotated text by Todd Harra, for whom funerals—both the idea of the things and the things themselves—are worthy of a life's work and serious scrutiny. Humanity is never so manifest as when a human dies; what we do about mortality separates us from other species. *Last Rites* is for mortals and mortuary sorts, the reverend clergy, and reverential humanists. And Harra is the most reliable kind of witness: a practitioner, scholar, and storyteller."

THOMAS LYNCH
author of *The Depositions* and *Bone Rosary*

Last Rites

Also by Todd Harra

NONFICTION

Mortuary Confidential: Undertakers Spill the Dirt
Over Our Dead Bodies: Undertakers Lift the Lid

FICTION

Grave Matters
Patient Zero

Last Rites

The
Evolution
of the
American
Funeral

Todd Harra

sounds true
BOULDER, COLORADO

Sounds True
Boulder, CO 80306

Published 2022

Book design by Linsey Dodaro

The wood used to produce this book is from Forest Stewardship
Council (FSC) certified forests, recycled materials, or controlled wood.

Printed in Canada

BK06230

Library of Congress Cataloging-in-Publication Data

Names: Harra, Todd, author.
Title: Last rites : the evolution of the American funeral / Todd Harra.
Description: Boulder, CO : Sounds True, 2022. | Includes bibliographical
   references and index.
Identifiers: LCCN 2021039101 (print) | LCCN 2021039102 (ebook) | ISBN
   9781683648055 (Hardcover) | ISBN 9781683648062 (eBook)
Subjects: LCSH: Funeral rites and ceremonies--United States--History.
Classification: LCC GT3203 .H37 2022 (print) | LCC GT3203 (ebook) | DDC
   393/.930973--dc23/eng/20220223
LC record available at https://lccn.loc.gov/2021039101
LC ebook record available at https://lccn.loc.gov/2021039102

10 9 8 7 6 5 4 3 2 1

For Melissa, who puts up with
the undertaker lifestyle.

To the dead . . . in our own beloved country, we owe, not only the foundations of the great fabric of our liberties, but those lessons of wisdom, justice, and moderation, upon the observance of which alone can depend its stability.

CHARLES FRASER

Dedication of Magnolia Cemetery, Charleston, South Carolina
November 19, 1850

Contents

The Dark Arts: An Introduction   1

Chapter 1   A Seismic Shift: Lincoln and
                the New Sanitary Science   5

Chapter 2   The Book of the Dead   25

Chapter 3   Lethal Combat and Other Roman Obsequies   37

Chapter 4   The Bloody Barber-Surgeons:
                Embalming Emerges from the Dark Ages   51

Chapter 5   Mourning Gloves and Liquor:
                Early American Burial Practices   65

Chapter 6   Embalming Surgeons   85

Chapter 7   Gone to Their Sleep: Victorian Sensibilities   107

Chapter 8   Resurrectionists: Advent of the Burial Vault   127

Chapter 9   Vessels of the Dead: Coffins, Caskets,
                and the Hysteria Surrounding Grave Alarms   147

Chapter 10   The Temple of Honor: Vehicles of the Dead   169

Chapter 11   Mourning the Great War   183

Chapter 12   Flame Burial   203

Chapter 13   Mushroom Suits and the Future
                (of Funeral Service)   223

Acknowledgments   237

Notes   239

Index   273

About the Author   277

The Dark Arts

An Introduction

We die. We're embalmed. We're waked. There's public notification. The community comes together for a service, then we're burned or buried. This is the American funeral.

Our death rituals, like all things American, are unique to the culture, but they share connective tissue with the far corners of the globe dating to antiquity. These often strange rituals, and by extension the men and women plying the dark arts, are almost as mysterious as death itself. *Last Rites* lifts the curtain and offers a glimpse of why we bury our dead the way we do.

The American funeral rite coalesced in a single moment involving a marble-sized piece of metal.

Ever since the first permanent settlement was established at Jamestown, the American death rite was a simple, austere event, borrowing heavily from English burial traditions. The remains were washed and dressed at home. A local cabinetmaker furnished a custom-made coffin, and the remains were carried by hand and immediately buried in the town's commons or on family land. The family and townsfolk gathered for the repast, and the funeral service was delivered after the burial.

Overnight, the tectonic plates shifted.

A seventeen-gram lump of Britannia metal—about the weight of an AAA battery—forever altered the American funeral experience, at least once John Wilkes Booth loaded it into his derringer and fired it into President Lincoln's head.

Lincoln's death was merely the catalyst for brewing changes coming on the heels of the Civil War's turmoil. A nation was in intense mourning, grieving its 650,000 dead sons. But there were other, external pressures being put on the old funeral traditions. Population centers were exploding, America was building its infrastructure, and the Industrial Revolution—put into overdrive by the recent war—was luring Americans off their farms and into cities and factories. Americans were more mobile, goods were becoming cheaper and more plentiful, and Americans were outsourcing the care of their sick . . . and their dead.

However, the thing that set America on a unique trajectory, casting off the vestiges of the old ways from across the Atlantic, was embalming. During the war, embalming surgeons had been practicing the new sanitary science of embalming, an archaic anatomical technique imported from Europe, thrust into the spotlight by necessity—for shipment purposes—and legitimized by Lincoln himself. Lincoln ordered the embalming of his good friend and former law clerk Colonel Elmer E. Ellsworth after he was killed during the war, and was so astounded by the results that when his beloved son Willie died of typhoid, he had him embalmed as well. This progression of events made it such that when Lincoln was martyred, it was only natural that Mary Todd Lincoln had him prepared the same way, thus thrusting this obscure wartime technology into the face of a nation.

An astounding 880,000 Americans cast their eyes upon the martyred president, a feat that hasn't been surpassed in a single untelevised funeral since, thanks to the newly adopted sanitary science of embalming. It was nothing short of a miracle, and it set the stage for the American funeral.

In the next three and a half decades leading up to the end of the century, the pieces fell into place. Factories started churning out ready-made caskets, replacing the old tradesman undertaker making coffins in his workshop; hearses morphed into specialized vehicles; extravagant floral displays became *de rigueur*; and the fear of body snatching led to the advent of the burial vault. In a sleepy little town in western Pennsylvania, a man built a personal crematorium. And Americans shifted the care of their sick and dead from the home to institutional settings such as hospitals and funeral parlors. From this vacuum stepped the funeral director, a man (almost always a man in those times) versed in all the necessaries needed to properly get someone in the ground.

One such man, James White, was a cabinetmaker in rural Milford, Delaware. My great-great-great-grandfather.

I've been plying the dark arts my entire professional career, and have found that people tend to view undertakers with suspicion: *Who would choose to work in death and misery?* Sure there's grief and sorrow and pain at a funeral. Sometimes a lot. Sometimes enough for a lifetime. But there's something else if one does it right: closure. Not closure in the sense of "that's done with and I can move on" but rather in that the instinctual need to care for our dead brethren has been fulfilled: the dead are where they need to be. With that closure comes hope—the hope to find the way forward. It's the same hope found at other rites—baptisms and weddings—but without the accompanying joy.

There's that old adage about asking a barber if you need a haircut. The same goes for asking the undertaker about needing a funeral. But I hope these pages make clear we're not here to sell you anything—the rituals surrounding the burial of the dead have been around long before the occupation.

The idea for this book came to me after reading David Oshinsky's *Bellevue: Three Centuries of Medicine and Mayhem at America's Most Storied Hospital.* Oshinsky made the story of a hospital—and in the same sense, the men and women who pioneered modern medicine—leap off the page for a layperson. Nothing like that has been done for funeral service. I find when I'm in mixed company and someone finds out what I do for a living, the questions start, and it's not because I have anything particularly interesting to say but rather people are honestly curious about the dead and the events and people surrounding them. So, I thought I'd break down the story of the American funeral and answer *the* questions: Why do we embalm? Why casket and not shroud, or vice versa? Where did the practice of cremation come from? Why is it customary to send flowers to a funeral? The aim is to demystify our death rituals and maybe make funerals a less intimidating experience.

An article from a funeral trade magazine, *The Casket*, a century and a half ago sums up well the historic underpinnings of the funeral: "The human family have in all ages found it imperatively necessary, if not gratifying, to bury or burn their dead, and have naturally sought to rob the unpleasant task of its most disagreeable features. The embalming process of the Egyptians, the cremating practices of the Romans, and the burial customs of other nations all attested to the existence of a sentiment that had reference to the affections and sympathies of the living as well as the character and the future of the dead."[1]

CHAPTER 1

A Seismic Shift

Lincoln and the
New Sanitary Science

I t was Good Friday, 1865, and Mary Todd Lincoln was vacillating between *Aladdin!* playing at Grover's Theatre or actress Laura Keene's one thousandth performance as the lead in *Our American Cousin*. *Aladdin!* had added a rousting patriotic grand finale and thus she was torn. Mrs. Lincoln decided she and her husband would attend Keene's millesimal, and last, performance at Ford's Theatre.

It would prove to be a fateful decision.

The Lincolns and their entourage arrived late to Ford's Theatre, and the actors paused so the orchestra could play "Hail to the Chief." Everyone then settled in to watch the comedic play. After intermission, Lincoln's bodyguard, John F. Parker, inexplicably decided to go next door to the Star Saloon for a drink. The state box was left completely unguarded. During the third act, a Confederate sympathizer and well-known actor, John Wilkes Booth,* entered the dimly lit state box and shot President

---

* This being a funeral book, it is pertinent to add that Booth's body was buried under the Old Penitentiary storeroom floor. The remains were moved in 1867 and reburied at the Arsenal. In 1869, President Andrew Johnson released Booth's remains to John H. Weaver, a sexton undertaker, from Baltimore. He was casketed in a mahogany casket designed by Weaver and moved to a holding vault in Green Mount Cemetery, Baltimore. On June 26, 1869, Booth was interred. Terry Alford, *Fortune's Fool: The Life of John Wilkes Booth* (Oxford: Oxford University Press, 2015), 323–31.

Lincoln in the head. A .44 caliber ball plowed through seven and a half inches of the president's brain tissue, coming to rest behind his right eye.[1] Booth leaped onstage, yelled "*Sic semper tyrannis*,"* adding "The South is avenged!" and put events in motion for a funeral that forever changed the way Americans bury their dead.[2]

Charles Augustus Leale, a young surgeon just months out of Bellevue Hospital Medical College, was in the audience at Ford's Theatre and immediately rushed to tend the wounded president. After an examination in the dim state box, Leale offered his prognosis: the president was alive but mortally wounded. Not believing Lincoln was stable enough for a journey to the White House, Leale ordered him moved across the street to a boarding house.

For the next nine hours Lincoln's medical team toiled in vain at the Petersen House. He died at 7:22 a.m. on April 15.

Mary Todd Lincoln was delirious with grief.

A nation was stunned.

What happened next with President Lincoln's body—preparation by the new sanitary science of embalming—was a novel precedent set by Lincoln himself four years prior during the infancy of the war when Colonel Elmer E. Ellsworth was killed.

Ellsworth was the poster boy of a young American hero. With dashing good looks, Ellsworth was an attorney and had commanded a company of National Guard cadets in Illinois. In an 1861 portrait, Ellsworth stands with his hand on his hip, campaign cap perched at a jaunty angle over a head of curly hair, eyes intently focused on something behind the camera. It's the portrait of a man destined for greatness.

The day after Virginia seceded from the Union, May 24, 1861, Ellsworth led the Eleventh New York Volunteers into Alexandria. They encountered no resistance until Ellsworth entered Marshall House, an inn, to take down the massive Confederate battle flag, so big it could be seen from the White House.[3] After removing the flag, innkeeper James Jackson shot Ellsworth at point-blank range with a shotgun. He was killed instantly.

---

* Not only is "thus always to tyrants" the Virginia state motto but that phrase would've appealed to Booth, a Shakespearean actor, because it is the shortened version of what Brutus reportedly said after assassinating Julius Caesar: *Sic semper evello mortem tyrannis*, or "Thus always I cause the death of tyrants."

Ellsworth had clerked for President Lincoln in Springfield, Illinois, and accompanied him to Washington in 1861. Lincoln, through the urging of the secretary of state, commissioned Thomas Holmes, an embalming surgeon, to embalm Ellsworth.[4] The procedure took place at the Washington Navy Yard.[5] Holmes's secret embalming fluid, "Innominata," was likely used to prepare Ellsworth.

Lincoln ordered that Colonel Ellsworth be laid out in the East Room where Mrs. Lincoln was quite taken with how well the dead soldier looked, despite a traumatic injury that would've rendered normal remains unviewable in a short time due to decomposition. She remarked that Ellsworth appeared "natural, as though he were only sleeping."[6] Ellsworth was subsequently conveyed back to New York City (en route to his eventual burial in Mechanicville) where thousands of mourners lined the streets to welcome home the fallen hero.

It was the visage of Ellsworth that was on Mary Todd Lincoln's mind when scarcely nine months later a calamity rocked the White House. At 5:00 p.m. on February 20, 1862, the Lincolns' third son, William Wallace, "Willie," succumbed to typhoid fever and died. The president, sitting vigil at his bedside, cried, "My poor boy, he was too good for this earth. God has called him home!"

The firm of Brown & Alexander Surgeons and Embalmers of 523 D Street N., was summoned to preserve the Lincolns' precious child. Henry Pratt Cattell, the stepson of Dr. Charles Brown, performed the embalming.[7] Cattell, twenty-three years old, was unlike many of the embalmers working at the time in that he had no previous medical training.*

Willie was laid out in the Green Room in a plain metallic coffin wearing what the Washington *Evening Star* described as "the usual every-day attire of youths his age, consisting of pants and jacket with white stockings and low shoes—the white collar and wristbands being turned over the black cloth of the jacket."[8] His right hand clutched a small bouquet of camellia and azaleas.[9] The mirrors in the reception rooms of the White House were draped† in appropriate mourning: black crepe over the frames and white crepe over the glass.[10]

---

* Cattell would go on to have a long career with the District of Columbia's Metropolitan Police. He was buried December 10, 1915, in Congressional Cemetery.

† This Victorian-era custom seems to be rooted in the superstition that the deceased's spirit couldn't be allowed to "see" they were dead and thus their spirit would be free to leave.

At no time in history had the presidency of the Union been more uncertain, assaulted by external and internal forces. The nation was torn apart by civil war, Jefferson Davis having just been inaugurated as the Confederacy's president, and based on the resolve shown by Confederates during the previous summer's campaigns, it promised not to be a short war. At home, the Lincolns had already endured the loss of a son, Edward, a decade prior. Tad, their youngest, lay sick with typhoid fever—possibly dying too*—upstairs in the White House, and the president's wife, overcome with grief, had sequestered herself.

At 2:00 p.m. the Reverend Dr. Phineas Gurley, pastor of New York Avenue Presbyterian Church, led the assembled family and government officials in a service. Afterward, two white horses† pulled the hearse, leading the funeral cortege through the frigid winter evening to Oak Hill Cemetery, located off R Street in Georgetown. Willie's coffin was entombed in the Carroll family vault. William Thomas Carroll, a clerk in the Supreme Court, loaned the vault space to the Lincolns until they could take their child's body back to Illinois.

Lincoln would often visit his son's crypt in the ensuing years, and he "requested the coffin be opened on at least two occasions."[11] The president sat for hours perched on the granite bench, the weight of the nation pressing down on his broad shoulders, and talked to his son. His words echoed off the stone walls dug into the hillside as he peered at the tiny form nestled in the metallic enclosure. The impulse of the living is to touch the hand of the dead, and it's not a far stretch to imagine the president patting the hand of his beloved son and smoothing his hair, maybe even providing fresh flowers for young Willie's hands.

Three years and two months after Willie's death, a grief-stricken Mrs. Lincoln once again called upon the services of Brown & Alexander Surgeons and Embalmers and Henry Cattell.

The president's body was returned to the White House directly from the Petersen House under the direction of Frank T. Sands, the government

---

* Tad recovered.
† Typically, white horses were used to denote the deceased was a woman or child, and black horses for men. (Sometimes it was the color of the hearse itself, if the undertaker was wealthy enough to have several hearses.) This tradition is correlated to weepers, or mourning armbands. White weepers meant the death of a woman or child in the family; black were for men.

undertaker, and taken to the guest room located on the second floor in the northwest corner for preparation.[12]

Nine men were in attendance for the cranial autopsy, including Surgeon General Dr. Joseph K. Barnes and the Lincoln family physician Dr. Robert King Stone. The autopsy was so rushed—it took place five hours after the president expired—that there wasn't even a proper autopsy set available. One of the surgeons (it is unknown who) offered up his private surgical kit.[13] Two men performed the prosection: Army Assistant Surgeons Edward Curtis and Joseph Janvier Woodward. The room was mostly silent as Curtis and Woodward went about their somber task. Despite four years of unimaginable bloodshed and hardship, this was the most difficult moment in the careers of all assembled. The only sounds were the scrape of saw blade teeth on bone, cascading water from the surgical sponge into the porcelain basin, and the occasional hushed remark.

In a letter to his mother, Curtis described the scene: "Stretched upon a rough framework of boards and covered only with sheets and towels, lay—cold and immovable—what but a few hours before was the soul of a great nation."[14]

In the autopsy report, written to the surgeon general by Woodward, there are some telling details about the president's wound: "The eyelids and surrounding parts of the face were greatly ecchymosed* and the eyeballs somewhat protuberant from effusion of blood into the orbits . . . both orbital plates of the frontal bone were fractured and the fragments pushed upwards toward the brain . . . the orbits were gorged with blood."[15]

The orbital plates of the frontal bone form, essentially, a vault in which the eye structure sits. When the vaults were broken by Booth's bullet, they more than likely pushed the eyes anterior, causing the protuberance Woodward reports. Modern postmortem reconstruction techniques could mitigate the issues caused by the broken orbital plates and return the eyeballs to their normal size. Additionally, modern specialty embalming fluids would be able to successfully bleach the purplish or black stains left by the ecchymosis, and cosmetics could cover the bleached areas.

Autopsy complete, Undertaker Sands sent for the embalmer.†

---

* Purple or black skin discoloration resulting in blood leaking from the capillaries. Unlike bruising, which is caused by mechanical injury, ecchymosis can be caused by disease.

† Like many facts surrounding Lincoln's assassination, there's debate over what occurred first, the embalming or the autopsy. While there's no clear answer, the author is choosing this version of events based on Dr. Stone's testimony at the trial for the conspirators.

Inexplicably, Cattell, now twenty-six years old and bearing some practical experience, was sent *alone* to the White House to embalm the leader of the nation without, as he stated in an interview with the Washington *Evening Star*, "even an assistant" despite the fact Dr. Charles Brown, an accomplished embalmer and namesake of the firm, was present in the office when the courier arrived with the summons.[16]

Cattell, working methodically, made an incision in the president's thigh and likely used a hand pump to inject an embalming solution of zinc chloride.[17] Zinc chloride has many modern commercial applications, but historically it was used as a disinfectant. Probably unknown to Cattell was how lethal to the living this concoction was. Even short-term exposure can cause ARDS—adult respiratory distress syndrome—which is treated by modern medicine with intubation.[18]

The method of injection by hand pump* was common at the time. A hose attached the container with the embalming solution to a hand pump. Another hose attached to the container terminated with a metal cannula— or thin tube—inserted into the vessel. The embalmer pushed the plunger on the hand pump to create pressure in the container and move the embalming solution into the circulatory system, simultaneously forcing blood out of the veins, Cattell choosing to drain from the jugular.†

Lincoln's body "hardened like a marble."[19] This may have been unintentional. The desired outcome of embalming is some firming of the tissues, but too much preservative will lead to over-firming of the tissues and accompanying discolorations.‡

Cattell may have miscalculated the solution concentration, which was made by dissolving zinc strips in hydrochloric acid. The *New York Times* later reported on the president's appearance: "The color is leaden, almost brown."[20] In an interview for the *Cincinnati Enquirer* twenty years after Lincoln's death, an unnamed undertaker, who, based on his comments, clearly had viewed the body, said the president's face appeared to have "been injured by gun powder," which was most likely caused by the dehydrating effects of a too-strong embalming solution.[21]

---

* As was injection by bulb syringe, a method where the embalmer squeezed a rubber bulb to move the fluid into the circulatory system.

† The right jugular vein is still the favored drainage site for embalmers.

‡ "Embalmer's gray" is the resultant discoloration when too much formaldehyde is used. Cattell wasn't using formaldehyde, as it hadn't yet been positively identified.

The science was still in its infancy at this point, and the fluid miscalculation isn't surprising. With all the different preservatives being used—many much harsher than what's available today—embalmers were probably feeling their way forward by trial and error. The firm of Brown & Alexander billed the government one hundred dollars for their service.*

At the conclusion of the injection, Cattell shaved Lincoln's face, leaving a small tuft of hair on the chin. He composed Lincoln's mouth in a manner described as "one who had put the foot down firm" and closed his eyes so they looked "calm as slumber."[22]

Later, Lincoln's body was dressed in the same black suit he had worn to his second inauguration on March 4, 1865.[23] The Great Emancipator was ready for the funeral rites.

Rev. E. D. Daniels wrote, "There was a panic over the whole county. People could not rest. They knew not what was coming next. People thronged the streets and waited for news, but there was no hope. The sister cities were draped in black."[24] Though his comments were specifically regarding La Porte County, Indiana, they echo the larger national sentiment. The nation needed a funeral so it could begin to heal.

What happened next was perhaps the greatest funeral conducted on American soil, a funeral that stretched across almost seventeen hundred miles and included *millions* of funeral-goers. The steady hand that had guided a people through four dark years and saved the Union had been suddenly and inexplicably taken. The only thing the nation's people could do in return was offer their presence in gratitude that his man laid down his life on the altar of freedom.

The War Department was busy but efficient, organizing a state funeral of the grandest magnitude with only the telegraph at their disposal to communicate. It took them three days to plan. Funeral services began Wednesday, April 19,† at noon in the East Room of the White House, the same place Colonel Ellsworth had laid in repose. Lincoln's coffin was placed on a grand catafalque—a raised dais—built for the occasion.

The coffin was designed and built by John H. Weaver, an undertaker in Baltimore, and ironically the same undertaker who would bury Lincoln's assassin, Booth, the final time in 1869. According to Cattell,

---

* Plus an additional $160 to accompany the remains by train to Springfield.
† There was an initial public viewing on Tuesday, April 18.

the coffin was "fitted up" (meaning, trimmed and finished) at the firm of Harvey & Marr in Washington.[25] The grand receptacle was six feet six inches* long to accommodate the president's six-foot-four frame. It was constructed of solid walnut covered in black broadcloth, lined in lead covered by white satin, and decorated with silver nailheads and stars adorning the head and foot end. Each side had four silver bail handles for the pallbearers, and there was an engraved silver nameplate on the lid. It cost $1,500, which would be $24,500 in today's dollars.[26] To put Lincoln's coffin cost in perspective, Weaver had furnished a "finished" (i.e., fitted up) coffin with handles six weeks earlier for Stephen Merrill, a soldier with the Thirty-Ninth Massachusetts Infantry, who died from wounds sustained at Hatcher's Run, and charged twenty-six dollars. It likely wasn't made of walnut, covered in expensive broadcloth, lined with lead and satin, or trimmed with silver ornamentation, all extras that exponentially increased the cost.

Admission tickets were printed and distributed to six hundred people. George A. Townsend,† the Washington correspondent for the *New York World*, described that afternoon in the East Room: "Death has fastened into his frozen face all the character and idiosyncrasy of life. He has not changed one line of his grave, grotesque countenance, nor smoothed out a single feature . . . No corpse in the world is better prepared according to appearances."[27] Services took place with every ticket holder in attendance, as well as in houses of worship around the nation. The acting secretary of state commissioned all religious houses to meet at the appointed hour and "solemniz[e] the occasion by appropriate ceremonies."[28]

Following the "private" services at the White House, the funeral cortege got underway on Pennsylvania Avenue at 2:00 p.m. The procession to the Capitol contained over five thousand members of the military as well as members of Congress and distinguished members of the executive and judicial branches, including the new president, Andrew Johnson. Lincoln's hearse was elevated so the crowd could see the coffin, the floor covered with a mixture of evergreens and white flowers, and pulled by six horses.[29] The hearse was followed by a riderless horse with boots reversed in the stirrups

---

* This is a standard-length casket now, but 150 years ago people weren't as tall (and coffins were almost exclusively custom built), and this would've been an extraordinary size.
† Like many bizarre coincidences associated with the Lincoln assassination, Townsend died on the forty-ninth anniversary of Lincoln's death.

symbolizing a fallen warrior. The first presidential funeral to feature the riderless horse was George Washington's in 1799, and a caparisoned horse[*] is now part of full military honors at Arlington National Cemetery.[30]

The coffin was borne into the Rotunda where Lincoln would lie in state until the morning of April 21, 1865. Lincoln was the first president, and second person, to lie in state in the Capitol whose construction had been completed in 1800. At the time of writing this work, thirty-four people, twelve of them presidents, have lain in state in the Capitol Rotunda.[†] At midnight a message was telegraphed from Secretary of War Edwin Stanton to Major General John Adams Dix. Regarding Lincoln's funeral train it read, "It has been finally concluded to conform to the arrangements made yesterday for the conveyance of the remains of President Abraham Lincoln from Washington to Springfield by way of Baltimore, Harrisburg, Philadelphia, New York, Albany, Buffalo, Cleveland, Columbus, Indianapolis, Chicago to Springfield."[31] Those listed were the larger cities designated for offloading the remains for funeral rites and viewings. The train would pass through 404 cities, towns, villages, and junctions during the seven-state, 1,662-mile journey—an almost facsimile reverse of Lincoln's inaugural train ride from Springfield to Washington in February of 1861.[32]

The Lincoln Special, as the officially named presidential hearse car came to be known, wasn't built for the occasion it was pressed into service for, though it was built for presidential use. It contained a "parlor, sitting room, and sleeping apartment, all of which are fitted in the most approved modern style."[33] It's rumored but unconfirmed that Lincoln was supposed to inspect the finished coach car Saturday, the day after he attended Ford's Theatre.[34] After the assassination, the coach was hastily outfitted with appropriate mourning drapes and black crepe and bunting. During the journey back to Springfield, the Lincoln Special would remain the second-to-last car, the caboose being last. In addition to Lincoln, the funeral car would also hold the remains of Willie. Secretary Stanton could only get Mary Todd Lincoln to agree to the train obsequies if her beloved son accompanied her husband back to Springfield for burial together. Mrs. Lincoln also stipulated that "no display be made"

---

[*] The riderless horse came to the attention of the nation during the broadcast of President John F. Kennedy's funeral, as millions of viewers watched a nervous quarter horse named Black Jack prance behind the caisson. Black Jack is one of three horses to be buried with full military honors.
[†] The caskets (or coffins) were displayed on the Lincoln catafalque.

of Willie.[35] Stanton held to Mrs. Lincoln's wishes. Willie wasn't included in the rites conducted along the journey except for entombment at Oak Ridge Cemetery in Springfield.

In addition to the honor guard, three hundred passengers rode on the train, mostly ranking government officials and military, as well as the press. The only family member on the train was the president's son, Robert, and he rode a total of two hours to the first stop, Baltimore, before returning to Washington (later meeting the funeral cortege in Springfield for the interment). Also on board and in charge of perhaps the biggest funeral of the century* was Undertaker Frank Sands, a mere thirty-one years old, accompanied by Dr. Charles Brown, the embalmer from Brown & Alexander Surgeons and Embalmers.

While many states issue dual licenses, some states today still issue separate licenses for "funeral director"† and "embalmer." A funeral director is someone who handles all the ceremonial arrangements, while the embalmer only does body preparation. This would've been the case with Undertaker Sands and Dr. Brown. Sands oversaw the ceremonial arrangements at each stop, and Dr. Brown (along with an assistant) was in charge of keeping Lincoln's appearance up. No easy feat with the many hundreds of thousands of mourners about to view him over a period of just seventeen days. This would be no easy task with modern chemicals and cosmetics, but in the dark ages of embalming, it was a Herculean feat.

At 8:00 a.m. on the morning of April 21, the Lincoln funeral train pulled out of the Baltimore and Ohio Railroad Company on New Jersey Avenue, leaving Washington, DC. A pilot engine navigated ten minutes before the funeral train, and would continue to do so for the duration of the journey. Its purpose was twofold: it was an early warning system to any potential danger, but it also allowed funeral parties time to assemble properly before the arrival of the chief magistrate. As a rule, the train wouldn't exceed twenty miles per hour to avoid possible calamity, but most of the time maintained a much slower speed to accommodate the droves of mourners who assembled trackside, day or night, braving the chilly, rainy April weather to catch a glimpse of history.

---

* And the author would argue the most elaborate in American history.
† *Undertaker* is the old-fashioned term for funeral director. In 1882, at the first annual meeting, the National Funeral Directors Association officially changed the title from undertaker to funeral director. Though outmoded, it is still an acceptable term.

After a procession in Baltimore, the body lay in the rotunda of the Exchange Building for a short hour-and-a-half viewing, before being taken to the Calvert Street Station. Of all the cities the Lincoln Special stopped at for official funeral ceremonies—eleven total—this viewing time proved to be the shortest, with only an estimated ten thousand people getting to view the body.[36] It's pertinent to note that Lincoln's coffin had a "lift-panel" lid— what might be colloquially called a "priest's casket" today. A lift-panel casket is one in which the entire lid* comes off; the lid isn't hinged at the top body molding like most caskets seen at contemporary funerals. The lid would be secured with screws (as in Lincoln's case), nails, or pegs. Though they are rarely seen in American funerals, with the exception of the Jewish Orthodox *aron*, lift-panel coffins offer the benefit of viewing the body from both sides. Thus two lines were able to file by Lincoln's coffin simultaneously, doubling the amount of people that could view the remains.

The Lincoln Special eased through hamlets, all draped in mourning and displaying patriotic banners, arriving in Harrisburg at 8:30 p.m. amid a deluge. Despite the rain, what was described by the *Philadelphia Inquirer* as an "immense concourse" escorted the remains while minute guns fired and lightning flashed to the State House.[37] Lincoln was placed in the House of Representatives chamber, and the gathered crowd was so immense the guards struggled to maintain order against the crush of humanity—losing control when the doors were thrown open and the crowd rushed through. During the evening and morning viewings, an estimated twenty-five thousand people filed past the coffin.[38] Like many future stops, there was still a massive line when the undertakers screwed the lid back on the coffin the following morning at 9:00 a.m., but there was a strict schedule to keep. The Lincoln Special left the station at 11:00 a.m. bound for Philadelphia.

After stopping in Lancaster, with the former president James Buchanan in attendance, the train arrived in Philadelphia around 4:30 p.m., where crowds crowded the tracks for miles outside the city and the "tracks were so heavily strewn with flowers that the train was almost stalled."[39] The coffin was escorted by a detachment of cavalry, two artillery batteries, and three regiments of the army, navy, and

---

* It should be noted that not the entire lid came off. The lid was cut so only the top portion of Lincoln's remains were viewable, much like a modern half-couch (split-lid) casket.

marines, as well as countless local government and civic leaders, to Independence Hall in a black hearse constructed by undertaker E. S. Earley. The hearse, specially constructed for the event, was drawn by eight black horses, each led by a groom in a top hat, for which the city paid Earley $4,000.[40] Lincoln was laid out in the Assembly Room where the Declaration of Independence was signed, with his head symbolically pointing toward the Liberty Bell.[41] Saturday evening's viewing was reserved for invited guests only, and it continued until nearly 1:00 a.m. Sunday morning. The public was admitted at 5:00 a.m.

Based on the average speed the guards moved mourners through the viewing lines throughout the thirteen-day train journey, it's likely that 150,000 people[*] viewed the remains, some standing in line for seven hours. At 2:00 a.m. Monday, the coffin was closed and taken to Kensington Station.

The ride through New Jersey was short, only lasting about five hours, with no stops to offload the coffin. The train arrived around 10:00 a.m. at Jersey City with the station clock stopped at 7:22 a.m., the time of Lincoln's death—a popular Victorian-era superstition to ward off bad luck. The coffin was loaded onto a ferry to cross the Hudson where it was met at the Desbrosses Street terminal by the undertaker Peter Relyea with another custom-built hearse. Glass-sided, the hearse was fourteen feet long and eight feet wide. So substantial a vehicle, it required sixteen "handsomely caparisoned" gray horses to pull it, each horse with its own groom.[42] Relyea, the creator of the hearse, was a sexton-undertaker. He, like his father, G. W. Relyea, was the sexton of the Willett Street Methodist Episcopal Church in the Lower East Side of Manhattan. Only seventy-two hours prior, on the morning of April 21 (the telegram from Secretary Stanton with the itinerary didn't go out until midnight, the morning of April 20), had a committee from the Board of Aldermen charged Relyea with such a nerve-racking task.[43]

Relyea was up to it.[†] A carpenter by trade, he labored for three straight days, employing sixty men and women to build the magnificent vehicle

---

[*] Estimates vary wildly from 30,000 to 300,000.
[†] Relyea later moved his practice from Manhattan to Williamsburg in Brooklyn. His business cards for the rest of his days advertised him as a "practical undertaker" who was the "Undertaker for President Lincoln, New York, April 26, 1865." It is unknown why April 26 was used. Lincoln's body left New York City April 25. Relyea is buried in Green-Wood Cemetery in Brooklyn.

that cost the city a staggering $9,000.[44] The canopy of the hearse was fifteen feet high and supported by columns, each column's base covered with three American flags covered in crepe.[45] Inside was a raised dais so the coffin sat a full five feet off the street, allowing the crowd to clearly view their slain leader.[46]

The New York Seventh Regiment, known as the "Grey Jackets," and the Veteran Reserve Corps escorted the hearse on a four-hour procession that meandered from Hudson Street to Canal Street, then Broadway, ending at City Hall where a great banner reading "The Nation Mourns" was mounted over the entrance.

The coffin was placed on an angled, raised dais and the viewing began around 3:00 p.m. and went until noon the following day, Tuesday, April 25. The line stretched down Broadway for blocks, people standing in tense silence. Inside City Hall was stuffy and dim, illuminated by the watery glow of gas lamps, the ethereal sound of the eight-hundred-person chorus swelling in the background as mourners wound up the curved staircase to the bier containing the Great Emancipator.

The sheer number of mourners, many who tried to touch or kiss the president despite the best efforts of the guards, coupled with exposure to air, flower dirt, and interior pollutants, was taking its toll on the remains despite the best efforts of the undertakers. The *New York Herald* reported, "The catafalque and its attendant hangings were thickly covered with dust, the face and beard of the corpse were powered over the same impalpable material." It continued on to describe the closing of the coffin: "With practised [*sic*] fingers the undertaker, Mr. F.G. Sands, of Washington, and his assistant Mr. G.W. Hawes,* removed the dust from the face and habilaments [*sic*] of the dead . . . and a few minutes later the lid was silently screwed down."[47]

The *New York Herald* estimated "nearly one hundred a minute [in] an unbroken stream of mourners flowed past each side of the impassive corpse" and "over one hundred and fifty thousand persons must have seen the body."[48] Major General John Dix, in command of the cortege while in New York State, estimated a hundred thousand people viewed Lincoln's body.[49] It's likely the real number lies somewhere in between.

---

* It is unknown who G.W. Hawes is, if he was a local hired to assist Sands and Brown or Sands's permanent assistant.

The Lincoln Special was waiting at the 30th Street Depot to convey Lincoln to Albany. According to Major General Dix, a half million people clogged the streets to witness the funeral processions in New York City.[50]

In Albany and Buffalo, massive crowds met the Lincoln Special's arrival. The *Buffalo Morning Express* reported that the remains looked "slightly discolored, but not as much as many had been led to expect," certainly a more favorable description than the New York papers allowed.[51] In response to the unfavorable reports, and in an attempt to quell the anxieties of the midwesterners who were about to receive the president's remains, Brown and Sands told the press in Albany, "No perceptible change has taken place in the body of the late President since it left Washington."[52]

The whole ordeal is a testament to Sands's and Brown's resourcefulness and skill. The president's remains were undoubtedly jostled around by the pallbearers and the constant transfer from train to hearse to catafalque and back again, not to mention the constant motion of the train or iron carriage wheels over cobblestone streets. The undertakers also had to deal with members of the processions or public touching the president if they were allowed, or in the case of those that weren't, sneaking a touch or a kiss.

And there was all the pollution to contend with. Oil and gas lamps used for indoor illumination put off an oily, sooty smoke (as would've the Lincoln Special putting off coal smoke) and the mounds of flowers heaped upon the coffin and remains would've generated lots of what is colloquially called by undertakers "flower dirt," a combination of pollen, petals, and the like. In short, it was a momentous task to keep the remains looking as fresh as possible for so many people, many of them prominent and powerful citizens. Thankfully Lincoln's suit was black and the pollutants didn't show, but before unveiling the president to the public, Brown changed Lincoln's shirt, if needed, and put on a crisp new white collar (men's collars were detachable then).[53]

The former president Millard Fillmore was among those who viewed Lincoln in Buffalo, as did the future president Grover Cleveland, who was then assistant district attorney for Erie County. As was becoming commonplace, crowds had to be turned away disappointed. There were simply too many citizens who wanted to lay their eyes on Lincoln.

At many of the stops where the coffin wasn't offloaded, such as Dunkirk and Westfield, societal and religious groups of ladies entered the hearse car to offer immense floral tributes. Prior to this, funerals in America were austere events with floral tributes rarely seen. But the Lincoln funeral was a turning point in this tradition, with copious flower tributes becoming the norm at funerals. Newspapers began to note the pieces and their donors as if "keeping score."[54]

The innumerable flower tributes offered at every stop of Lincoln's journey served the dual purpose of a tangible show of grief from the mourners as well as "bathing the hearse car in a continuously pleasant scent," and it can be extrapolated that the flowers kept the public viewing areas smelling fresh too.[55]

In Cleveland, the train pulled into Euclid Avenue Station Friday morning at 7:00 a.m. by the William Jones, one of the engines that had pulled Lincoln's inaugural train.[56] The citizens of Cleveland had erected a pavilion, an elaborate catafalque with a pagoda-style roof, in Public Square. The Cleveland stop is unique because it was the only stop along the funeral route that elected to hold the services outdoors. The *Cleveland Daily Leader* predicted crowds of 120,000 mourners to view the president. Theoretically, the outdoor venue could've allowed the guards to more quickly marshal through a larger volume of people than dealing with the confines of a building. Torrential downpours dampened the expected crowds. Still, sixty-five thousand hardy Ohioans braved the weather during the twelve-hour viewing.[57] The coffin was closed at 10:00 p.m. and the Lincoln Funeral Train pulled out of Cleveland at midnight.

The next stop was Columbus, where the body was borne to the state capitol building by yet another hearse specially built for the occasion. The vehicle, which was pulled by six gray horses wearing black plumes, had gathered black broadcloth trimmed with silver fringe and tassels and black plumes making it reminiscent of a royal litter. The coffin sat, angled, six feet off the ground so spectators could catch a glimpse of the president's coffin.[58] The entrance to the capitol bore a banner from Lincoln's second inaugural address, reading, "With malice toward none, with charity for all."

The city had erected a catafalque in the rotunda, unique from all the others, in that it was the only one not constructed with pillars and a canopy. The coffin sat about waist high on a dais surrounded by a bed of moss and flowers sloping away from the coffin, giving it an almost pastoral appearance. Carpeting was laid over the capitol's marble floors and stone steps so to muffle footsteps; it gave the normally cavernous chamber an intimate, hushed atmosphere.[59] The Lincoln Special left the station at 8:00 p.m. for Indianapolis.

Because of the immense crowds, extra train service was added to bring mourners into the population centers designated on the funeral route, but it was the crowds in the rural areas that shocked the passengers on the funeral train. The area between Columbus and Indianapolis in the mid-nineteenth century was very rural. Before the advent of electricity there would've been no light pollution in those pastoral areas cut only by railroad tracks, but passengers on the Lincoln Special said that "the night sky was almost continuously lit by lingering torches and bonfires," so numerous were the citizens assembled trackside.[60]

Heavy rains greeted the train in Indianapolis. Instead of the planned procession, the coffin was conveyed directly to the elaborately draped state capitol. The hearse was drawn by eight white horses, draped in black, six of which had pulled the president's carriage four years earlier during the inaugural train stopover.[61] The coffin lay in state for the next fourteen hours as people braved the deluge and passed the coffin at an estimated brisk pace of 155 per minute for a total of 130,000 viewers.[62]

The Lincoln Funeral Train pulled into the Twelfth Street Station in Chicago at 11:00 a.m. on May 1 and was met by hundreds of thousands of people. The *New York Herald* estimated the crowd size at "the time the [funeral] procession moved, could not have been less than two hundred and fifty thousand."[63] The immense procession of forty thousand people, led by Major General Joseph "Fighting Joe" Hooker, was divided into five divisions comprising police, firefighters, military, civic, religious, and fraternal organizations, as well as academic institutions, who escorted the remains from the station to the Cook County Court House.[64] The coffin was placed in the rotunda next to a banner that read "We Mourn. Liberty's Great Martyr has sunk to rest by his country blest," and it was opened to the public at 6:00 p.m. where it remained so for the next twenty-six hours, with only breaks for Brown and Sands to attend to things.[65] An estimated 125,000 Chicagoans filed past the coffin to catch a glimpse of the Great Martyr.[66] Despite time and distance, the remains had endured.

The *Chicago Tribune* was kind, concluding, "No corpse in the world is better prepared, according to appearance."[67]

At 8:00 p.m. the coffin was sealed and borne back to the train station by torchlight, reminiscent of a Roman funeral.

The president was headed to his final stop, Springfield, his hometown.

The Lincoln Special pulled into Springfield on Wednesday, May 3, at 9:00 a.m., amazingly only an hour later than the projected timetable from when the train left Washington twelve days prior. This near perfect timing was not just a by-product of meticulous planning but also due to the fact that the entire railway system in the country was under military rule. Brigadier General Daniel McCallum, the general who directed all railroad activities for the Union during the war, personally supervised all railroad functions during the time the funeral train was operational. General McCallum was also a member of the honor guard, a group of high-ranking military personnel who accompanied the body everywhere during the funeral journey.

Springfield's budget had been strained by the decorating costs associated with readying the city for Lincoln's return and, unlike the other cities, it couldn't afford to finance the commissioning of a grand hearse for the occasion. The mayor of St. Louis offered to loan a hearse to Springfield. The cash-strapped city gratefully accepted.

The hearse, which had been used previously for the funeral of Missouri Governor Hamilton Gamble, was owned by liveryman Jesse Arnot.[68] It had been built in Philadelphia by the famed coach builder William "Old Billy" Rogers for $4,000.[69] A grand vehicle* with three panes of glass on either side, giving a full view of the coffin, it was ornamented with "gold figures burned into the surface," silver wreathes and torches, and topped with "[e]ight majestic plumes, dark as the raven's wing."[70] A team of six black horses came with the hearse, and Arnot himself drove the president from the Chicago & Alton Railroad Station to the statehouse, where volunteers had been toiling to prepare since the news of Lincoln's death. The public was admitted at 10:00 a.m. and for the next twenty-four hours eighty thousand mourners streamed past. This final stop was different,

---

* The hearse was destroyed in 1887 in a fire that also killed four people and eighteen horses. Jesse Arnot claimed, at the time of its destruction, that the hearse hadn't been used for a funeral since Lincoln. "A St. Louis Holocaust," *St. Albans Daily Messenger* (St. Albans, VT), February 11, 1887.

more personal. The big halls of the chamber were thick with silence, except for the murmured "move a little faster please" from the guards urging on the endless line.[71] Many of the people viewing Lincoln knew him personally, were neighbors in the city where he raised a family and practiced law for almost two decades.

At 10:00 a.m. the coffin was closed for the final time* and the procession to Oak Ridge Cemetery began with General Hooker in command. The procession passed Lincoln's house at the corner of Eighth and Jackson, the home having been heavily draped with mourning fabric and adorned with flower arrangements.

Mourners gathered crypt-side at the receiving vault where Lincoln's and Willie's coffins were placed side by side on stone slabs. The vault, built in the side of the hill, had been decorated with black mourning crepe and many flower arrangements. Receiving vaults were common in cemeteries of this era. Before mechanized equipment, remains reposed in receiving vaults while grave preparations or mausoleums were completed. In northern areas of the country, the remains reposed in the vaults during the cold months until the ground thawed enough to be dug. Lincoln's body would remain there for eight months before being moved due to security concerns. He was later moved to his permanent tomb, also in Oak Ridge Cemetery, on September 19, 1871, where after several failed grave robberies in 1901 he was buried under the burial chamber floor under ten feet of concrete.

Five members of the clergy participated in the committal service to give the chief magistrate over to his maker. After the opening prayers and scripture, the funeral oration was given by Rev. Dr. David Simpson, a bishop of the Methodist Episcopal Church. After making some remarks about Lincoln, he said, "Such a scene as his return to you was never witnessed among the events of history. There have been great processions of mourners. There was one for the Patriarch Jacob, which came up from Egypt, and the Egyptians wondered at the evidences of reverence and filial affection." He continued, "Far more have gazed on the face of the departed than ever looked upon the face of any other departed man. More races have looked upon the procession for 1,600 miles or more, by

---

* The coffin was opened again in 1901 and twenty-three people viewed the remains.

night and by day, by sunlight, dawn, twilight and by torchlight, than ever before watched the progress of a procession."[72]

It is hard to estimate how many millions of Americans actually took part in the funeral processions or wept as the Lincoln Special swept past them trackside. About 880,000 people laid eyes on the slain president, or just under 3 percent of the nation's entire population—a staggering figure. Bishop Simpson was correct: more people gazed upon Lincoln than any other person in history, and it's a number that hasn't been surpassed since.*

After Bishop Simpson finished, the Reverend Dr. Phineas Gurley, the Lincoln family minister and the same clergyman who officiated Willie's funeral, offered the benediction. Then George Willis, the cemetery sexton, locked the receiving vault's heavy iron doors and handed Robert Lincoln the key.

The obsequies were over.

Prior to Lincoln's extravagant funeral, Americans buried their dead in a simple, austere manner reflecting the nation's Puritan roots. The deceased were waked, or viewed, but typically for only a short period before decomposition set in. It was astonishing—a miracle almost—that someone who had died nineteen days prior and was viewed by hundreds of thousands of people was still viewable. Embalming, something previously reserved for anatomists, roared into the forefront of American culture as Americans wholeheartedly embraced the new science. But embalming is just one piece of the modern American funeral experience.

To understand contemporary burial customs, one must first look into the past to grasp the *why*. The modern American funeral begins its story well before the Civil War. It begins five thousand years ago, and across an ocean in ancient Egypt.

---

* Vladimir Lenin has been viewed by more people but his remains have been on public display since his death in 1924.

CHAPTER 2

The Book of the Dead

At banquets thrown by wealthy Egyptians it was common for a servant to carry around an eighteen-inch model of a corpse in a coffin and proclaim to each guest, "Drink and make merry, but look on this; for such shalt thou be when thou art dead."[1] In contemporary society, most folks would agree it sounds like dreadful dinner conversation (unless, of course, you're an undertaker), but to the Egyptians it was the norm. Nowhere in history are life and death as intertwined as in ancient Egypt. Death was viewed as a natural part of life, and life was to be spent planning and saving for continued existence in the afterlife. The key to successfully navigating the *duat*, or underworld, and achieving immortality was the preservation of one's earthly remains. Enter the science of embalming.

Embalming and religion in ancient Egypt are a causality dilemma, essentially the chicken-and-the-egg paradox. Was the theology created to explain a phenomenon or was the science of embalming developed to explain the theology?

A curious thing happens when someone is buried in the sandy soil and arid climate of North Africa. There's no putrefaction and decomposition. Rather, slow desiccation and decay occurs, leaving preserved remains—mummified remains—for the tribes living in Kemet, what is now known as Egypt, to ponder.

The upper and lower regions unified as one kingdom around 3100 BCE to give rise to the Egyptian civilization. Like all civilizations, they shared a culture and had a predominant religion, one that was polytheistic. Over the course of the thirty-one ruling dynasties spanning three millennia, their religious beliefs morphed. The outside influences brought by invaders and traders explain those changing beliefs. Gods and demigods rose and fell from favor, except one: Osiris, the god of the underworld.

Much of the recorded knowledge of the Egyptians comes from the Greek historian Herodotus. He noted during his visit around 440 BCE, "No gods are worshipped in common by the whole of Egypt save only Isis and Osiris."[2] Knowing the mythology behind Osiris gives a better understanding of why this culture chose to spend so much time and treasure on perfecting their mortuary arts.

Nut, goddess of night, bore five children: Osiris, Horus the Elder, Set, Isis, and Nephthys. Osiris married Isis,* and Set married Nephthys. Osiris and Isis ruled over Egypt, but his brother was jealous and wanted to be king. Set threw a banquet and held a contest where he presented an ornate chest and told the attendees that whoever could fit in the chest would win it. When Osiris climbed in, Set sealed it and threw it in the Nile. The chest washed ashore and a tamarisk tree enveloped the chest. The massive tree was felled as the pillar for a king's house. When Isis heard about this pillar, she knew the reason the tree had grown so large, and she retrieved Osiris.[3] Before she could bury the chest, Set found it, cut Osiris into fourteen pieces, and scattered him over Egypt.[4]

Isis was able to recover thirteen of the fourteen pieces, except his penis, which was eaten by a fish.[5] She fashioned a penis out of gold and brought Osiris back to life long enough to conceive a child, before enlisting Anubis (her stepson and the jackal-headed god of embalming) to embalm him, creating the first mummy.

Osiris became the ruler of the *duat*, and his son, Horus, defeated Set to become king of Egypt. When Horus died, he became Osiris and the new pharaoh "became" Horus—the ultimate manifestation of kingship. Thus, the ruling pharaoh was a demigod, a god on earth, linking royalty to the afterlife.

To the Egyptians, to be embalmed was to be almost godly. In fact, in the early days of the practice, it was reserved exclusively for the nobility,

---

* The marriage of brother and sister Osiris and Isis set the precedent for royal incestuous relationships.

but by the Middle Kingdom—beginning roughly 2050 BCE—the practice of mummification spread to anyone who could afford it.[6]

So, exactly what happened when someone died? Much like today, the bereaved family called the undertaker. Back then, the high priest of the mortuary temple fulfilled the role. Herodotus, sometimes called the "Father of History" for his historical accountings, recorded, "Whenever a man of note is lost to his house by death, all the womenkind of the house daub their faces or heads with mud; then, with all the women of their kin, they leave the corpse in the house, and roam about the city lamenting, with their garments girt round them and their breast showing; and the men too lament in their place, with garments girt likewise. When this is done, they take the dead body to be embalmed."[7]

The high priest, the *kher-heb*, was summoned to the house. He brought with him painted wooden models of the three different types of embalming offered. Once the price was agreed upon, the decedent was removed to the *per ankh*, or "house of life"—the mortuary temple.[8] According to Herodotus, if the decedent were a beautiful woman or the wife of a wealthy man, the family would wait three or four days before summoning the *kher-heb*.[9] This waiting period allowed the remains to sufficiently decompose and prevented necrophilia. It's unknown if this was a regional concern during the specific time Herodotus visited Egypt or the information given to him was lost in translation and he misconstrued the meaning.

When the decedent arrived at the *per ankh,* there in temporary structures—likely tents, or *ibu*—located on the west bank of the Nile, the body was washed with wine and water from the river.[10] The first washing is known as primary disinfection, and is a practice still used in modern embalming. The ethyl alcohol in the wine would've had a similar antimicrobial effect as present-day germicidal soap. After the washing, the body was moved into a permanent structure called the *wabt wat*, or "pure place," for the embalmers to begin their work.[11]

The embalming the Egyptians practiced was mummification. Modern embalming has three goals: disinfection, preservation, and restoration—in that order. Mummification was only concerned with one thing: preservation. Today, embalming is meant as temporary preservation for the purpose of viewing before final disposition. Mummification was meant as preservation for eternity.

After the mummification process was complete, the remains would've ended up disinfected (by ancient standards) as a by-product of the process, but the harshness of the methodology—necessary for *eternal* preservation—wouldn't allow for a suitable viewing experience (in the modern sense) afterward. The process was a closely guarded trade secret, passed down from master craftsman to apprentice in a similar fashion of feudal gilds. The Egyptians left no written record. In fact, it was expressly forbidden. A rule from a Book of the Dead warns embalmers against divulging the tradecraft.[12] What is known about the process comes mainly from Herodotus's firsthand account, as well as a few other historians, coupled with archaeological study.

The process took seventy days. Like everything in the culture, this time period had religious significance. It's speculated this time interval was chosen because the star Sirius, associated with Anubis, disappeared from the night sky for seventy days each year.[13] There was a lot to be done while the body preparations were underway. In the meantime, according to funeral historians Robert Habenstein and William Lamers, "The tomb was properly inscribed . . . with text and scenes of the departed's life, tomb furniture was built . . . and a group of professional mourners was immediately organized to sing funeral dirges throughout the city."[14]

The trade of embalming was highly specialized, with many different artisans* performing the necessary tasks. Thomas Greenhill, an eighteenth-century English surgeon, postulated five distinct specialties based on the writings of Herodotus and Diodorus: designer, dissector, apothecary, embalmer, and priest.

In the *wabt wat*, the decedent was laid out on a sloped wooden table, to allow for drainage, and blocked up to allow packing material to be placed around the remains. The first step was to draw out the brain. Using an iron hook, the embalmer† smashed through the cribriform plate of the ethmoid bone, at the base of the nose, and pulled the brain out by scraping. The embalmer, or *hery seshta*—meaning "he who controls the mysteries"—wore a

---

* Embalmers occupy a unique niche. Though they were a subsect of priests, because of their technical skill they were considered craftsmen.
† Most likely it was the embalmer's servants doing the actual physical work. Greenhill wrote, ". . . that were his Assistants and Servants, commonly Dissected, Embowell'd, Wash'd, Anointed and Embalm'd the Bodies of the meaner sort of People, yet when any Prince of Nobleman was to be Embalm'd . . . he perform'd the chief part of the work." Greenhill, quoted in Robert W. Habenstein and William M. Lamers, *The History of American Funeral Directing*, 8th ed. (Brookfield, WI: National Funeral Directors Association, 2014), 14.

jackal mask to simulate the presence of Anubis.[15] The purpose of the brain was unknown to the Egyptians and it was discarded. The cranial cavity was washed with palm wine and packed with linen or filled with resin.

After brain removal, the designer indicated the path of evisceration on the lower-left area of the abdomen. The dissector, using a knife of "Ethiopian stone," made the incision and immediately fled, being chased and stoned by his colleagues for defiling the body.[16] The organs were removed, treated, and separated into four vessels called canopic jars, though in some accounts the viscera were presented to the sun—as an apology of sorts for the impurities they'd consumed—and then cast into the Nile.[17]

There remains a mystery surrounding the treatment of one organ: the heart. The Egyptians believed it was the seat of intellect and feeling. A major part of their belief in the afterlife centered around the heart being weighed by Anubis in a "scales of justice" type of way. In their writings, the ancient philosophers Plutarch and Porphyry don't specifically mention the heart, but they imply it was cast into the Nile with the rest of the viscera.[18] The heart, if removed, was replaced with an amulet, an artificial scarabaeus beetle, carved from green stone, representing rebirth.[19] The fact remains that about 25 percent of mummies that have been examined have been found with their hearts.[20]

Once the organs were removed, the abdominal and thoracic cavities were washed again with palm wine and packed with spice blends compounded by the apothecary and fillers such as sawdust and straw to regain shape. The body was then immersed in natron, a naturally occurring mineral that's a mixture of mostly sodium carbonate and sodium bicarbonate, for forty days. The salt drew out all remaining moisture from the body; it was really a sped-up version of the dry burial, leaving desiccated remains that were no longer a suitable growth medium for the bacteria that causes decomposition. A lesser priest then wrapped the remains in yards of linen or silk strips, sometimes up to a thousand yards of cloth.[21] During the wrapping, amulets were tucked into the folds of the linen. The amulets' magical powers further assisted in the preservation of the dead. The deceased's station in life would determine the number of amulets, which could easily number over a hundred for royalty.

The embalmers covered the head with cartonnage, a decorative mask. Depending on the wealth of the family, the cartonnage could be made of different materials. Most often it was made of linen and painted plaster, but royalty and members of the ruling class had gold cartonnage inset with precious and semiprecious stones. The use of cartonnage would see a resurgence in medieval Europe in the form of death masks.

For citizens who couldn't afford the most expensive treatment, Herodotus described a syringe filled with cedar oil that the embalmer would "inject the drench through the anus and checking it from returning."[22] After the prescribed time in the natron bath, the remains were unplugged and the cedar oil was drained out along with the dissolved organs.

The use of eviscerating oil, however, has been disputed. The Egyptians were known to embalm animals: bulls, crocodiles, cats, and other beasts—even scarab beetles. The embalmed animals were venerated in temples and also buried with the dead. Turpentine, similar to cedar oil, was used in the animal preparations. It's possible Herodotus confused the enema rigs for animal embalming for human use.[23] The British Assyriologist Rev. Archibald Sayce doesn't trust all of Herodotus's claims, stating, "It is frequently difficult, if not impossible, for us to tell whether Herodotos [sic] is speaking from his own experience or quoting from others, whose trustworthiness is doubtful or whose statements may have been misunderstood."[24] By "misunderstood" Sayce is likely referring to the fact that Herodotus didn't speak Egyptian, and he was at the mercy of translators for information.

The final method, for the poorest citizens, was to "cleanse the belly with a purge," immerse it in the natron, and give it back to the family after the seventy days.[25]

It should be noted that there was no standard for mummification, the complete opposite of the acceptable standard of embalming taught in American mortuary schools. This book makes a sincere effort to present the process in a digestible manner, but the truth is the process changed and evolved over three thousand years. The methodology was passed down by word of mouth, *and* there were regional variations. It's unlikely that any two mummies discovered by archaeologists will ever reveal the exact same preparation.

Once the decedent was mummified and encoffined, the funeral procession could commence to the tomb that had been under construction for much of the person's lifetime. It was a bad omen to finish a tomb while one was still alive. To do so was to invite death. As such, tombs were finished during the embalming period. If one was a poor noble—of the class expected to have a tomb—it wasn't uncommon for the family to commandeer an ancient tomb of a family who had died out, and repaint and re-plaster it.[26] Tomb funerary maintenance, such as bringing the ritual offerings of food and drink, was performed by a special priest who was maintained by an endowment, much like how the price of a grave purchased in a modern cemetery includes a perpetual care fund. However, the famed Egyptologist Adolf Erman admits that once a family's fortunes waned or were stretched too thin with many tombs to maintain and the endowment ceased, "doom was certain."[27] Meaning, once someone stopped keeping an eye on a tomb, it was fair game for tomb robbers or a new family to come set up shop.

One of the funeral preparations that needed completion during the seventy-day period was finishing the Coffin Texts. Coffin Texts were spells, or instructions on how to successfully navigate the afterlife, inscribed inside the coffin. In the beginning of the First Intermediate Period, around 2200 BCE, Coffin Texts begin appearing in the tombs of nobility. It's no coincidence that this is around the time the nobility begins to dabble in mummification, something originally reserved for royalty. From there, there's a gradual slide toward mummification becoming available to any citizen who can foot the bill. Half a millennium after Coffin Texts appear, the Book of the Dead emerges. Written on papyrus scrolls, the book was called "Book of Going Forth in the Day" and was renamed with its new, rather morbid title in the nineteenth century. Typically commissioned while the person was alive, the book isn't a single text but rather a customized compilation of spells required to navigate the afterlife as well as a written record of the decedent's accomplishments in life. In order to have them handy in the afterlife, some mummies have been uncovered with the Book of the Dead wrapped in their hands.[28] Not much has changed since then. Today, it's not uncommon for the decedent to be buried with a Bible or other religious text in their hands.

The funeral procession was a great cortege—at the direction of the *kherheb*—with the sarcophagus* placed on a sledge drawn by oxen and

---

* The stone outer container that the "nesting doll" series of coffins would be placed in. Literally translated, *sarco* means "flesh," and *phagus* means "eat." The ancients called these "flesh eaters" because it was thought the stone would eat the flesh of the dead, as evidenced by only bones when sarcophagi were unsealed.

trailed by family, enslaved people, and professional mourners. At the tomb the most important ceremony was performed: "Opening the Mouth." Until this point, the dead was considered, well . . . dead. The Opening the Mouth ceremony reanimated the decedent, giving them back their senses for the beginning of their journey through the *duat*.

Once the decedent was "brought back to life," the sarcophagus would be entombed in the sepulcher* along with all the grave goods the deceased would need in the afterlife. These grave goods included furniture, games, jewelry, even beloved (of course, mummified) pets and little models of servants called *ushabti*. Models of wailing mourners were also placed in the tomb, their number determined by the importance of the decedent.[29]

If the tomb were that of a wealthy person, there would be a chapel above the sepulcher where the funeral concluded with a funeral feast with musicians and wine that often degenerated into an orgy.[30]

The chapel was an important feature of the tomb if one could afford such a thing. Later, family members or a specially hired priest visited the chapel with food offerings for the deceased's *ka*. Though it is sometimes tough to extrapolate the ancient Egyptian belief systems to current day understanding, the *ka* would be akin to the soul. The *ka*—whose hieroglyphic symbol looks like an upside-down staple symbolizing the two arms of humans—was an independent spiritual being living inside of a person, giving the flesh intelligence and health.[31] The *ka* was bound to the tomb, near the body, requiring offerings of food and drink to stay alive.

The *ba* was the spiritual manifestation of the deceased that came in existence after death. At the end of the deceased's journey through the afterlife, the *ka* and *ba* united to form the *akh*, the being that existed in the afterlife, or the Field of Reeds.[32]

Like Christianity's heaven, Islam's Jannah, or Hinduism's Svarga, the Egyptian religion had a heaven, typically referred to as the Field of Reeds. Whereas in Christianity the only criterion for admittance is accepting Jesus Christ as the savior, the path to gaining entrance into the Field of Reeds was a bit trickier. Navigating the *duat* involved almost a quest-like adventure with caverns, gates, and encounters with interesting creatures such as "eater of blood," "leg of fire," "breaker of

---

* A room or chamber in a tomb.

bones," and "eater of shadows." But as long as one had their Book of Going Forth in the Day—a crib sheet, essentially—overcoming the obstacles was no problem. At the end of the journey, the deceased arrived at the House of Osiris and the Hall of the Two Truths where Osiris, Thoth,* Anubis, and forty-two judges would hear the Negative Confessions, or a list of forty-two sins the deceased didn't commit. This is, of course, a theme later found in Christianity in the form of Saint Peter guarding the gates to heaven, allowing some in and casting others into hell. If the tribunal decided the deceased was without sin, Anubis weighed the deceased's heart against the feather of truth. If the person was pure, their heart was lighter than the feather and they were allowed to pass into the Field of Reeds, paradise.

Reflecting back on the finding that only 25 percent of mummies found retained the heart is interesting in light of Egyptian religious beliefs. If the heart was so important in the final step of the journey through the afterlife, it would make sense that every mummy should've retained their heart to be weighed against the feather of truth—unless the carved scarabaeus amulet was a good enough substitute for a real heart. There's no indication as to what happens if the deceased doesn't have a heart to offer to Anubis for weighing, but it stands to reason they met with the same fate as those who weren't pure and their heart was heavier than the feather of truth. Ammut, a goddess who is part crocodile, lion, and hippopotamus, ate those poor, unfortunate souls. The torture didn't stop there. The lost were sent to the Slaughtering Place, overseen by Sekhmet, where "demonic servants hack the damned to pieces, burn them with unquenchable fire, and submit them to all sorts of eternal tortures."[33] It would stand to reason that the average Egyptian would do anything to avoid Sekhmet and her machinations. And it was possible—for a price.

A person's chances of making it to the Field of Reeds was increased by how complete their Book of Going Forth in the Day was. A book could be as long or as short as one could afford. The complete book contained 190 spells (in 650 BCE).[34] Other factors, such as the quality of papyrus, number of illustrations, and texts the commissioner of the work wanted

---

* Aside from maintaining the universe, he was a judge of the dead. Talk about a multitalented god.

included, also determined the cost. Paying for a complete book seems a small price to pay to ensure eternal paradise, but there were also other funeral expenses to consider.

To get a grasp on simply how much money was spent on a funeral, a surviving record shows one family paying 370 drachmas* for mummification.[35] To put it in perspective, 400 drachmas could purchase a small house.[36] That's just the cost of the body preparation. There were all the other additional costs of the funeral: the building of the tomb, the scribe to compose the book of spells, the carpenters to build the tomb furniture and coffins, food for the funeral feast, as well as all the other ancillary costs to execute a fitting funeral.

Egyptian tombs were constructed sturdier than regular dwellings, using stone rather than the unbaked mud brick used for homes.[37] This practice hasn't changed much in four thousand years. Contemporary single-family homes are often stick construction, while mausolea are granite block. But a mausoleum costs about as much as a single-family home. Add that to the cost of the mummification and everything else and you have a funeral that costs several houses.

It may seem shocking to spend such a disproportionate amount on the dead, but this was the norm in their culture. In modern mortuary law in the United States, when the courts examine the reasonableness of a funeral bill, some of the factors they consider are "the station in life of the decedent, the decedent's religious faith, and local and contemporary custom."[38]

A person's "station in life," of course, refers to the fact that a more elaborate funeral is more reasonable for a wealthier person. This hasn't changed. In ancient Egypt there would've been a direct relationship between a person's wealth and their funeral. We know this because three different kinds of mummification were offered. The other two factors, "religious faith" and "local and contemporary custom," refer to the fact that the (contemporary) courts recognize some groups (religious or ethnic) will customarily spend a disproportionate amount of their income on funeral rites.

For example, funerals in Indonesia involve the entire village and can last for days or more. Families have to save for long periods to pay for all their neighbors to party. And in Ghana, fantasy coffins are popular.

---

* A Greek unit of currency used during part of the Greco-Roman period of the Egyptian empire.

A pilot may be buried in one made to look like a plane, and an author buried in one to look like a pen.* It comes at a steep price. In a country where the average salary for a doctor in 2017 was about $14,000, a fantasy coffin starts at $1,000, over 7 percent of a professional's annual gross income.[39] If an Indonesian in America threw a lavish post-funeral reception or a Ghanaian bought the most costly casket a funeral home offered, they would be normal funeral expenses because it's part of their culture, much like it was the Egyptian custom to spend so lavishly on funereal accoutrements.

In 1996, a large cemetery, covering 2.3 square miles, was discovered in Bahariya, an oasis located in Egypt's Western Desert, containing an estimated ten thousand mummies from the Greco-Roman period, the last period of pharaonic culture.[40] The lack of canopic jars and encoffined remains, and multiple remains piled in single graves sounded the death knell for mummification.[41] The mummies uncovered at Bahariya signal a dilution of the ancient art by outside influence or the sloppy work of hurried and harried embalmers and funerary priests. Either way, mummification was on its way out. The practice was largely abandoned as the pharaonic culture collapsed in the fifth century with the spread of Christianity.

Despite the disappearance of mummification, anatomists working to preserve specimens centuries later in the Middle Ages and the Renaissance would study the scant evidence left behind by Herodotus and Diodorus for clues to the ancient art of preserving the dead. The type of embalming practiced today doesn't use any of the methods pioneered by the Egyptians. Advances in chemicals, instruments, and technique have completely changed the procedure,† but one of the end goals, preservation (the other two for contemporary embalming being disinfection and restoration), is the same as it was five thousand years ago.

The practice of embalming itself isn't their only legacy. The mythology behind the practice—pieces of their theology—is evident in many mainstream religions. The Egyptians had the Field of Reeds and the Slaughtering Place. Many religions incorporate some version (or versions)

---

* Begs the question: What does the undertaker's coffin look like?
† And shrunk the timetable from seventy days to two or three hours.

of a heaven and hell. The *ka* was a key element to one's achievement of immortality after death, and that divine piece, or soul, is almost universal in mainstream religions.

Furthermore, the widespread practice of inhumation burial may be a result of Egyptian influence. The burial customs of Christianity, Judaism, and Islam—all religions originating in the Middle East—have traditionally called for inhumation for the purpose of resurrection. The land mass of Africa touches the Middle East where the present-day Israeli-Egyptian border is, and the Egyptians traded on the Mediterranean and Red Seas. It's not a far stretch to imagine the Osiris funerary cult spreading with such booming commerce and having some influence on their creation mythology.

The contribution of the ancient Egyptians to the modern funeral rite is indisputable, and the grandness of their funerary practices—still evident today by the great pyramids*—may never be surpassed.

---

* The Great Pyramid at Giza is the only surviving structure of the Seven Wonders of the Ancient World.

CHAPTER 3

Lethal Combat and Other Roman Obsequies

When Emperor Titus celebrated the Amphitheatrum Flavium's inaugural games in 80 CE, he slaughtered nine thousand exotic animals captured from the far corners of the empire in a *venatio*—wild beast hunt.[1] Over half—five thousand— were butchered in a single day.[2] And the bloodshed didn't stop there. The *ludi meridiani*—the midday games—featured the execution of criminals and prisoners of war in cruel and creative ways, such as placing a prisoner on a trapdoor platform and dropping him into a cage of wild beasts to be torn limb from limb.[3] But the animal hunts and executions were merely an entrée into the bloody main event: gladiatorial combat—*munus*—in the afternoon.

For well over three centuries, the sand of the Colosseum, as it's now known, soaked up the blood from man and beast and served to quench Rome's almost unslakable bloodlust. It may be lost to history how many gladiators died during the hundred days of the inaugural games, but comparing that event to a major *munus* that happened about thirty years later may give us a close approximation. A fragment from a recovered Roman calendar—*fasti ostienses*—records 4,941 pairs of gladiators squared off over the course 117 days.[4] That's quite a brisk pace of forty-two fights per day, or forty-two corpses dragged off the arena sand each and every day.

Gladiatorial combat, and quite possibly the main arena—the Colosseum—where it was featured, came about as the result of a funeral.

When Decimus Junius Brutus Pera, a consul,* died in 264 BCE, his son Decimus Junius Brutus Scaeva decided to attract more attention to the public spectacle with a new funeral game—death matches.[5] Funeral games, known as *ludi novemdiales*, were nothing new. They generally consisted of feats of strength and athletic competitions, and concluded the funeral rituals on the ninth day after burial.[6] But Decimus Junius Brutus Scaeva decided to bring the obsequies—and the prestige of his family—to a whole new level. He ordered three sets of his enslaved peoples to square off against each other in a cattle pen as the grand finale.

The citizens were enraptured by the bloody combat in a filthy cattle pen.

Other aristocratic families quickly moved to not only copy Decimus Junius Brutus Scaeva but outdo him, and thus gladiatorial combat was born. In 200 BCE at the funeral of Consul Marcus Valerius Laevinus, twenty-five gladiatorial matches—the gladiator pool largely consisting of condemned criminals and prisoners of war—celebrated his death.[7] Seventeen years later, 120 pairs of men fought to the death at the funeral of Consul Publius Licinius Crassus Dives.[8] *Munera* were so popular that politicians hijacked the idea. Candidates for election to magistracies began giving them.[9] Officials began literally buying votes with blood. The Senate was forced to pass a law in 63 BCE disqualifying any candidate who financed a show within two years of an election.[10] This didn't mean the end of gladiatorial combat, in fact, the opposite: the Republic (and later the Roman Empire) used it as a political tool but in a different way than to garner votes. The rulers used *munera* to maintain public favor because there was no public spectacle Romans loved more.

Fast-forward a little over three hundred years from the beginnings at Decimus Junius Brutus Pera's funeral and gladiators have become the preeminent form of entertainment for Roman citizens (as well as big business), with Emperor Titus dedicating a grand stadium where the main event is the *munus iustum atque legitimum*, or "a proper and legitimate gladiator show."[11] The last gladiator spectacle happened at the turn of the fifth century as the empire crumbled. There is no vestige of post-funeral games,

---

* In the Republic, consuls were elected annually and wielded considerable power, comparable to the US president in that it was the highest elected office.

human sacrifice, or gladiator combat in the American death ritual today, but plenty of Roman funerary customs survived long after Odoacer deposed the last emperor Augustus Romulus in 476 CE.

The Roman Empire is the gorilla in the room when examining the history books. At its peak, the empire covered a swath of territory around the Mediterranean Sea stretching from Spain to the Middle East and Britain to North Africa. Though the empire existed a much shorter time than pharaonic Egypt, the Roman influence on economics, politics, jurisprudence, social institutions, and, yes, funerary practices reverberates into time immemorial.

Prior to Emperor Constantine's conversion to Christianity in 312 CE,[*] cremation was the preferred method of disposition since the late Republic. The almost immediate shift from cremation to inhumation is attributed to the influence of mystery religions popular in Rome at the time, as well as Christianity's emphasis on bodily resurrection.[12] There's also the argument that the Roman inclination for ostentation moved the needle toward burial. The wealthy could flout their affluence in the form of expensive mausoleums and sarcophagi.[13]

The fact that an archaic Roman form of disposition aligns with a contemporary American one (cremation is now the chosen method of disposition) isn't what makes Roman funerary practices worth mentioning. It's the fact that they had a secular funeral director, the *libitinarius*—derived from Libitina, the goddess of corpses.[14] Nowhere before in recorded history had control of funeral ceremonies been at the hands of a professional and not a religious man. In fact, the priests of Rome avoided all contact with the dead, fearing that contact with a corpse would pollute them.[15]

According to the British scholar Bertram Puckle, "The word funeral, properly speaking, denotes a torchlight procession, for it is derived from the Latin 'funeralis' from funis, a torch" because the majority of funerals were at night for the practical purpose that Roman funeral processions were so grand and they would disrupt normal daytime commerce.[16] The string of bobbing torches signaling an approaching funeral procession had the added benefit of warning off priests and thus avoiding impurity. Daytime services weren't unheard of, but they were reserved for wealthy patricians.

---

[*] Although it wasn't adopted as the official state religion for another sixty-eight years, in 380 CE.

When a Roman died, the nearest relative immediately kissed their lips in hope of receiving their soul, and all the assembled relatives called out the dead by name.[17] Then the *libitinarius* was summoned to the home. At the temple of Venus Libitina, the undertaker registered the names of all those who died.[18] It's interesting to note the dichotomy of the undertaker operating out of a temple, yet he wasn't a holy man. It also bears pointing out how the fastidious Roman bureaucracy even applied to the dead: every name* was duly recorded. Centralized (by state) birth and death records didn't start in America until the twentieth century—well over two thousand years after the Romans kept a death roll. Before American states began collecting vital statistics, births were recorded in family bibles, and deaths were recorded only in undertakers' ledgers.

The *libitinarius* brought with him a *pollinctores*, an enslaved person who was the embalmer. The historian John Lanktree states, "In the art of embalming the Romans were greatly superior to the Egyptians."[19] Lanktree's conclusion is likely based on appearance. Certainly, the Roman corpse looked more natural in repose after preparation than that of the Egyptian, but their goals were vastly different. The Egyptians spent seventy days preserving the body for eternity, whereas the Romans only needed a state of semipreservation for up to seven days for the lying-in-repose. As such, the definition of Roman embalming was that the body was washed and anointed with myrrh and aloe.[20] Then the body was dressed and a coin was placed in the deceased's mouth to pay Charon, the ferryman who ushers souls across the River Styx.[21] The remains were laid on a couch with the feet toward the door, and the door to the home was adorned with a cypress bough.[22] Cypress symbolizes death, and it would let neighbors know that it was a house of mourning. This passive method of notifying the community of a death translated to Victorian-era Americans placing black crepe on their front doors.

The lying-in-repose lasted from three to seven days, depending on the social status of the decedent (the greater your status, the longer the lying-in-repose). From the home, the *designator*, an employee of the *libitinarius* whose job it was to direct the actual event, organized the funeral procession.

---

* Of citizens, certainly not enslaved peoples.

If the decedent were a person of means, the *libitinarius* enlisted a *praeco*, or herald, to summon folks. The role of funeral herald continued unabated until daily newspapers made them obsolete.

In contemporary times, the funeral cortege is simply a functional means to get from one service, the funeral, to another, the committal. In Rome, the procession was the event.

Under the direction of the *designator*, the decedent was carried from their home on their funerary couch—the *feretrum*—set upon a bier carried by, depending on their status, as many as eight bearers. Bearers were often male relatives or freed slaves. A funeral band including pipers, horn blowers, and trumpeters led the *pompa* (procession) followed by persons singing dirges. Hired mourners, *praeficae*, were a common part of funeral processions, and they followed the band. The *praeficae*—the number attending depended on the wealth of the family—were hired by the *libitinarius*. These mourners-for-hire wailed, tore their hair, and rended their garments in great theatrical displays of grief. Their grief intensified as the funeral unfolded, and as the ceremonies neared an end, the women would tear at their faces until bloody.[23] The mourners serviced a Roman superstition that the dead would become jealous if they bore the death in too stern a fashion, and thus a niche industry was born.[24]

Professional mourners were prevalent in America in the late nineteenth century, though their histrionic displays of grief were mostly limited to wailing, and not the physical disfigurement of tearing their hair out and clawing their faces to ribbons. The Jewish faith has long rended their garments based on a Hebrew Bible story that predates Romulus marking the sacred boundary—*pomerium*—of Rome. The story tells that Jacob tore his clothes in grief when he believed his son Joseph to be dead. Jewish people still practice the tradition but now use a *kriah* ribbon, a little black ribbon pinned over regular clothing. *Kriah* means "tearing." In contemporary funerals they tear the ribbon instead of actual clothing. Professional mourners in America all but disappeared by the time the Great War changed mourning customs.

Following *praeficae* came the jesters, or mimes, with one wearing a mask of the decedent and clothes signifying the highest rank the deceased achieved in life. This mime imitated the decedent's gait, speech, and gesticulations, even going so far as to "[pass] jests on his character and life."[25]

Funerary mimes are a fascinating piece of the Roman funeral rite as they weren't comical or theatrical like performance artists today; their dancing was described as "grotesque" and their actions coarse.[26] It seems contrary for someone at a supposedly somber occasion to jest with the audience or ridicule the character of the dead, but there was a method to the comedic mockery. The classics professor Geoffrey Sumi postulates in the *American Journal of Philology* that Romans engaged in inversion behavior, like mourners wearing ragged clothing or mimes engaging in jesting, as part of ritualized disorder to control the uncontrollable—death.[27] It can also be explained by a phenomenon called "ceremonial acting out" where an acquired meaning is attached to acting out deep emotions when words don't suffice.[28] The mechanism of attaching meaning to ceremony is used in modern times for funerals, weddings, graduations, and even sporting events. In Roman antiquity, jesting and abusive language were part of the culture. As such, the mockery has been recorded taking place at weddings, triumphs, and banquets.

Of course, not everyone included a mime in their funeral rites; even royalty was known to abstain from this tradition. Caligula seemingly lacked a sense of humor. He once burned a poet* for a double entendre contained in a verse, and his sternness translated to his funeral.[29] A mime was conspicuously absent from his *funus imperatorium*—royal funeral—as it was from the funeral of his successor, Claudius.[30] But by and large, most Romans employed a mime to literally bring to life the words and works of their dearly departed. Usually an enslaved person who was of similar height and weight was tapped to play the role of dead. Diodorus wrote that wealthy Romans used actors who were part of their retinue and had spent time to "carefully observe his carriage and several peculiarities of his appearance."[31] The mask, gait, and verbosity of the mime were all secondary to the main purpose, that of displaying the rank of the deceased. The mime wore the garb of the highest rank the deceased achieved. Status was important to the Romans, and since death is the great equalizer, the funeral-goers could see just how important that family was by the pomp of the procession

---

* Talk about poetic justice. The cremation of Caligula was botched. He was only half cremated—on purpose— due to a poorly constructed funeral pyre. Hugo Erichsen, *The Cremation of the Dead: Considered from an Aesthetic, Sanitary, Religious, Historical, Medico-Legal, and Economical Standpoint* (Detroit: D. O. Haynes, 1887), 16.

and significance in the social hierarchy of the funerary mime-as-the-dead. Funeral mimes were quickly phased out when Christianity was adopted as the state religion due to the mime's association with theater, which was considered a pagan vice.[32]

After the mime came the *imagines*, or ancestral masks, worn by actors. The *pompa* would literally contain a parade of dead ancestors—the family tree, if you will—in the form of waxen masks that had been worn by mimes at previous funerals. Masks were kept in a wooden shrine in the household, and were taken out and decorated on public holidays and for funerals of family members.[33] According to Servius, six hundred *imagines* were paraded out for the death Augustus's favored nephew, Marcellus.[34]

Imagines were similar to cartonnage, the Egyptian death masks, even though the cartonnage was meant to be buried and the *imago* was to be retained by the living as a keepsake. As we will explore in later chapters, death masks stayed in vogue for centuries and likely only fell out of favor because of photography. Unlike the European death masks later in history, *imagines* were mostly sculpted pieces and not cast directly from the deceased's face.

In the modern American funerary tradition, the same objective is achieved as the mimes and *imagines*, not through theater but photography. The Romans used the actors to reestablish familial links during the uncertainty surrounding death just as Americans use photographs. It's common for families to display photo collages or slideshows showing the decedent in business and pleasure activities, but also older photographs with long-dead relatives. The Romans had no choice but to use theater to renew these ties, whereas the modern funeral can use technology to achieve the same ends.

Next in the procession came the bier bearing the decedent, followed by family with the chief mourner wearing a laurel crown to designate their status, freemen, enslaved people, and friends, all wearing black.

When the procession arrived at the place of burial or cremation, a bit of earth was thrown on the deceased, or if the person was to be cremated, a finger was cut off to ensure death.[35] In Rome, all burials, whether burial of a body or cremains, had to take place outside the *pomerium* (sacred boundary of Rome), for sanitary reasons. The vast majority of citizens were buried on the roads leading into the cities except vestal virgins. They were special. Vestals were allowed sepulture within the city.[36]

Vestal virgins were the priestesses of Vesta, the god of the hearth and home.[37] Vestals entered into the priesthood at the age of six, and they took a vow of chastity for thirty years, after which they could marry.[38] The Romans revered vestal virgins, and the order enjoyed many privileges. Praetors and consuls—powerful political men—had to lower their faces in submission when they encountered one. Vestals could immediately pardon criminals sentenced to death.[39] The penalty for insulting one of the high priestesses was public whipping to the death.[40] Their exalted status extended to funeral rites. Whereas a priest was forbidden to approach a corpse for fear of pollution (hence the torchlights for warning them away), vestals had no such restrictions.[41] Vestals were allowed to participate in the *pompa*; it's documented that they participated in the statesman Sulla's funeral.[42] But their exalted status and privileges came with a high price if they broke their vows. Punishment was live burial.[43]

Keeping with the Roman law of extra-municipal burial, the roads leading to the city were lined with ostentatious and simple tombs, many still standing today. The tombs vary wildly in architectural design, running the gamut from pyramids, to tower tombs, to circular tombs, and the popular house tombs. Some were so lavish they included gardens that could be up to an eighth of an acre; one man built a vineyard enclosed by a wall at his tomb.[44] The inscription V.F.—for *vivus fecit*—means the occupant erected it in their lifetime, much like the Egyptians who began construction on their tombs while alive.[45] The famed Roman mausoleums weren't just for bodily entombment; cremated remains were placed in them as well. Tacitus, the Roman historian, described cremation as the "Roman style," and for five centuries, beginning in the fourth century BCE, many of the tombs were columbaria, or tombs constructed with niche spaces to place cinerary urns.[46]

In the case of cremation, the place of burial was where the pyre was constructed. The same disposition theory is true today in America: the crematorium is the place of disposition* in the eyes of the state.

---

* Instead of the name of a cemetery, the funeral director lists the name of the crematorium on the death certificate as "place of disposition."

In Rome, the decedent was laid on the pyre still on their funerary couch, their eyes were opened, and the chief mourner ignited the pyre.[47] Perfumes and personal articles were added to the pile—including pets killed on site.[48] The point of the perfumes is obvious, but adding personal articles to the burning pile is more than likely some sort of reconciliation (as opposed to mounding them in a tomb) with sending items for the deceased to use in the afterlife.

After the fire was doused with wine, the family would pick through and sort the decedent's remains from the combustibles; sometimes the remains were wrapped in asbestos prior to burning so the family could be sure.[49] The charred bone fragments were placed into ash chests or urns. Much like today, urns came in a variety of styles and were made from a variety of materials including marble, terracotta, and glass.

A marble, stone, terracotta, lead, or wood sarcophagus was used to enclose the body for inhumation or entombment.[50] The material of the vessel depended on the wealth of the decedent. The wealthier would be buried in ornately carved marble and stone sarcophagi in private family mausoleums with more modest families having wooden burial cases in communal hypogea (what the Christians would later call catacombs) or simpler in-ground burial.

To add to the mayhem when the *pompa* reached the place of disposition—as the dirges reached fever pitch and *praeficae* clawed at their faces and tore clumps of hair from their heads—a squealing shoat would be brought forth to have its throat slit, signifying the grave to be a legal grave under Roman law.[51]

After burial or cremation, the family and the household underwent ritual purification. This was practical as much as it was ceremonial. In the hot Mediterranean climate, by the time the *pompa* happened, as long as a week after the death, the remains were likely in a state of advanced decomposition. The Romans didn't shy away from death; as such, the family members were in close contact and quarters with the decedent during that weeklong period. Once the family was pure, the funeral meal was eaten at the grave.

The funeral meal, though not strictly compulsory in the modern American funeral rite, is still an important piece of the ceremony. The ritual of breaking of bread with friends and family reaffirms emotional ties, and the meal itself is a tacit declaration of nourishment, or life. Since Roman antiquity, the funeral meal has been a staple of the Judeo-Christian tradition. Bereaved Jews still eat the *seudat havra'ah*, a repast consisting of hard-boiled eggs and other cylindrical items to symbolize the circularity of life. Medieval European Christians gathered for the "funeral baked meats."[52] The tradition continued in America, partly out of necessity. Many colonial funeral-goers traveled a distance to pay their respects and the bereaved family was obligated to feed them before their journey home.

The grand mausoleums of the rich contained kitchens elaborate enough to have wells and ovens for preparing the funeral banquet.[53] The added expense of the mausoleum kitchen wasn't put in for the single use after burial. Romans gathered at the crypt on many anniversaries throughout the year to feast where they shared the feast with the deceased. Pipes connected the encrypted dead with the living. The Romans made no distinction between regular burials and cremations; the pipes are almost ubiquitous. Their purpose was to keep the dead "alive" with nourishment in the way of food and drink.[54] This has a striking similarity to the Egyptian's belief in the *ka* and their nourishment of the *ka* with offerings. It isn't inconceivable that this Roman tradition is one they absorbed and appropriated from the Egyptians. Some Romans practiced the Egyptian mystery cult, inscribing petitions to Osiris on their tomb.[55]

The ninth day after burial, which concluded the period of full mourning, the family gathered at the burial site for the *cena novendialis* feast where nourishment for the *manes*—or spirits—was first offered through the libation pipes. The *cena novendialis* was the occasion to host funeral games, including gladiatorial combat.

The annual public commemoration of the dead was Parentalia, occurring February 13–21 with the last day being the public celebration where citizens made pilgrimages to ancestral graves with offerings.[56] The obvious correlation to Western religion is the absorption of Parentalia by the Roman Catholic Church in the form of All Souls Day, which occurs November 2.* It's unlikely the Catholic Church commandeered the Roman holiday because its observance wasn't formalized until

---

* In the Eastern Orthodox faith there are many observations of All Souls Day throughout the year. Most of them occur on a Saturday—the day Jesus lay in his tomb.

nearly six centuries after the fall of Rome in 1048 by a Benedictine abbot name Odilo.[57] The more likely explanation is that church leadership saw the human need for ancestral veneration and created a formal holiday with echoes from Roman past in a phenomenon known as convergent evolution, where two things evolve independently and end up with the same functionality.

The grandest Roman funeral spectacles were the imperial ones—*funus imperatorium*. Similar to the pomp and ritual of a state funeral in America that might include lying in state or honor in the Capitol Rotunda (or state capitol building), a religious service, a procession, and a committal service, the Romans had their version: *apotheosis*. Like lying in state in the US Capitol must be granted by Congress, *apotheosis* had to be conferred by the Senate as it was reserved for those entitled to enrollment among the gods.[58] Essentially, service to the state deified the decedent.

After the funeral ceremony, a waxen effigy was placed on a couch in a public place for a period of seven days. During this interim, physicians would periodically approach the effigy and declare it to be getting worse. On the final day the physician declared the patient dead.[59] Lanktree refers to this drama in *A Synopsis of Roman Antiquities* as a "ridiculous farce," and, yes, it does seem a bit farfetched by modern standards.[60] This bit of theater was likely a version of a coping mechanism now known as "anticipatory grief," where the grieving process starts before the person dies so that it's less severe when death occurs. In a time in history when people died young and suddenly with a high frequency, this mourning over a waxen dummy could offer a glide path of grief for a stricken populous.

From the public place of repose, the effigy was borne along the Via Sacra to the Forum, where the successor in whatever office the deceased occupied delivered a *panegyric*, or public speech of praise that today would be called a eulogy.[61] From the Forum, the *pompa* advanced to the place where a four- or five-story funeral pyre had been erected, usually Campus Martius. The pyre was made to look like porticos stacked upon one another and were decorated lavishly with "gold, ivory, and paintings."[62] After the pyre was lit, an eagle was released if the deceased was an emperor* to transport the soul to the Blessed Isles, or Roman heaven.[63]

---

* If an empress, a peacock was released.

The poor didn't fare so well. Slaves, prisoners, gladiators, and plebeians were carried to the burial site on a litter by *vespilliones*, or tattooed men, who lived on the outskirts of town near the cemeteries.[64] Their bodies were thrown into the *puticulus*, or common burying place, which was nothing more than a trench grave. Despite the distastefulness of seemingly body disposal, this may be the social underpinning for state burials (i.e., indigent burials) that modern civilizations have adopted. The Romans were obsessed with cleanliness and order, and devoid of religious orders that absorbed disposition duties during the medieval era, the state had to do something to ensure all dead bodies were disposed of in the manner prescribed in the Twelve Tables, the foundation of Roman law. This method of ensuring burial correlates loosely to the way counties contract with modern funeral establishments to guarantee indigents are buried properly. Most municipalities have a *puticulus* called "Potter's Field"* for the burial of indigents. The most famous contemporary example is New York City's Hart Island that opened in 1869† and has more than a million people buried there.[65] The difference is the Department of Corrections, which oversees Hart Island, documents the known names and locations of burial, whereas the unfortunates buried in the *puticulus* couldn't hope for that much.

The Roman state also contracted with local *libitinarii* for the disposal of gladiators, which was probably a lucrative contract based on the number of gladiators killed per day at the average *munus*. After a match had been decided, attendants, disguised as Charon, approached a dead or dying gladiator and smashed him in the head with a mallet. Reassured he was actually dead, they waved over the *libitinarius* to cart off the slain warrior.[66] The *libitinarius* then turned the corpse over to the tattooed men who carried it to the common burying place.

By the reign of Constantine (in 306 CE), when Christian values begin to permeate Roman bureaucracy, even the poorest citizens were guaranteed to be "followed to the grave by a crossbearer, eight monks, and three acolytes."[67] After the fall of Rome, the occupational undertaker, the *libitinarius*, disappears for nearly thirteen centuries as the

---

* The name Potter's Field is biblical. Matthew 27:7 King James Version, ". . . and bought with them the potter's field, to bury strangers in." The field referred to had ample red clay used by potters before being used as a burial ground.
† The original Potter's Field in New York City is now Washington Square. Most of the estimated twenty thousand people buried there died of yellow fever during the late eighteenth century.

church steps in to fill all the necessary duties pertaining to funerals. The Roman Catholic Church solidified its position during the Black Plague in the fourteenth century when only religious orders would care for the dying and tend to the dead.[68]

Some death rituals, such as the post-funeral games and torchlight processions, ended along with the Roman Empire, but many continued. As the once mighty empire was carved up and its subjects dispersed like seeds in the wind, they took with them their culture and spread many Roman funerary practices. Europe as well as parts of North Africa and Asia Minor continued to wake their dead, have corteges to the place of disposition—albeit without the pageantry—and conclude with a post-funeral banquet. Granted, the Romans appropriated many pieces of their funeral rites from the Egyptians, though notably absent was the appropriation of the closely guarded secret of mummification-style embalming.

The occupational undertaker—the European version of the *libitinarius*—wouldn't surface until the late seventeenth century in England. Before that, curious men, who read works by the famed Greek surgeon Claudius Galenus—also known as Galen—and the historian Herodotus, began experimenting with human preservation, trying to unlock the secrets of the Egyptian embalmers.

CHAPTER 4

The Bloody Barber-Surgeons

Embalming Emerges
from the Dark Ages

D r. Martin Van Butchell was an eccentric London dentist who rode around Mayfair on a purple-spotted pony wielding the jawbone of an ass to defend himself.[1] It wouldn't be unfair to accuse him of being a quack for advertising pain-free dentistry in the late eighteenth century, nearly seventy-five years before anesthesia was commonplace. In addition to his pain-free dentistry practice, Van Butchell was a truss maker* and renowned fistula curer.

A fistula is an infection in one of the glands surrounding the anus that causes a painful abscess. Given the diet and personal hygiene of Europeans during this time, fistulas were a common affliction, and good fistula curers would conduct a brisk business. Van Butchell is said to have learned fistula curing from a Dutch physician who was "ruptured" (an eighteenth-century term for herniated) and came to Van Butchell for a truss. In exchange for successful treatment, the physician taught Van Butchell the secret art of fistula curing.[2] A later advertisement of Van Butchell's would read: *Fistulae— Patients—Fee is according to ability!*[3]

---

* Corrective bands used to treat patients suffering from rheumatism.

However, what propelled Van Butchell into fame was neither his purported healing powers nor his personal peculiarities but rather the fact that his late wife lay embalmed in his living room in perpetuity.

Van Butchell's reasons may not have been motivated by anatomical study as one might assume of a medical man. No, it was rumored to be a financial decision. Van Butchell was purportedly able to control some property as long as Maria Van Butchell "remained *above ground*."[4] Though this probably wasn't the first time someone was preserved through the new method of arterial injection for purposes other than anatomical study in post-medieval Europe, it's one of the well-documented early cases. Van Butchell himself not only documented the case but he also participated.

Maria Van Butchell, age thirty-six, died January 14, 1775, of empyema—a condition where the area outside the lungs fills with pus.[5] Dr. Van Butchell called on William Hunter and William Cruikshank to embalm her. Van Butchell had studied medicine and anatomy under Hunter's brother, John Hunter. The brothers were well-known Scottish anatomists who were experimenting with the cutting-edge method of arterial injection to preserve tissues for dissection demonstrations. In 1695, Gabriel Clauderus, a German physician, published his method of arterially injecting the "balsamic spirit."[6] Frederick Ruysch, a Dutch botanist, is credited with inventing arterial injection, but his methods were a closely guarded secret and died with him. Hunter's embalming procedure, using Clauderus's methods, had three distinct parts and was outlined in Van Butchell's diary as noted by Jessie Dobson in the *Journal of the History of Medicine and Allied Sciences.*

Van Butchell wrote, "At half past two this afternoon Mr. Cruikshanks [*sic*] injected at the crural arteries 5 pints of Oil of Turpentine mixed with Venice Turpentine and Vermilion*."[7] *Crural* is a term relating to the leg or thigh. It is assumed Cruikshank was specifically injecting the femoral artery, a favored injection site of the Hunter brothers. In lecture notes from 1776, Hunter instructed his students during this first step to "fill the Arteries and Veins and go further to produce extravasation to every part of the Body, i.e., til the face and all the flesh swell."[8]

---

* Oil of turpentine is a solvent, and Venice turpentine is an essential oil used as a sealer (and it has a history of being used to toughen horse's hooves). Vermilion is mercury sulfide, a scarlet-colored pigment that Cruikshank added for internal colorization.

For some reason, Van Butchell had a death mask made prior to embalming. This is interesting from the standpoint that Van Butchell was embalming his wife to keep her viewable, making a facsimile of her face redundant, unless it proves he wasn't confident in the embalming outcome.

The following day the body preparation continued when both Hunter and Cruikshank "began to open and embalm the body of my Wife."[9] Van Butchell is referring to the second phase of Hunter's method in which the viscera are removed and placed in water, and the blood is then pressed out of the viscera, face, and extremities, and then the viscera washed in wine. The last phase is a second arterial injection followed by replacement of the viscera along with camphor, nitre (what the Egyptians used), and resin.[10]

Three days later, on January 18, Hunter and Cruikshank returned to place Mrs. Van Butchell in a box containing 130 pounds of plaster of paris as well as three bottles of scented distillates to mask any foul odors.[11] The plaster of paris would've acted as an absorbent in the event of leaking.

Van Butchell kept his wife in his sitting room wearing her black wedding dress* with—of all things—an embalmed green parrot between her feet.[12] If she was part of an unusual advertising campaign, for which Van Butchell was well known, it worked. The hordes of curious Londoners—including nobility and gentry—that flocked to Van Butchell's house forced him to post a sign announcing "No stranger can see my embalmed wife unless it is between nine and one . . . Sunday excepted."[13]

Van Butchell's second wife's† protestations about her predecessor displayed in their parlor fell on deaf ears. The original Mrs. Van Butchell wasn't moved to the Hunterian Museum until 1815 after Dr. Van Butchell's death.

Although Mrs. Van Butchell certainly wasn't the first documented case‡ of embalming using vascular injection, it proved to be a watershed moment in embalming. Whether it was financially motivated or a guerilla marketing scheme, the case of Maria Van Butchell not only reinforced

---

* Van Butchell gave his wives a choice of color they could wear: black or white. Once they chose, that was the only color they were allowed to wear from then on. His first wife chose black, and his second wife chose white.
† Who was previously a servant in Van Butchell's household.
‡ A full seventeen years before Van Butchell, Dr. Charles White embalmed Miss Hannah Beswick, who became known as the Manchester Mummy, likely using the Hunter brothers' techniques. He kept her body in a clock case in his home until his death in 1813.

to the scientific community vascular injection as a means for maintaining anatomical specimens but also proved to the public (who flocked to his home in droves as evidenced by his sign) that this was a viable technique of preservation for viewing and thus funeralization purposes.

Previous to the Renaissance, embalming was limited to preservation for anatomical dissection and for royalty, clergy, military leaders, and select noblemen. Much like the goal of the Egyptians, preservation, not restoration, was the key. Often the body was so badly mutilated by the procedure that the remains were rendered all but unviewable. With the monarchial system the prevalent form of government in Europe, it was critical to preserve the remains of monarchs long enough for relatives to make a positive identification and allow the rightful heir to be acclaimed.[14]

Royal funeral ceremonies often lasted for many days or as long as a week. Given the rudimentary nature of preservation, the first order of business was usually to cast a death mask. The mask, sometimes used in conjunction with an effigy—especially during hot weather—was typically displayed on the catafalque during the services.[15] The death masks were an aesthetic necessity because the preservation techniques practiced by the trade guild of embalmers, called barber-surgeons, were so drastic that if preservation was achieved, it was at great cosmetic cost.

When Henry I of England died in 1135, he was buried in the Church of Reading Monastery. He was embalmed by "removal of the brain, tongue, heart, eyes, etc. by means of incisions, and the use of various drugs."[16] The salted, eviscerated body was wrapped in a tanned bull's hide for shipping.[17] After such an invasive procedure, it's almost certain that Henry I's remains weren't viewable, hence the popularity of death masks. Despite the restorative limitations on embalming at the time, the preservative results were sometimes documented to be exceptional. When King Edward I's tomb at Westminster Abbey was opened in 1774, 467 years after his death, his remains were "found in perfect form and good preservation."[18] The last documented case of royalty using a death mask for viewing purposes was Anne of Austria, who died in 1666. Her waxen effigy was placed on display at the Louvre immediately following her death.[19] The practice of casting death masks didn't cease after the mid-seventeenth century, as evidenced by Van Butchell making one of his first wife over a hundred years after Anne of Austria's death. The practice migrated to America, and was occasionally employed, like casting Presidents Garfield's and McKinley's faces postmortem. The methodology is still taught in mortuary colleges. Death masks may once again become commonplace as the medicine behind face transplants continues to advance. The modern death mask—latex instead of wax or plaster—would allow the donor's family to still have a viewing prior to final disposition.

Until the twelfth century in England the clergy practiced surgery and medicine.[20] In 1163 the Council of Tours decided that the practice of shedding blood was incompatible with the role of the clergy and banned the practice of surgery, though priests were allowed to continue healing through the practice of medicine.[21] Barbers, who had previously assisted clergymen throughout the Dark Ages with "bleeding, tooth-drawing, cauterization, and the like," assumed the vacated role and dubbed themselves barber-surgeons.[22] It's with this unlikely group of shavers and blood-letters that control of the dead was wrested from the church's grip and back into a secular group—much like during Roman times.

The Barbers were a trade guild who, aside from their vocation, feasted once a year and were required to attend members' and wives' funerals.[23] They began to organize as early as 1308, appointing a master of the company, Richard le Barber.* This was their first step toward legitimization and self-governance as London had passed an ordinance in the year prior forbidding barbers from displaying blood in their shop windows or publicly dumping buckets of blood into the Thames.[24] Perhaps it was a wise move; nothing engenders confidence in a surgical practitioner as much as a pool of congealing blood in front of his doorstep.

In 1540 the incorporated Company of Barbers (who were already well known as barber-surgeons) joined with the unincorporated Guild of Surgeons. It seems discordant to join such dissimilar crafts, but Henry VIII's rationale was consolidation of surgeons, some who "practised [sic] under the name 'Barbers'."[25] Though some practitioners of surgery may have chafed at the idea of being lumped in with "shavers and hair-dressers," the move was partly political, aimed to elevate the status of surgeons.[26] The Company

---

* Surnames in medieval Europe often described one's trade: Carpenter, Smith, Cook, Chandler, Cooper . . . In the case of Richard, his name translates to Richard the Barber. Nifty coincidence for the first master of the guild.

of Barbers was well connected and had considerable assets. The Guild of Surgeons brought no property to the union.

In an ironic twist after combining barbers and surgeons, King Henry VIII's Act of 1540 also *separated* the trades within the company so that "no one using the faculty of Surgery should practise [*sic*] Barbery, and that no Barber should practise [*sic*] any point in Surgery, the drawing of teeth excepted."[27]

The king's act also assigned four "malefactor" corpses to the company annually for public dissection. The malefactors were executed criminals, dragged from the executioner's block directly to the dissection table to be carved up immediately before the tissues started to putrefy. A professor or physician* would read the lecture in anatomy while a barber-surgeon labored over the mahogany dissection table in their operating theater on Monkwell Street.[28] The company was allowed to perform private dissections if a surgeon had an interesting case or a professor wanted to demonstrate to his students, as long as it was performed in the theater of the Common Hall. This regulation, which applied to embalming too, wasn't often enforced as evidenced by the home embalming of Maria Van Butchell. Interestingly enough, item 60 of the 1604 bylaws stipulate, "Anatomies to be decently buried," which could be interpreted to mean anything, but probably was a better lot than the usual disposition a criminal could hope for.[29]

The malefactors, and the additional private anatomies, may be the reason the company felt like they could lay a legitimate claim to embalming, for purposes of preservation for scientific study—in addition to their intimate knowledge of the human body through their study of the "mystery" of surgery. It was during this time period that anatomists such as Leonardo da Vinci tinkered with embalming methods to preserve the structures they were studying, but there is no surviving record of the British barber-surgeons actually embalming a malefactor prior to dissection. Despite this fact, the company saw other trades such as butchers, smiths, and chandlers encroaching on their territory and decided to put a stop to it. In 1604, the company applied for a new charter, in which clause 16 declares, "The openinge,

---

* The College of Physicians was a separate guild that practiced medicine and thought themselves superior to surgeons. The two companies clashed occasionally, and as evidenced by a 1595 letter to the master of the Barber-Surgeons cautioning them against "practising [*sic*] physic." Sidney Young, *The Annals of the Barber-Surgeons of London* (London: Blades, East, & Blades, 1890), 125.

searinge and imbalmeinge of the dead corpes to be p'ply belongeinge to the science of Barbery and Surgery."[30] Clause 16 enumerates the reason the other "mechanical" trades shouldn't be entrusted with the preservation of human remains in graphic detail: "Theire unskillfull searinge and imbalmeinge, the corpes corrupteth and groweth p'nthe contagious and ofensive to the place and p'sons approachinge."[31]

The embalming and "searing" techniques practiced by barber-surgeons in the Middle Ages and early modern periods were far more rudimentary than what anatomists such as William Hunter later employed after the discovery of vascular injection. The differing methodologies were ostensibly linked to Egyptian embalming by the medical practitioners, who were educated men that could read Greek and Latin and had studied Herodotus's account. However, Hunter disputed any connection between the new methods and the ancient ones. He was critical of Egyptian methods, saying in his embalming lecture:

> [T]he embalmer had taken out all the Viscera of the head, Thorax and Abdomen and cut all the flesh off the bones, and cavities of the Thorax & Abdomen were filled up with Tar, Pitch &c and the form of the leg, Thigh &c were altogether made up of linen Rigs dipp'd in Tar, Pitch &c so that I have the Opinion that they were allow'd to carry the dead Body home by pretending to embalm it to preserve the Flesh &c, but you see they either buried or burnt the Flesh.[32]

Despite Hunter's objections—Hunter, in fairness, may not have completely understood or appreciated from observation alone the seventy-day process that occurred at the *wabt wat*—there are certainly similarities to the Egyptian methodology. There also seems to be a conscious effort to improve on the Egyptian paradigm using "modern" techniques and chemicals. In addition to disembowelment (which would remain part of the process until the mid-nineteenth century when strong fluids such as zinc chloride and arsenic were able to arrest decomposition in the soft tissues by vascular injection alone, and later aided by the invention of the trocar by Samuel Rogers in 1880), the barber-surgeons achieved preservation in the appendages by making deep longitudinal cuts and packing them with spices and powders.[33] The procedure was documented in the sixteenth century by the French barber-surgeon Ambrose Paré:

> [T]he bodie which is to bee enbalmed [*sic*] with spices for very long continuance, must first be embowelled, keeping the heart apart that it may be embalmed and kept as the kinsfolk think fit . . . Then you shall make deep incisions along the arms, thighs, etc., to let out the blood and give space for putting in the aromatic powders. The whole body should be washed over with aqua vitae and strong vinegar . . . then the spices . . . shall be stuffed in and the incisions sewn up, and then let the whole bodie bee anointed with turpentine dissolved with oil of roses and camomile . . . then let it be strewed over again with the fore-mentioned powder, then wrap in a linen cloth and then in searcloths.* Lastly let it be put in a coffin of lead and filled up with dry sweet herbs.[34]

The "aromatic powders" described by Paré were most likely a proprietary mixture he devised through experimentation. In 1562, the Dutch physician Peter Forestus† documented his embalming of Countess Hauterkerken. His recipe for aromatic powders included "two and a half lbs. aloes; myrrh, 1½ lbs.; ordinary wermut, seven handsfull; rosemary, four handsful; pumice, 1½ lbs.; marjoram, 4 lbs; storacis calamata, 2 loht; the zeltlinalipta muscata, ½ loht."[35]

Despite the burgeoning interest and advances in embalming technology, there was little that could be done throughout the Middle Ages and Renaissance for the aristocracy, royalty, and military leaders who died abroad. It would be well into the mid-nineteenth century by the time scientific and medical advances, coupled with shrinking travel times, made shipping human remains great distances a reality. As it still is today, getting the remains home for burial is a critical step in the grieving process. That's the reason the American military's Mortuary Affairs Operations

---

* *Searcloth* is a Middle English term that morphed into *cerecloth*. Cerecloth is a waxed sheet that was waterproof, thus making it the choice for wrapping human remains before they were encoffined. The cerecloth wrapping was made airtight with beeswax, thus further keeping the remains preserved. Shakespeare mentions in act 2, scene 7 of *The Merchant of Venice*, "To rib her cerecloth in the obscure grave."

† Forestus also documented the embalming of Pope Alexander V.

goes to such exhaustive lengths to recover the remains of fallen soldiers and return them home, even if multiple decades have elapsed.

Medieval Europeans devised a simple remedy: *mos teutonicus*, otherwise known as independent bone burial. This elegant solution, if not a gruesome process, prevented the spread of disease associated with shipping decomposing remains and precluded burial on foreign soil.

Throughout history there have been exceptions to shipping human remains, usually for great leaders. The Spartans used honey in 380 BCE to preserve King Agesipolis I to transport him home for burial.[36] This wasn't necessarily novel thinking on the Spartans' part as Herodotus had previously recorded the Assyrians using honey to embalm their dead. But the sticky, viscous liquid works if you can get enough of it. The Macedonians filled a golden sarcophagus with honey to transport Alexander the Great home from Babylon in 323 BCE.[37] Alcohol works well too. Two millennia after Alexander the Great was shipped in honey, the highly decorated Major General Edward Pakenham, who commanded the British forces during the War of 1812, was shipped home* in a cask of rum.[38] Typically, the resources (even for royalty) simply weren't available to ship a whole body hundreds or thousands of perilous miles. Enter independent bone burial. The practice appeared in the late eleventh century, around the time of the First Crusade because crusaders wished to have a Christian burial in home soil and in consecrated ground—a paramount concern to Christians during the Middle Ages.

The process of independent bone burial involved "disemboweling and disarticulating the body, cutting off all soft tissues, and then boiling the bones until free of soft tissues."[39] The soft tissues and broth were discarded or buried at the site. Then the dried bones were wrapped in bull hide or placed in a chest and shipped home. Like the reader will see later as embalming was offered only to officers during the American Civil War, this service was only available to people with means. The *best* the rank and file could hope for was to be buried where they fell.

Independent bone burial was denounced by Pope Boniface III in 1300 about the time the Crusades were petering out. The Holy See said the practice was "an abuse of abominable savagery, practiced by

---

* When the cask arrived back in England, it was accidentally shipped back to the United States, where thirsty Charlestonians drank the tapped keg. It wasn't until the keg was empty that Pakenham's body was discovered.

some of the faithful in a horrible and inconsiderate manner."[40] But Pope Boniface only made things worse. Monks were the only ones at the time who possessed the knowledge and skill for *mos teutonicus,* and after the edict they were unable to continue to practice. The practice of slicing up and boiling a human devolved to the camp butchers.[41]

The arrival of the butchers and the promise of eternal damnation in hell did little to stem the practice. Edward of York and the Earl of Suffolk, who died at the Battle of Agincourt in 1415 during the Hundred Years War, were boiled and their bones returned to England.[42] Later, when King Henry V of England, who was celebrated as the victor of Agincourt, died in France in 1422, his bones were boiled to "obtain a perfect skeleton" and placed in a coffin for burial in Westminster Abbey, but not before the coffin containing the bones was taken into Notre Dame for a Requiem Mass—a mass for the dead.[43] Papal dispensation in cases like these was sought after the fact (and granted). And like most royalty of the time, Henry was buried *in* the church.

Emperor Constantine set the precedent in 337 CE when his remains were buried in the vestibule of the Church of Holy Apostles in Constantinople.[44] This concept of burial within the church wasn't entirely new. Christians had already begun erecting churches over the sites of martyrdom such as St. Peter's Basilica in Rome where Saint Peter was crucified or the Church of the Holy Sepulchre in Jerusalem where Jesus was crucified. But Constantine's burial in the Church of the Holy Apostles marked the start of a trend of Christians—non-martyr and nonclergy—opting to be buried within the walls of an established church. This was a natural progression for Christians, who before Constantine were forced to worship in secret, often at altars constructed in the necropoli such that they were literally surrounded by their dead.

Soon after Constantine's death, the pious were clamoring for space within the church walls—the closer to the altar, the closer to God. Burial within the church became a common practice for anyone who could afford it, and something that created controversy within the Roman Catholic Church for hundreds of years. During Roman times, burials were relegated to outside the city walls, as public health officials feared the spread of disease, for good reason. Intramural burial, as burial inside a church is called, polluted the space with foul odors for worshippers and certainly led to undocumented health issues. The Italian physician Bernardino Ramazzini noted in his seminal work *De Morbis Artificum Diatriba*, "There are so many tombs in the church, and they are so often opened that this abominable smell is too often unmistakable. However much they fumigate the sacred edifices with incense, myrrh, and other aromatic odors it is obviously very injurious to those present."[45] Despite the misgivings of church and government officials, the faithful dead continued to be entombed and inhumed within the church walls, spilling out into churchyards called "God's acre." The demand for burials on church property gave rise to another vocation that further wrested the control of the dead from the grip of the church to laity: the sexton. The sexton was an under officer of the church whose main duties included digging graves and tolling bells. In a time before mass communication and when much of the population was illiterate, the church bells alerted the community to important events—including announcing deaths and Requiem Masses.

The sexton is a role that would continue for centuries and morph into the role of the sexton undertaker in colonial America. Because the sexton made the grave preparations (and controlled the permitting process, essentially giving them a burial monopoly), families began calling on the sexton to handle the other funeral details, such as laying out the body and presiding over the procession.[46] Peter Relyea, the sexton of the Willett Street Methodist Episcopal Church in Manhattan, who was called upon to handle President Lincoln's funeral, evidences this.

Other vocations, following the sexton's lead, began to dabble in undertaking. Carpenters, cabinetmakers, drapers, heralds, upholsters, and chandlers started advertising the accoutrements (coffins, mourning cloth, shrouds, carriages, and candles) and services needed to bury the dead. William Boyce, the proprietor of Whight Hart & Coffin, was the first recorded undertaker in 1675 offering complete furnishings: "You May Be Furnished with all sort & sizes of Coffins & Shrouds Ready Made And all other Convenience Belonging to Funerals."[47]

The odd amalgam of barber-surgeons finally split in 1745. It appears that embalming, protected by the barber-surgeons' great political clout for the previous two centuries, was largely forgotten by the Company of

Surgeons* as they moved to pursue the exciting scientific breakthroughs happening in medicine.

Certainly, The Barbers' Company (as they were known after the split), who was now only officially acting as hairdressers and shavers, couldn't lay claim to this "medical" practice. Thus embalming falls by the wayside only to be picked up by the funeral furnishers, many of whom were operating within the Upholders' Company. *Upholder* is an antiquated term for a furniture dealer and repairer. Because of their trade reupholstering furniture, it was a natural fit for them to buy coffins from the coffin maker and line them.

In 1722 London undertakers attempted to form their own trade group, the United Company of Undertakers, but it was not admitted to the guildhall, and the association slowly began to dissolve, disappearing altogether in 1748.[48] British undertakers continued to offer their burial services in conjunction with their regular trade for the next century and a half—and to slowly wrest control of embalming† from anatomists and surgeons—until the undertakers formally organized in 1894 to form the British Institute of Undertakers.

The funeral furnisher's counterpart in America was the tradesman undertaker, emerging around the same time, at the end of the seventeenth century. The benefit the tradesmen undertakers had was they didn't have to work within the confines of the trade guilds like their English counterparts. The tradesmen undertakers didn't take up embalming in earnest until the outbreak of the Civil War, when Americans adopted the new sanitary science as part of the American burial tradition. With no such conflict in England, embalming never quite caught on with the same ferocity as in America.

The anatomists and barber-surgeons of England and greater Europe took the scant recorded knowledge of the Egyptian embalmers and classical anatomical teachings of Galen, and using the explosion of knowledge and ideas of the Renaissance, developed and refined techniques and chemicals for preserving tissues that would lead to the rise of modern embalming.

But nothing fired up the public's imagination and interest like Dr. Van Butchell's embalmed wife on display in his home. Mrs. Van Butchell

---

* Now called the Royal College of Surgeons.
† The British Embalmers' Society was formed in 1900.

remained on display in the Hunterian Museum for 126 years after her husband's death. A fire in 1941 caused by a Luftwaffe bombing raid destroyed her.[49] Though he's gone down in history books as somewhat of a quack, Van Butchell can't be accused of being a poor dentist. A man viewing Mrs. Van Butchell's remains eighty-two years after her death marveled at "[her] remarkably fine set of teeth."[50]

CHAPTER 5

Mourning Gloves and Liquor

Early American Burial Practices

L ucas Wyngaard died in 1756. He was unmarried and the last of his lineage, leaving an estate of some size. The Wyngaards were of Dutch descent, having settled in the Albany, New York, area. The Dutch explorer Adriaen Block, who explored the coastal area off New England between 1611 and 1614, is said to have named Martha's Vineyard* after one of Lucas's ancestors, Martin. Skipper Block named it Martin Wyngaard's Island. The name was later bastardized to Martha's Vineyard.[1]

The Wyngaards aren't remembered for their Vineyard claim to fame. No, they're remembered because Lucas's repast devolved into uncontrolled debauchery. A piece published in *Harper's New Monthly Magazine* recounted that the mourners returned to Lucas's home and consumed a pipe of wine.[2] A pipe is an old-fashioned cask size, equal to a butt, which holds 126 gallons.

The article goes on to describe "dozens of pounds" of tobacco consumed. This was an Irish tradition, in which even nonsmokers were expected to offer at least a ceremonial puff at wakes.[3] The revelers, thoroughly intoxicated on wine and nicotine, smashed "grosses" of pipes as

---

* Other sources claim the island was named as early as 1602 by the eventual founder of the Jamestown Colony, Bartholomew Gosnold, after his eldest daughter, Martha.

well as every single glass and decanter in the house. The party ended when the inebriated pallbearers kindled a fire with their scarves, which had been given to them as mourning gifts.[4]

The actual services aside, Wyngaard's funeral neatly encapsulates the funeral experience: a booze-soaked repast and mourning gifts.

The journey from cradle to grave took a scant thirty years in colonial America.[5] Infant deaths went unrecorded, so their numbers can only be guessed at.[6] Three out of nine children (the average number of births in a Puritan family) died before their twenty-first birthday, and a child only had a 74 percent chance of making it to their tenth birthday.[7] Death literally lurked around every corner for the colonists. Childhood illnesses such as measles, whooping cough, and mumps, and other diseases such as malaria, yellow fever, consumption, typhoid fever, dysentery, and influenza were common. Farming and manufacturing accidents, wars, and general lawlessness were other causes of death high on the list. Most deaths took place in the home. As such, colonists had a frequent and intimate relationship with death.

Early funerals in America were very different than the extravagant affairs they morphed into in the Gilded Age. Puritan burial customs were based on *A Directory for the Publique Worship of God*, a worship manual that replaced the Book of Common Prayer in 1644. It stated, "When any person departeth this life, let the dead body, upon the day of burial, be decently attended from the house to the place appointed for publick burial and there immediately interred, without any ceremony."[8] Essentially, there was no service, but the community would come together in solidarity. Eliu Lechford wrote in 1645, "At burials nothing is read, nor any funeral sermon made, but all the neighborhood or a goodly number of them come together by the tolling of the bell, and carry the dead solemnly to his grave, and then stand by him while he is buried."[9]

If a family was unsure of how to handle their dead, a local woman was called to wash and dress the body. These women, who often functioned as midwives as well, came to be called layers-out of the dead. *The Philadelphia Directory for 1810* lists fourteen such layers-out, all women, a role that was their entrée as tradesman undertakers.[10] In contemporary America, families wishing assistance of a home funeral can call on a death doula or layperson versed in home funerals for verbal instruction* on how to perform the washing and dressing, similar to the role of layer-out of the dead.

In colonial America, the family took the local carpenter a piece of knotted string cut to the length of the decedent, and spacing of the knots representing the width at the elbows.[11] Coffins were single-break, flat-lidded affairs slathered with pitch on the interior joints to seal them with four inches of bran and sawdust placed in the bottom.[12] The purpose of the pitch sealant and sawdust was to prevent leaking until the burial. The carpenter included all wood scraps and shavings in the completed coffin, as the superstition was that if another person touched the wood scraps they would become death's next victim.

An article from the undertaker's journal *The Sunnyside* describes typical coffin construction of the time:

> Coffins were mostly made of wild cherry half-inch board . . . the sides and ends stained red with cam-wood whisky [*sic*] stain and rubbed off with shavings, which soon dried. The lid was polished with beeswax, which was applied with a hot smoothing iron . . . coffins were without any lining, and a handful of the softest [wood] shavings were saved for a pillow with a piece of course [*sic*] muslin tacked over it.[13]

Death notices weren't printed due to the fact that most newspapers were weeklies. The dead were usually in the ground within a day or two, so notification was made by word of mouth. In villages and towns the news spread naturally by local gossip. Larger colonial cities had a death crier to roam the streets. In New York, the "Inviter to Funerals," as the death crier was called, ensured citizens knew the details of the obsequies. The first "Inviter," John van Gelder, was approved by the "court of mayor and alderman" in 1684 to "comport himselfe Civilly" by those who enlisted his services.[14] Van Gelder and his successors were licensed by the city and could charge eight to eighteen shillings depending on the age of the person. Any family member caught inviting friends to a funeral was

---

* With current state licensing laws, a person assisting in a home funeral can only offer verbal instruction to family members or run the risk of providing unlicensed funeral services.

subject to a forty-shilling fine.[15] In Pennsylvania, where the population was more spread out, men on horseback called "warners" took to the countryside with the grim news.[16] A family of means might send a set of mourning gloves along with a printed card that read "Invitation to follow the corps [*sic*]" to a prominent citizen or local dignitary whose attendance was especially desired.[17] The invitation didn't preclude others from showing up to follow the corps as the privatization of funerals—by invite only—didn't begin until the early nineteenth century. Funerals in early America were very much a community affair.

The decedent was laid out for viewing in their bed or in the parlor on a newly constructed coffin resting between sawhorses. The Scotch tradition of providing guests liquor when they crossed the threshold of a house in mourning, and then again when they viewed the decedent, immigrated across the Atlantic.[18] So, at funerals like Lucas Wyngaard's, the guests began to get tipsy before the body was even in the ground and the repast began.

The body was carried—if the pallbearers were still ambulatory after consuming copious amounts of funeral liquor—from the house to the place of burial on the "herse," which bore little resemblance to the modern, motorized hearse. This "herse" was a draped litter upon which candles were mounted. Copying English fashion, elegies—or poems lamenting loss—were tacked to the herse for the journey to the grave.[19] The coffin was draped with a pall, a cloth sometimes called a bier-cloth or mort-cloth, owned by the town and stored on the porch of the meetinghouse.[20] The pall is a carryover from the Greek *pallium*, or cloak, when the dead were carried on a litter to their burial place enshrouded by their pallium.[21] In Nicolas Poussin's painting *The Funeral of Phocion*, two body bearers carry the Athenian statesman who was sentenced to die by drinking hemlock. Phocion's body is wrapped in cloth, his pallium. Even when "chested" burials became *de rigueur*,* the tradition of the pall remained. The purpose morphed from the simple dignity of covering the dead to a symbolic one that reminds mortals that everyone is equal in the eyes of God.

Two sets of bearers were assigned to the procession. The bearers bore the actual weight of the coffin—as well as the "herse" upon which it rested—while the pallbearers, typically older men, held the pall in place.

---

* In England and Europe. We'll see in a later chapter that almost all American burials were "chested."

Ostensibly, the pallbearers had to guide the underbearers because custom dictated the massive piece of black cloth cover the heads and torsos of the underbearers. If the distance to the grave was significant, a second set of underbearers stood at the ready to fulfill their corporal act of mercy.[22]

The notion of the "rural cemetery"—what we think of in the twenty-first century when we hear the word *cemetery*—wouldn't be created until the mid-nineteenth century. Burial took place at the churchyard, in the town commons, or on in a private family lot, all places an ambulatory funeral cortege could easily access. There, the body was placed in a grave prepared by a sexton or family members and wordlessly filled.

A funeral sermon would be preached, but weeks after the burial and then printed for distribution, despite the fact that the majority of the population was functionally illiterate. The Puritan press specialized in mourning broadsides of funeral sermons and elegies. The gruesomely decorated pamphlets typically featured skeletons, scythes, hourglasses, and coffins, helpful reminders of the hellfire and damnation that awaited.[23]

By the turn of the eighteenth century, colonists began shedding the austere burial practices, even though the *Boston News-Letter* reported as late as 1730 that an address—a sermon—at a funeral was rare.[24] The earliest example of a "funeral address" was in 1683 during the funeral of Pastor Elam Adams in Roxbury, Massachusetts, who had prayers said at the house prior to the burial procession.[25] Robert Habenstein and William Lamers theorize in *The History of American Funeral Directing* that this shift was caused by "urbanization and its concomitant secularization, and the rapid expansion of industry and trade had begun to weaken the theocratic organization of the New England Colonies."[26]

The pendulum rapidly swung from austerity to vulgarity.

The expense of a colonial funeral far exceeded that of a modern funeral, as much as one-fifth of the entire estate in the case of Waitstill Winthrop, a magistrate in the Salem witch trials who died in 1717.[27] The expense of an eighteenth-century funeral had nothing to do with the costs typically associated with funerals today: casket, services of the funeral director, cemetery plot. No, the crippling costs arose from food, alcohol, and mourning gifts.

Mourning gifts—gifts given to attendees by the bereaved—were a vestige of the English feudal funeral.[28] Mourning clothes known as dooles were distributed.[29] The word is equivalent to *dole*, meaning a pittance, and is derived from the Latin *doleo*, "to grieve." Thus the custom of "giving doole" means to offer something in grief.[30] Giving doole made its way across the Atlantic and became a way of displaying social status in the colonies. Rings, scarves, gloves, brooches, pendants, bracelets, spoons, fans, and books were common luxury items distributed to funeral-goers.

Jonathan Belcher's wife, Mary Partridge Belcher, died on October 6, 1736, while he was concurrently serving as the royal governor of the Massachusetts Bay Colony and New Hampshire. Unlike most royal governors, Belcher was American. Born to an extremely wealthy Boston merchant, Belcher attended Harvard, and in 1729, at the age of forty-seven, received royal appointment from King George II to govern both colonies.

Belcher was a member of the gentry with significant political clout, so it was natural for him to reinforce his social position by giving away over a thousand pairs of gloves while Mary lay in repose for two days at Province House (the governor's mansion).[31] On October 8, the procession commenced "thro Cornhill Street went down fro[m] our front into Kingstreet went as far as Colo[ne]l Fitche['s] house turn'd up street on South side off Town house to burying Ground."[32]

Belcher would marry again, and later died in Elizabethtown on August 31, 1757, while governor of New Jersey.* His will stipulated he be buried in Cambridge with his cousin Judge Jonathan Remington. The distance between the two towns is well over two hundred miles, and traveling the rustic colonial roads—that were nothing more than muddy tracks through wilderness—the journey would've taken days. Given the distance and "hot, sultry season" as recorded by Caleb Smith in the postscript of Belcher's biography, Belcher was likely "emboweled and put in a Cere-cloth," as Judge Samuel Sewall of Boston noted in his diary as the procedure for delayed burials.[33]

His dear and visibly ill friend Aaron Burr,† the second president of Princeton University, preached Belcher's funeral sermon on September 4 in Elizabethtown. Despite protestations from his wife, Burr made the forty-mile journey in the sweltering heat to lead the funeral and was described as

---

* Belcher founded the College of New Jersey that was later renamed Princeton.
† Father of the third vice president of the United States, Aaron Burr. When Burr, Sr., died, his son wasn't yet two years old.

"fitter for a sick bed than to have been in the pulpit."[34] The description was accurate. Burr died twenty days later. He was forty-one years old.

After services in New Jersey, Belcher was transported to Cambridge and buried at Old Burying Ground. It's unknown the extent of the mourning gifts distributed at the governor's funeral.

A year and a half after the death of Mary Belcher, a rich slaver named Andrew Faneuil died in Boston in February of 1738. Faneuil was an odd bachelor, stipulating to his nephews Peter and Benjamin that he'd leave his fortune to them as long as they didn't marry.[35] Benjamin decided he enjoyed the company of the fairer sex, and he got hitched, leaving Peter to inherit most of Uncle Andrew's staggering fortune of £50,000, or roughly $7.7 million in today's money. In light of his windfall, Peter threw his dear uncle a funeral worthy of royalty. The *Boston News-Letter* reported, "[A]bove 1,100 Persons of all Ranks, beside the Mourners, following the Corpse, also a vast Number of Spectators were gathered for the Occasion."[36] Over three thousand pairs of gloves were given away by Peter to commemorate the event.[37] Peter was only able to enjoy the fortune for five years before dying, but not before erecting Faneuil Hall for the city of Boston. Peter left his uncle's fortune to his sister, and, ironically, Benjamin.

Mourning gifts weren't solely for the wealthy. Even working-class families were expected to at least provide gloves for the minister and pallbearers. This tradition led the Reverend Dr. Andrew Eliot, pastor of New North Church (not be confused with the "one, if by land, and two, if by sea" church made famous by Paul Revere which is Old North Church) in Boston, to keep scrupulous records. In his thirty-two years he collected a staggering 2,940 pairs of gloves.[38] Granted, a minister could expect to receive gloves for marrying a couple and baptizing a baby. Even if only a third of the gloves were from funerals, that means Eliot averaged 2.5 funerals a month his entire career, which lends credence to his popularity. Eliot was one of the few clergy who remained in the city during the siege of Boston. He sold the gloves, of varying quality, to local milliners for the tidy sum of $600.[39] Eliot also left a mugful of mourning rings when he died.[40]

The earliest known dated mourning ring in America is a braided gold ring manufactured by the Boston jeweler Jeremiah Dummer in 1693 to commemorate James Lloyd, who died August 21.[41] It's a simple ring of crossed lines to form a diamond pattern with some of the original black enamel still visible. As mourning gifts became the norm, mourning jewelry embraced the Puritan fascination with death. Winged skulls, a coffin with a skeleton in it, and gemstones cut into the shape of a coffin were all popular designs. The finger jewelry often featured cheerfully morbid mottos such as "Prepare to follow me" or "Death conquers all" to remind the wearer of their proximity to the grave.

Later in the century, when Andrew Eliot would've been preaching, rings featured the hair of the decedent and neoclassical mourning motifs such as cinerary urns and weeping willow trees. One of the earliest known hair jewelry pieces dates from 1704. A century later, hair jewelry was wildly popular and jewelers were paying cash for twenty to thirty inches of hair.[42] Finely chopped hair was incorporated into the pigment used to paint the mourning scene or the hair became the feature itself, braided or woven.

Jewelers were known to have premade mourning rings, and would often get orders for rings of different weights. The closer kinship received the weightier rings. It was common for different quality mourning gifts to be distributed. In 1633, Samuel Fuller, a respected physician in Plymouth Colony who made the journey to America on the Mayflower, died. He stipulated in his will that his sister was to get gloves worth twelve shillings, while Rebecca Prime, a commoner, was to get gloves worth two shillings, sixpence.[43]

Judge Samuel Sewall amassed quite a collection of mourning jewelry. In addition to being a prosperous Boston merchant, he was a justice of the Superior Court of Judicature. He even served as a magistrate (along with the aforementioned Waitstill Winthrop) on the convened Court of Oyer and Terminer during the Salem witch trials. Sewall is possibly best remembered for his later voiced public regret for his role in the kangaroo court that executed twenty innocent people, including Giles Corey, who was subjected to the particularly barbarous method of pressing.

Sewall's greatest historical legacy was his diary. He chronicled daily life and happenings in the Massachusetts Bay Colony (including many, many funerals) from 1674 to 1729, including comments about the mourning gifts, such as this entry from April 19, 1717, writing about the funeral of a friend's grandmother: "I had a Scarf and Ring.

Coming and going were in danger of oversetting the Calash.* But did not through the goodness of God. Got home well. *Laus Deo.*"†⁴⁴ It's no surprise with all the funerals he attended that when Sewall died in 1730 he left fifty-seven mourning rings to his heirs.⁴⁵ Undoubtedly, many of them were weightier ones, given Sewall's lofty position.

Mourning gifts still exist but in a much more economical fashion. Memorial cards and folders are handed out as mementos at funerals today. It's also common for the family to give packets of seeds at the funeral, so the blooming flowers are a reminder of the deceased in the same way mourning scarves were meant to be sewn into shirts after the funeral to be a daily reminder. The cost of a little cardstock or packets of seeds is much more manageable to the bereaved than rings costing a pound apiece, about sixty dollars in today's money. Of course, leaving a drawerful of prayer cards as a (monetary) legacy isn't the same as a "mugful" of pricey mourning rings.

Gifts weren't the only financial hardship associated with colonial mourning. Often their cost paled in comparison to the ruinous costs of the repast. Gathering for a post-funeral meal is nothing new; the practice dates back to antiquity. The act of communing over food has emotional and spiritual benefits, which why it's common in many cultures. It also serves a practical purpose: to refresh the weary traveler.

In colonial America, friends and family braved treacherous travel on the rutted tracks that passed for roads on journeys that might take days. Rightfully, they expected to be housed and fed. Most of all they looked forward—and expected—to be lubricated with liberal amounts of booze. A funeral was the one occasion when colonials broke from the daily monotony of work to gather and socialize, and the only time Puritan forefathers condoned alcohol consumption. Nathaniel Hawthorne observed, "[Funerals were] one of the only class of scenes, so far as my investigation has taught me, in which our ancestors were wont to steep their tough old hearts in wine and strong drink, and indulge an outbreak of grisly jollity."⁴⁶

There was a colonial aphorism that when a child was born, the parents began stockpiling wine for the wedding or the funeral.⁴⁷ Given the

---

* An open carriage with facing passenger seats.
† "Praise be to God."

custom of getting mourners good and lubricated, sage prerevolutionary parents were smart to squirrel away an extra spirituous jug if they could spare it, especially given child mortality rates. Lucas Wyngaard's funeral, though perhaps an extreme example, evidences the proportion of the funeral bill tied up in intoxicants, as does David Porter's funeral.

Porter hailed from London. While visiting friends in Hartford on a steamy June day in 1678, he decided to go for a refreshing swim in the Connecticut River. His swimming skills didn't match the current and he drowned. The circumstances of his death aren't that unusual, nor did Porter leave a lasting legacy. The bit of immortality he achieved has to do with the estate inventory presented in Hartford court on December 5, 1678:

By [*sic*] a pint of Lyqr to those that dived for him 1s

By a qrt of Lyqr to those that brought him home 2s

By 2 qrts of wine & gall of sydr to ye Jury of Inquest,. 5s, 4p

By 8 galls & 3 qrts wine for the funeral cost £1, 15s

By a barrel of sydr for do. [funeral?] Cost 16s

By a coffin, cost, ...12s

By a winding sheets, cost, ...18s

By to pay for the grave, &c . . . . .5s[48]

It cost Porter's estate almost twice the amount to lubricate everyone involved with the obsequies than it did to furnish poor Porter with a coffin and winding sheet. Winding sheets are no longer used, but to approximate them to the cost of a casket and vault in modern times would mean the liquor bill (at double the combined cost of the casket and vault) for a funeral would be in the high four or low five figures. That's a lot of "lyqr."

In the event of a pauper's death, the town provided the libations—two or three gallons of rum or a barrel of cider—to those townsfolk who pitched in to provide the corporal act of mercy.[49] When a minister died, the church was responsible for providing the liquor; the vestige of the tradition survives today.[50] Some congregations will provide a repast for members (often without the booze). By 1741, a large enough majority of people were fed up with the exorbitant cost to die that a Massachusetts Provincial Enactment was ordered that stated that "no

Scarves, Gloves (except six pair to the bearers and one pair to each minister of the church of congregation where any deceased person belongs), Wine, Rum, or rings be allowed to be given at any funeral upon the penalty of fifty pounds."[51] Old habits die hard, especially when the only bit of joy and sanctioned inebriation comes from a funeral (of all occasions). An unnamed citizen was quoted as saying bitterly, "Temperance has done for funerals."[52]

Of course, some citizens simply ignored the new laws.

Caleb Davis died July 6, 1797, at the ripe old age of fifty-eight in his house on Common Street (now Tremont) across from what is now the Wilbur Theatre in Boston. Davis was described as a "capable, public-spirited citizen," having been elected to the general court as a representative several times, and he held many other political appointments, including ratifying the Constitution at the Massachusetts Convention in 1788.[53] In his private life, he was equally as prolific, having interests in sugar refining and banking.[54] In short, Davis was an important citizen of Boston when he died. As such, his funeral reflected it.

The repast menu included beef, fowl, Spanish *and* French bacon, ham, fish, oysters, 150 eggs, peas and onions, and twenty-five pounds of potatoes; for dessert: cheese, fruit, raisins, and sweetmeats. The menu also included rum, wine (122 bottles total), beer, gin, and brandy. Based on the number of chairs rented for the event, it's estimated 110 people—all men—attended the repast.[55] Each guest was allotted at least one 32-ounce bottle of wine—unlike today's standard bottles that hold 25.3 ounces. There's no doubt the mourners left revelers.

The total bill of fare was $420. Davis's coffin cost $16—about six times the normal price of the time, but less than 4 percent of the cost of the funeral dinner and less than 2 percent of the total funeral bill.[56]

In an interesting little incestuous funereal twist, Davis's first wife (of three) was Hannah Ruggles, daughter of Samuel A. Selectman, the master builder who constructed Faneuil Hall.[57] Of course, it was Peter Faneuil—who distributed three thousand pairs of gloves at the funeral of his uncle—who donated Faneuil Hall to Boston.

The cost of a funeral wasn't only gifts and liquor. Feeding the masses wasn't cheap. The repast wasn't simply a kindness to travelers; it was another feudal tradition the settlers brought from the old country. People have been using food to commune with the dead at ancestral burial places for thousands of years. The Egyptians and Romans formalized the practice with kitchens at the mausoleums, and that tradition morphed into the *averil* in feudal Europe. *Averil* translates literally to "heir ale," meaning it was the banquet not necessarily only to commemorate the dead but also to welcome the successor, or heir.[58] Puckle quantifies the averil as "an unrestricted gorge, wherein the honour of the bereaved family was thought to depend much upon the quality and above all the quantity, both of liquid and solid."[59]

As soon as the British, Dutch, French, and Scotch-Irish settlers gained some stability and prosperity, the averil intercalated itself as a tradition into the colonial funeral experience, though in many instances the repast wasn't paid for in sterling but rather the common colonial trade method of bartering goods and services.

John Griggs died in Virginia in 1676 at the age of twenty-three. His father (also John Griggs, who died at age twenty-two) had been granted land in York County as well as a home upon his arrival from London. Young Griggs, at two years old, inherited the land upon his father's death. The parcel was sizeable enough that when young Griggs died, he warranted a considerable funeral feast. The repast consisted of "turkeys, geese, other domestic poultry, a pig, several bushels of flour, twenty pounds of butter, sugar and spice and six gallons of cider and six of rum."[60] The total bill of fare cost the estate 1,750 pounds of tobacco.[61]

It wasn't unusual in agrarian areas for goods and services, even funeral expenses, to be bartered for, like in the case of Griggs, well into the twentieth century. The post-funeral meal is a piece of the funeral rite that's survived more or less unchanged since antiquity: friends and family gathering after the last clod of sod has been tamped into the earth to commune over food and drink. The shift is the proportion of the total funeral expenses. The modern repast typically runs in the neighborhood of 10 to 20 percent of the total funeral expenses, whereas three centuries ago that percentage would be flipped, the food and liquor comprising 80 to 90 percent of the total expenses. It's almost become a colloquialism, as I hear people say on a weekly basis: "When I go, I told my family just have a big party for me." It certainly seems, at least anecdotally, that there's a cultural momentum toward this retro-funeral practice of the funeral meal playing a larger role in the obsequies.

Mourning fell out of fashion for several decades as a result of the sumptuary laws. In the course of history this is nothing new—a government regulating the amount (the excessive waste!) its citizens can spend on the dead. The Athenian statesman Solon decreed no more than three robes and a bull could be placed on a cremation pyre, and the Romans enacted regulations during the reign of Constantine to prevent excessive spending on paraphernalia and funeral-procession ostentation.[62] In the sixteenth century, England passed laws "restricting the use of mourning as to quantity and dictating also the quality of the materials."[63] It was funerals like that of John de Vere, the thirteenth Earl of Oxford, where nine hundred mourning cloaks were distributed that led to the passage of mourning restrictions.[64] A century later, England passed the Burial in Woolen Act in 1666 that required burial shrouds to be made from wool rather than the traditional linen. This wasn't a direct sumptuary law but something dreamed up by wool merchants that had the same effect of regulating the amount a person could spend on a shroud.

The American efforts of regulating funeral costs came to a screeching halt on a wintry day on the eve of the nineteenth century. George Washington died and mourning came roaring into fashion, with patriotic fervor.

Washington, fastidiously punctual, remained in wet riding clothes on December 12, 1799, after a day inspecting his farm in sleet and snow so he wouldn't be late for dinner.[65] The decision killed him.

The following day brought a sore throat.

The day after, Martha sent for Washington's personal physician, Dr. James Craik, when he awoke with labored breathing. Washington was bled, a treatment he demanded, the fourth and final bleeding drawing off two pints of blood. "Blood ran very slowly—appeared very thick," a witness in the sickroom recorded.[66] Approximately four pints were bled from Washington that day. A modern blood donation collects two pints. If Washington had a fighting chance prior to the bleeding, it was gone. It is unknown exactly what Washington contracted, but based on this sore throat, it was likely the flu, strep throat, or even diphtheria, a common bacterial killer at the time.

Around 10:00 p.m. Washington called Tobias Lear to his bedside. "Have me decently buried," he said to his secretary, "and do not let my body be put in the vault in less than three days after I am dead. Do you understand me?"

To which Lear replied, "Yes."

"'Tis well," Washington replied.[67]

Washington died minutes later. It was Saturday, December 14, 1799.

Martha directed his body be moved to the New Room, the drawing room, to lie in repose.

Washington's relatives began arriving the next day. Due to the suspicious nature of his death, Craik and Dr. William Thornton[*] lobbied for a speedy burial lest Washington died of something contagious. Wednesday was settled upon.[68] That date would fulfill Washington's request of waiting at least three days before burial, certainly a common practice at the time, and a request Martha was intent on honoring.

Lear dispatched the farm manager, Mr. Anderson, to Alexandria with orders for the Ingle brothers. Joseph and Henry Ingle were undertakers and cabinetmakers located at 112 South Royal Street.[69] Lear contracted them to build a lead-lined mahogany coffin. As was the norm, the coffin was to be built to order. Before the former president was moved from his deathbed, Dr. Elisha Dick, one of the three treating physicians, took measurements.

The Ingle brothers labored around the clock. Around 1:00 p.m. on December 17 the brothers arrived at Mount Vernon in a wagon with George McMunn, a local plumber who built the lead liner, in tow.

The coffin featured two silver plates, the one at the head reading *surge ad judicium* (rise to judgment), and at the midpoint *gloria deo* (glory to God). The Ingle brothers also built a cloth-covered outer burial case. Accompanying the Ingles and McMunn was Michael Gretter, who brought the burial shroud and black pall he and his wife had sewn.[70]

It's unknown who coffined Washington, but it was probably his staff under the direction of Lear. The Ingles were tradesmen undertakers, furnishing a product and not a service, as they have no further documented involvement with the obsequies.

Washington's coffin was placed in the piazza around 11:00 a.m. on the morning of December 18. Despite Dr. Craik's and Dr. Thornton's earlier reservations of Washington dying of a contagious disease, the coffin was opened

---

* Thornton, the architect of the Capitol, had not been part of Washington's treatment team.

and mourners were allowed to file by until 3:00 p.m. when the procession got underway.[71] The "private" affair Washington wanted was anything but. It's estimated that a thousand people showed up at Mount Vernon.[72]

Led by local cavalry and infantry units and a military band, Washington's saddled horse, outfitted with holster and pistol, escorted the bier, borne by Freemasons and officers, as the procession wound down the lawn to the family burial vault near the Potomac.[73] In the background, a schooner anchored in the river fired minute guns.[74]

Crypt-side, Rev. Thomas Davis read a short service and then turned it over to the Freemasons. Three Masonic Lodges were in attendance. Dr. Dick and Rev. Dr. James Muir, minister of the Old Presbyterian Meeting House in Alexandria, recited the Masonic rite from memory, placing his white lambskin Masonic apron and sprig of acacia on Washington's body.[75] The coffin was closed and Washington was placed in the family vault.*

America's greatest patriot had been laid to rest.

The massive funeral party assembled back at the house for the repast. Unlike the tradition of serving mourners a meal, the Washington repast was finger food and, of course, booze. The spread consisted of forty pounds of cake, three large cheeses weighing a total of sixty-one pounds, and thirty-nine gallons of rye whiskey.[76] For the sheer number of people, it is suspected some, or all, of the sixty-seven gallons of apple brandy and sixty gallons of peach brandy that appear on an October 1799 inventory was served.[77] Thirty-nine gallons equates to five ounces of rye per person, not nearly enough to slake the thirst worked up by mourning the former and first commander in chief. It's safe to say Lear ordered some—or all—of the brandy stores released.

The Ingles billed Washington's estate $99.25 for their labors; of that, $88 was for the coffin.[78] Thomas Moyers and Fleming Rich, cabinetmakers in Wythe County, Virginia, charged $10 in 1834 for construction of an adult coffin made of walnut. Adjusting for deflation following the Revolutionary War and War of 1812, that same coffin would've cost $14.50 in 1800, meaning Washington's receptacle cost roughly six times more than the average (not including the cost of the lead liner). It's interesting to note that Moyers & Rich took a barter

---

* McMunn was summoned back Christmas Day, after all the relatives had a chance to view Washington in the vault, to solder on the lid.

payment of 7.5 gallons of apple brandy for a credit of $10.38, or the cost of a coffin.[79]

The Gretters were paid $12 for sewing Washington's shroud and pall. There were some other funeral expenses—namely, outfitting the staff in proper mourning attire. The repast cost a grand total of $7, the amount billed to the estate by George and Judy Edick for baking the forty-pound cake.[80] Unusual for a funeral of the time, as the repast typically weighed disproportionally in the expenses billed to the estate, Washington's repast cost less than 3 percent of the total expenses billed to his estate. The reason: Washington was a big producer of whiskey in Virginia. Twenty-nine gallons of the rye whiskey came from Washington's stills,* the other ten gallons were donated by George Gilpin. The cheese is thought to have come from Washington's farm, as there is no bill for it, so the only expense was for the massive cake.[81]

In Philadelphia, a public funeral was planned based on four resolutions presented by John Marshall, of later fame as chief justice of the Supreme Court, on behalf of the joint committee of both Houses. Marshall's plan would become the basis for the American state funeral,† designed to, as Marshall stated, "let the grand council of the nation display these sentiments of which the nation feels."[82]

In America, a state funeral is for presidents, president-elects, and other people designated by the sitting president. Upon death, the president issues a proclamation to fly flags at half-staff at all government buildings, and will issue an executive order for a national day of mourning. Elements of a state funeral include lying in state in the Capitol, lying in repose in the National Cathedral, a funeral procession along Constitution Avenue in a horse-drawn caisson, and a national funeral ceremony. State funerals are all slightly different because they are tailored to the wishes of the family, and they typically include private services and interment.

---

* A drop in the bucket. Washington's stills put out eleven thousand gallons annually. Richard Klingenmaier, "The Burial of General George Washington: The Lesser Known Participants," *Alexandria Chronicle*, Spring 2012, 8.

† The first official state funeral wouldn't be until 1841 for William Henry Harrison, the first president to die in office. Ten thousand people took part in the procession, of which was observed, "It was more imposing and better organized than that of the inauguration." Gilson Willets, *Inside History of the White House* (New York: Christian Herald, 1908).

The public memorial service* for Washington commenced at noon the day after Christmas with minute guns firing for an hour under the direction of Brigadier General William Macpherson. The military band—fifes and drums—playing Handel's "Dead March" led the cortege from Legislative Hall.[83] Following a sizable contingent of federal regulars and local militia came the riderless horse, escorted by two grooms. Army General Alexander Hamilton, who had served with Washington during the Revolution, played the role of the chief mourner—who traditionally *follows* the remains—and led the draped bier containing an empty coffin topped with Washington's hat and sword. Six army sergeants† carried the bier.[84] Members of the House and Senate, as well as members of federal executive departments and members of the Supreme Court representing the three branches of government, followed the bier.[85] Civic organizations and local government officials as well as Freemasons and regular Philadelphians also partook in the procession.

The procession ended at the German Lutheran Church located at Fifth and Arch Streets, where President John Adams and First Lady Abigail Adams waited. Washington didn't attend this particular church when he was in Philadelphia; rather, it was selected because of its size. Bishop William White, the rector of Christ Church, which was Washington's church when in Philadelphia, delivered the service. A dear friend of Washington's, General Richard Henry "Light Horse Harry" Lee, delivered the now famous eulogy. Lee said of Washington, "First in war, first in peace, and first in the hearts of his countrymen."

Because the federal government was nearly broke, the marble monument outlined in Marshall's resolution wouldn't be completed until 1884. In the meantime, a mausoleum was completed under the Capitol Rotunda in 1834. Martha, who had acquiesced to moving her husband's remains for the greater public good, was long dead. John Augustine Washington, George Washington's nephew, refused to allow the remains of George and Martha moved, citing that Washington's will stated he desired to be buried at Mount Vernon.[86]

The burial chamber under the Rotunda remains empty.

---

* The (corporeal) remains are present for a funeral; a memorial is a service where no remains or cremated remains are present.
† For a modern state funeral, the casket is borne by a nine-person casket team made up of all five branches of the military.

Washington's death set into motion the first display of public mourning. Services and eulogies were delivered across the nation during the
defined official mourning period that was to end on Washington's birthday, February 22, but more insidious waves reverberated through society
as Americans wanted to express their grief. As Anita Schorsch, author of
Mourning Becomes America: Mourning Art in the New Nation, writes, "To
mourn him [Washington] was an act of patriotism."[87] Thus, mourning
art became fashionable.

Angelica Kauffman, a Swiss eighteenth-century neoclassical painter,
is credited with creating the archetypal mourning scene that became the
rage in Federal-era America. Kauffman's mourning pictures, done on silk,
feature imaginary landscape scenes with four distinct elements: an urn,
a plinth, a tree, and a mourner. The urn—a nod to the Roman cinerary
urn—an interesting choice given cremation wasn't a choice of disposition
at the time—symbolizes the spirit of the departed, while the tree the
opposite, life.

A crown of laurel designates the chief mourner—another nod to
Roman antiquity—in Kauffman's scenes. The scenes are lush and serene
and calming.[88] Gone were the grim skulls and skeletons from earlier
American funerary scenes.[89] Americans appropriated the art form as the
way to memorialize General Washington, but the manner of grief expression was so pleasing that it morphed into a way to mourn the loss
of kin—but not always. So popular was mourning art that young ladies
diligently needlepointed or painted mourning scenes even if there *hadn't*
been a death in the house.

Mourning scenes were placed in the most prominent room of the
house, replacing the old ancestral portraits over the fireplace.[90] Many
of the pieces were personalized by mixing finely chopped hair of the
deceased with pigment to paint the scene.[91] And mourning art wasn't
limited to paintings. There was a surge of memorial products that
included textiles, ceramics, and jewelry that said, yes, the American
people want to spend money to memorialize their dead, sumptuary
laws be damned.

As Americans continued their fascination with mourning products,
something was looming on the horizon that would revolutionize funerary practices: the introduction of embalming. A bloody civil war was

about to ravage the nation, and as a by-product, preservation of the dead—available to all citizens—would change American funerals forever.

CHAPTER 6

Embalming Surgeons

lbert S. Dwight* was a mere twenty years old when he enlisted with the 155th New York Volunteers in the early fall of 1862. The regiment was mustered into duty November 18 in Newport News, Virginia. Private Dwight saw action immediately at the Battle of Deserted House west of Suffolk, Virginia. On May 18, 1864, the now veteran Corporal Dwight was wounded at Spotsylvania.[1] Dwight was patched up, promoted to second lieutenant on June 19, and sent back to his unit. Lieutenant Dwight got to enjoy his new rank for three days.

On a lonely, dusty road south of Petersburg called Jerusalem Plank, Dwight was killed in action. He was buried near where he fell.

While there's nothing unique about Dwight's short life and tragic end—the same fate that met some 250,000 combatants† during the bloody Civil War—the journey of his corporeal remains was distinct. In the fall of 1864 after young Albert's death, his father, Timothy Dwight, a commercial merchant, levied charges of fraud and extortion against embalming surgeon Dr. Richard Burr.

Burr, who had been previously accused of burning down a competitor's embalming tent, was specifically accused of inflating his charges and holding the remains hostage until his demands were met.

---

* Despite the fact that the army death register has him listed as J. Albert Dwight, and the 1850 census has him listed as Alfred, it is believed, based on his cemetery records, that his name was Albert S. Dwight.
† The estimates vary wildly, but about 650,000 soldiers died during the Civil War. About 40 percent died as a result of combat; the rest succumbed to disease.

Despite the brewing fight over Dwight's remains, he was actually one of the lucky dead. He made it home to rest soundly in the family plot in St. Johns Cemetery in Yonkers, New York. Most of his comrades didn't have that luxury—they never made it off the battlefield. Dwight's family not only had the means to pay to get him home but they also received word of his death in a timely fashion. Despite General Order 33 issued by the War Department early in the killing season of 1862, which ordered commanding generals to "secure, as far as possible, the decent interment of those who have fallen," in the chaos surrounding the ever-changing battle lines, the dead would lie for sometimes days waiting for "decent interment" by overwhelmed burial parties.[2] When the victor took the field, the best a slain soldier could hope for was burial by friends in his company, or in the case of the dead from the losing side, burial by prisoner-of-war comrades. At worst, it might be by soldiers on the opposing side on burial detail for punitive reasons.

General Order 33 went on to specify that graves have "headboards to the graves bearing numbers, and, where practicable, the names of the persons buried in them."[3] This was a sound practice in theory, but a bit harder in execution. Troops didn't wear standard-issue identification tags, and troop movements were mostly limited to fair weather—and the warm temperatures speeded decomposition. By the time burial details were able to reach the fallen, they were often greeted with bloated corpses whose personal (and thus identifying) items had long been looted, making personal identification difficult. Major Robert Stiles of the Army of Northern Virginia recalled the horrific scene at Gettysburg in the sweltering July heat in his memoir:

> The sights and smells that assailed us were simply indescribable—
> corpses swollen to twice their original size, some of them actually
> burst asunder with the pressure of the foul gases and vapors. . . .
> The odors were nauseating, and so deadly that in a short time we
> all sickened and were lying with our mouths close to the ground,
> most of us vomiting profusely. We protested against the cruelty
> and folly of keeping men in such a position. Of course to fight it
> was utterly out of the question.[4]

Troops would attempt to bury friends under the cover of darkness or the armies would allow the opposition to deploy burial parties and ambulances under a flag of truce to clear the fields. Frederick Brown, the chaplain for the Seventh Regiment, Ohio Infantry, wrote to his wife almost despondently early in the war about his feelings regarding the grisly work to be done under a flag of truce: "To-morrow morning Dr. Cushing and I go back to the field under a flag of truce, to see to the dead and wounded. I think we shall not be harmed; at any rate, it is our duty."[5]

The flag of truce often wasn't accepted by a commander fearing destabilization, as was the case of Major General Ulysses S. Grant refusing vanquished Confederate General P. G. T. Beauregard's request of allowing burial parties to return to the battleground the day after the bloody Battle of Shiloh. In Grant's refusal, the following day, he states the reason: "Owing to the warmth of the weather I deemed it advisable to have all the dead of both parties buried immediately. Heavy details were made for this purpose and it is now accomplished."[6] It seems unlikely this had been accomplished a mere two days after the conclusion of a battle that yielded an estimated twenty-three thousand casualties, especially given his remembrances of the aftermath of Shiloh in his 1885 memoir of "[a battlefield] so covered with dead that it would have been possible to walk across the clearing, in any direction, stepping only on dead bodies without a foot touching the ground."[7]

The bottom line is the armies, both North and South, were woefully unprepared to handle the carnage and often simply left the field in flight or pursuit. A nurse arriving at Antietam ten days after the battle still found rotting corpses aboveground.[8]

It was in these killing fields that embalming surgeons worked quickly against Mother Nature to ply their dismal trade and salvage the remains of as many boys as they could. Naturally, there would be misunderstandings between grieving families given the rudimentary communications of the time and their lack of comprehension of actual conditions. Complaints against embalmers weren't uncommon. Typically these complaints fell on deaf ears. The army had bigger issues to worry about than the men preserving the dead. But Timothy Dwight took his personal fight right to Secretary of War Edwin Stanton. Burr responded vigorously. He declared that his fee of ninety dollars was not only warranted but reasonable. His men located and dug up the body, then carried the decomposing remains several hundred yards to a waiting wagon under the threat of enemy fire.[9] Burr preserved the body with his proprietary embalming fluid and charcoal, sealed it in a zinc-lined coffin "which was exhibited to Mr. Dwight who expressed himself satisfied at the time," and provided drayage (transport to the train depot) for the fee.[10] Burr told the provost marshal, who was investigating the matter, the charges for Dwight were what he charged everyone, and "[my] books are open to your inspection at any time."[11]

Around one hundred dollars was the going rate, depending on rank. It was the methodology that got the embalming surgeons into trouble—what might be called consumer complaints today. They usually embalmed on spec, rescuing dead officers—whose families were of means and could pay their fees, or so they assumed. And the family, hundreds of miles away, received word that essentially offered their dead son back, for a price. In the case of Timothy Dwight, his dissatisfaction stems from the fact that he found a much lower price *after* having used Burr's services—or it appeared to be cheaper. The lower price, about half of Burr's price, was furnished to Dwight by William Bunnell, possibly in an act of revenge for burning down his tent and supposedly stealing his embalming cases (i.e., dead officers). Bunnell despised Burr, writing to him, "You are a man of no principle nor even a gentleman."[12]

The investigation concluded and nothing ever came of it, though the provost marshal, General Patrick, wrote shortly after the complaint levied against Burr, "Scarcely a week passes that I do not receive complaints against one or another of these embalmers. . . . I most honestly recommend that no further permits be given embalmers that come to the Army . . . those now with these Armies shall remain be referred to the Lieutenant General [Grant]."[13]

The complaints from families continued to pile up. By January, General Grant had had enough and withdrew all embalming permits, ordering the embalming surgeons behind the lines. It was too late. The war ended three months later.

The practice of embalming became part of the undertaker's proverbial tool kit as a direct result of the War Between the States. The war took an obscure technique used on royalty and for scientific tissue preservation and propelled it—literally (there were "examples" propped in Washington, DC; Georgetown; and Alexandria storefronts during the war)—into the face of a nation. Enterprising capitalists followed the Union army, to serve any family who could pay to have their loved one shipped home—as the railways wouldn't accept decomposing bodies. Meaning, the dead had to be encased in an expensive sealed transport case, or embalmed. There's a quote from Plato about necessity and inventions, and while it's true the War Between the States necessitated that this new invention be put to use, embalming had already gained a toehold in America.

Lincoln wasn't the first president prepared using the new sanitary science. The first president was embalmed* almost two decades before the Great Emancipator.

On February 21, 1848, the eve of George Washington's birthday, John Quincy Adams clutched his chest and fell across his desk in the House of Representatives while resolutions were being read. Adams was carried to the Speaker's room where for two days he lingered unconscious before dying. The firm of Lee & Espy was summoned to the Capitol to prepare the body. The embalming procedure used on the sixth president wasn't documented, but it was proficient enough to thoroughly preserve him. The funeral director and author Todd W. Van Beck wrote about Adams's funeral, saying, "The condition of Adams's remains when it [was viewed] three weeks later was reported as being excellent."[14] It's likely that Henry Lee and Benjamin Espy continued to do embalming touch-ups on the president—much like Dr. Charles Brown would do on the Lincoln Funeral Train—between funeral stops before his burial in Quincy, Massachusetts, on March 11. Adams's obsequies weren't nearly as grand as Lincoln's would be. After a funeral in Washington, he lay in repose in a receiving vault at the Congressional Cemetery until March 6. A funeral train made stops in Baltimore, Philadelphia, New York, and Boston before its final destination of Adams's hometown. For their trouble, the undertakers billed Congress sixty-five dollars for eleven days of professional services and "use of pall."[15]

---

* There is some scant evidence that William Henry Harrison was chemically prepared in some form in 1841. His remains spent more time—eighty days—in a receiving vault at the Congressional Cemetery than he did in office, thirty-two days. The burial in Ohio took place three months after death, at which point advanced decomposition should've set in. Reports of those viewing him prior to burial say he had a "natural expression." Todd W. Van Beck, Bob Inman, and Mac McCormick, "The History of Civil War Embalming" (unpublished manuscript in author's possession, April 29, 2020), PDF file.

The science of preserving the dead had been brought to the United States from Paris only eight years before Adams's death by a Philadelphia surgeon named Richard Harlan based on a technique patented in 1837 by French Chemist Jean Gannal.

Harlan had his curiosity piqued about epidemiology after being sent by the city of Philadelphia to Montreal to study techniques used to treat Asiatic cholera.[16] He toured Europe, visiting hospitals, for the first time in 1833. On his second trip five years later, he read Gannal's book, *Histoire des Embaumemens*, that had been published that year. Harlan, who was in charge of a private dissecting room in Philadelphia, was immediately taken with the Frenchman's tissue preservation method after visiting his museum where on display were human subjects from birth to six years, and various animals such as monkeys, dogs, and birds.[17]

The Medical Examiner, a Philadelphia medical journal, reported in their "foreign summary" in 1839 that "Gannal has recently published a pamphlet on the embalming of bodies, and the preparation of specimens of natural history and morbid anatomy. . . . After numerous trials with the salts of alum and various other substances, M. Gannal has selected the sulphate of alumina. . . . Two pounds of the sulphate of alumina dissolved in a quart of water, are sufficient to preserve a dead body in a state of freshness for at least three months."[18] Gannal's recipe for preservation for funeralization purposes was a bit different than reported in *The Medical Examiner* and included a small amount of red dye as well as arsenic. The red dye was for internal coloring, to give the skin ruddiness. Red dyes are still used in modern fluids to replace the coloring lost by the red blood cells and keep the deceased from looking washed out. The arsenic was a widely used chemical at the time, especially known in the medical community for its preservative qualities, despite its danger to the surgeons working on the anatomical specimens.

In 1846 France outlawed arsenic in embalming fluid in part because of Gannal. Gannal embalmed a member of the nobility whose mistress was later accused of poisoning him. Arsenic was identified in his tissues. Gannal testified on her behalf that the presence of arsenic was most likely due to the embalming, and she was acquitted of murder. The public was outraged that this defense could be used by anyone looking to get away with murder, and as such, arsenic as an additive was banned.[19] New York

State tried passing an anti-embalming bill* in 1887–1888 due to the fear of poisoners being able to get away with murder and blaming it on the embalming fluid. The bill flopped by a vote of thirty-one to fourteen.[20] The issue wasn't embalming itself; many embalmers were critical of the arsenic. Auguste Renouard, a successful embalming professor, was quoted in *The Casket* saying, "At the present moment it would seem that, if once the undertaker is allowed to enter the house, there is no chance for conviction in arsenic poisoning. This means that arsenic, being the most dangerous, is now practically the safest agent for committing murder."[21] Michigan was the first state to ban the use of arsenic in embalming fluids in 1901.

In 1840 Harlan translated Gannal's text to English, and the *History of Embalming* was published in Philadelphia. The text certainly didn't become a bestseller; in fact, it hardly made a splash. The only people interested were physicians for the purpose of preserving cadavers for anatomic study. Occasionally a diplomat might be embalmed for international shipping purposes.

Dr. Pilate, an agent for Dr. Jean-Pierre Sucquet of Paris, came to New York in 1842 and 1843 to demonstrate Dr. Sucquet's embalming fluid in hopes of licensing the product to an anatomist. The New York medical community was intrigued, and Pilate sold the rights to use Sucquet's embalming method to Drs. Charles Brown and Joseph Alexander in 1845.[22] The method calls for the injection of four quarts of the proprietary zinc chloride. This is significant because it's the patented method used on Abraham Lincoln twenty years later. Modern embalming is typically achieved with a *minimum* of twelve quarts of solution, but the chemicals are vastly different and not nearly as harsh as the fluids used in embalming's infancy.

For the next fifteen years embalming languished, unknown to the American public, but was practiced in the dead houses, or dissecting rooms, of hospitals. The first patent for an embalming process was issued to J. Anthony Gaussardia of Washington, DC, in 1856. There aren't many records of Gaussardia embalming soldiers during the war that soon followed his patent, probably because his process was not only very labor- and material-intensive, thus making it prohibitively expensive, but

---

* There were published rumors in the trade journal *The Sunnyside* that Thomas Holmes, "the Father of Modern Embalming," was responsible for promoting the anti-embalming bill.

also downright dangerous to the practitioner. *And* it required a generator (or battery), quite the contraption to lug around in the mid-nineteenth century, considering many bodies were embalmed in the field during the war. According to Gaussardia's patent, his method included injection of acidum pyroligneum arsenicalis (basically a solution of arsenic in wood vinegar) followed by electrocution until the "liquid matters and humors have become congealed." The body was then washed in a proprietary arsenic-based solution and sealed in a metallic coffin that was then filled with an arsenic and alcohol solution.[23] Easy, right?

Civil War embalming wasn't initially for the purpose of viewing the remains—this would be a later by-product of the wartime practice—but it was funereal in nature. Families from far-flung corners of the United States had that basic psychological need of closure simply by having remains—whatever state they may be in—returned to them so they had *something* to bury, something to give them closure. That impulse, to seek closure through seeing, is as old as humankind. Recall the practice of *mos teutonicus*, independent bone burial, by the medieval Europeans, and before that the Greeks cremated their fallen warriors so the cremains could be transported home.

Civil War soldiers shipped home by the embalmers were sometimes nothing more than skeletal remains. According to William Bunnell's embalming casebooks, he offered two kinds of embalming. One was arterial, injecting a soldier in an artery and sending a preserved body home. The other was essentially disinfection for advanced decomposition cases. These cases, swollen and unrecognizable, and crawling with maggots, were beyond the point where arterial injection was practical or possible. Bunnell treated them by removing the viscera and burying them, and placing the body in a sealed metal coffin with a layer of charcoal and several inches of sawdust saturated with embalming fluid.[24] Having something was far better than always wondering, a tragic fate that befell most families who didn't have the means to have their soldier shipped home. Many men—unskilled laborers—would've been happy to gather the remains of the dead for a price and place them in a cheap wooden coffin for the journey. It quickly became apparent that wasn't an option. The baggage carriers and freight men for the Adams Express Company, the railroad for the North, nearly mutinied handling the stinking, dripping wooden coffins at the outset of the war, and passengers complained bitterly of the stench.[25] Adams Express quickly ruled that remains had to either be embalmed or placed in an airtight metallic case. Either way, there could be no odor or the railway wouldn't ship the remains. Almost overnight Washington, DC, the jumping-off point for men and matériel, was crawling with men seeking their fortune. Some of those men had a very particular skill that could satisfy the railway's requirements.

One such man was Thomas Holmes. A man who by war's end embalmed a staggering 4,028 soldiers.

Holmes set up shop as a physician in Brooklyn, though there's debate if he graduated from the College of Physicians and Surgeons. It's likely he did because he was able to secure an endorsement in 1852 from the famed surgeon and professor Valentine Mott, for Holmes's "lying-in institute." A lying-in institute would be akin to a modern convalescent home since hospitals at the time were viewed as places of pestilence.

Holmes also made his living as a coroner's physician for New York City beginning in the late 1840s despite nearly dying after conducting a postmortem on a woman with a cut on his left hand. The *Evening Post* reported, "His sufferings are intensely severe, and unless he finds relief he will lose his life."[26] Holmes found relief and continued his adventures. The newspapers gleefully reported on Holmes's exploits, including his testimony regarding the carnage caused by an exploding boiler on Hague Street* in Lower Manhattan that killed nine and the bludgeoning injuries inflicted by a homicidal "maniac" in the Sixth Ward.[27] During his time with the coroner's office, Holmes—with unlimited access to cadavers in the city morgue—experimented with preservation methods and chemicals until leaving around 1856.

His whereabouts prior to the war are spotty, but he showed up in New Orleans in 1857 to conduct some kind of embalming demonstration that was more akin to a freak show when (much to the paper's delight) he unveiled a corpse he claimed he embalmed nine years prior and proceeded to saw his subject in half to prove the veracity of his methodology.[28] By the time the war broke out, Holmes had

---

* Hague Street no longer exists. It intersected with Cliff Street, near the base of the Brooklyn Bridge.

set up shop in Washington, DC—initially out of Anthony Buchly's undertaking shop on Pennsylvania Avenue—and positioned himself brilliantly to become the best-known embalmer of his generation and perhaps of all time.

Colonel Elmer E. Ellsworth sustained a fatal chest wound from a shotgun slug just a few weeks after the garrison at Fort Sumter surrendered to P. G. T. Beauregard, kicking off the bloody conflict. Holmes saw his opportunity and made a brilliant marketing maneuver. He approached President Lincoln directly, along with Secretary of State William H. Seward, and offered to embalm Lincoln's dear friend free of charge. Initially Lincoln balked. But eventually he, according to Holmes, "yielded through the solicitation" of Seward.[29] Lincoln was beyond impressed with the results, believing that every friend and family should have the chance to say goodbye in the same manner he was able to view his old law clerk. This goodwill garnered by Thomas Holmes paved the way for the multitude of embalmers setting up shop in Washington, DC.

Less than six months after Ellsworth was killed, another dear friend of Lincoln's, Colonel Edward Baker,* was killed mounting a Union defense. He'd been shot multiple times in the head and chest. Holmes embalmed him, and Lincoln went to view his friend at Buchly's undertaking shop before he was shipped home to California. The *Brooklyn Times Union* reported, "[H]e lay in the coffin not a ghastly and pale corpse, but as lifelike as we have seen him in all the glow of health . . . he would easily be mistaken for a sleeping soldier."[30]

It was Lincoln's approval that tacitly green-lighted the cadre of embalmers.

Most embalming operations had a Washington, DC, office because the city was where the lion's share of business was. Sick and wounded soldiers were carted from post and field hospitals near the front lines to the general hospitals in Washington and Alexandria where they succumbed to wounds and disease. It wasn't unusual for examples—the embalmed dead—to be propped in store windows, almost as a barometer of skill; or for the marquee to boldly advertise "Embalming the Dead" as did the firm of Brown & Alexander. Not all citizens were thrilled with the proliferation of undertakers that cropped up in the capital city to help with the dead. Toward the

---

* Baker holds the distinction of being the only sitting senator to be killed in action.

end of the war, the city aldermen, at the urging of local residents, passed a local ordinance licensing embalming establishments and making it unlawful to operate one within five hundred feet of a dwelling house.[31] The real issue was likely lack of common sense, much like the city of London passing an ordinance forbidding barbers from publicly dumping buckets of blood in the Thames. The heady pace of a city at war coupled with zero oversight made for an environment where a few bad actors ruined it for everyone. The ordinance passed unanimously, and it is one of the earliest examples of funeral facilities being regulated.

For the soldiers who perished in the field, the embalmers followed the army and set up operations in tents or abandoned buildings. A famous photograph of Drs. Chamberlain and Lyford's embalming tent at Gettysburg depicts the doctors busy at work. The tent is draped in evergreen and cypress, the ancient symbol of mourning, with two "examples" propped in coffins. The examples were actually live soldiers who volunteered for the exciting prospect of having their picture made. In another famous photograph, suspected to have been taken at Gettysburg by Mathew Brady, Dr. Richard Burr embalms a soldier on a table made of a plank resting between two barrels. Burr is operating a hand-pump injector. In the photo it's clear Burr is injecting via the axillary artery located in the armpit, unlike most of his contemporaries who injected via the carotid artery in the neck or femoral artery in the thigh. Burr's choice of injection site may not have been optimal for achieving the best preservation results, but from a cosmetic standpoint it was genius. Receiving families were amazed, as the incision was hidden in the armpit, and it was as if the body had been preserved by magic. Burr's technique fed into the Victorian concept of "people gone to their sleep."

The embalming surgeons either compounded their own fluid,* their vocational background in medicine giving them the chemical knowhow to do so, or they purchased it premade from enterprising men, such as Thomas Holmes, who made and sold their own ready-made fluids. Holmes likely never patented his formula, Innominata, for fear others would copy it. Despite Holmes's public protestations to the

---

* Mercury, arsenic, alcohol, creosote, and alkaline salts were all common ingredients used at the time.

contrary, Innominata was doubtlessly an arsenated compound as was later attested by his family members.[32] Arsenic was a popular ingredient in most early American embalming fluids due to its preservative and disinfecting qualities. And it was cheap. Thirty pounds of arsenious acid cost four dollars during the war.[33] An approximation of what might have gone into Holmes's formula can be guessed at by looking at another successful embalmer's fluid. Daniel Prunk was an embalming surgeon with a number of branch offices in Tennessee, Georgia, and Alabama during the war. Prunk wrote to Dr. J. P. Buckesto in San Jose, California, in 1872 of his wartime formula: "Embalming fluid: Arsenious Acid, 2 oz., Liquid Chloride of Zinc, 1 pint, Potassium Nitrate, ½-1 oz., boiled water—2–3 gallons."[34] The only drawback to using arsenic, aside from its toxicity to the practitioner, was discoloration. The renowned embalming professor Auguste Renouard wrote in *The Casket* several decades after the war, "This yellow tint [caused by an arsenated fluid] would gradually turn to a light brown in the course of time. No certain means have yet been found to remove this particular discoloration."[35] In reality, the battlefield embalmers weren't terribly concerned with the cosmetic effect of the fluid as much as they were with getting the remains preserved. Their successors, embalmers in the late nineteenth century—that is, community undertakers—relied on repeat business and took the utmost care to get the decedent looking as good as possible. Embalming surgeons, such as Holmes, were working against the clock to preserve the overwhelming casualties. It was like drinking out of a fire hose.

At the beginning of the war, embalming surgeons handed out handbills before a battle. The handbill gave instructions for anyone who came across a decedent with such a flier in their possession to convey the remains back to a specific embalming surgeon for preparation and shipment. It may have provided a modicum of consolation for some soldiers as a safety net that they wouldn't be lumped with the unknown, but the military quickly squashed the practice as demoralizing. An unnamed officer recounted seeing such a handbill a number of years later to the *New-York Tribune*: "The wounded in great numbers were being carried past us to the rear; their fate may be ours, was the thought of us all. At this moment when one's backbone need all the bracing possible, I saw on a tree, some little distance from me, a paper which looked much like a notice of a horse race . . . I read the following: BODIES OF OFFICERS CAREFULLY EMBALMED AND FORWARDED BY EARLY EXPRESS TO THEIR FRIENDS FOR $50."[36]

Aside from the ethics surrounding such a practice, handbills weren't wholly practical as many soldiers were stripped of their clothing and personal effects. Dog tags wouldn't be standard issue until the Great War, so many soldiers, in an effort to preserve their identity, abandoned the practice of pinning their name in their uniform and carved their names in pieces of wood and wore them around their neck, or purchased an engraved metal pin from *Harper's Weekly* magazine.[37] Some embalmers realized the usefulness of the identification tag and created a stamped metal medallion to be worn around the neck—almost like a modified version of the handbill—so the burial detail would know whom to contact.

Sometimes a company would scrape together the funds to have a friend embalmed and sent home, but often they simply couldn't afford the expense. At Seneca Mills in the autumn of 1862, Private Willard Thayer of Warren, Vermont, wrote home to his wife, "[There] was a young fellow just married the one that was buried here his foalks [*sic*] lived in the north part of the State the Co could not rase money enough to send him thare he had a brother in the same Co O he felt bad I tell you and who wouldent."[38]

Ultimately, it was the responsibility of the family to provide for recovery of a loved one, otherwise they'd fall under General Order 33's provision of "a decent burial" and be buried in a mass grave. Many times, the families wouldn't learn of a death until it was reported in the newspaper, sometimes weeks later, unless a friend, commanding officer, or chaplain sent word. In many cases, agents employed by families were sent back out into the field to recover remains weeks or months after an engagement, for shipment home. William Bunnell* recorded the longest interval in his embalming logs between burial and exhumation as six and a half months.[39]

---

* Bunnell was trained by his brother-in-law Thomas Holmes. They became estranged after Bunnell and Holmes's sister, Jane, divorced and as a result were competitors during the war.

Holmes rarely mentioned his wartime work. One of the few times he broke his silence was in a letter to *The Sunnyside* in October of 1885 where he addressed the difficulties with recovered remains:

> During the later war I have embalmed 4,028 officers and soldiers, most of them on Southern battlefields, in the hottest weather. At the battles of Fair Oaks and Seven Pines, the embalmed bodies were sunk under the water of the Pamunkey River to prevent capture, and were finally sent to their relatives North, East and West; they were received in as good a state of preservation as if they had died at home. The INNOMINATA has removed every vestige of offensive odor from bodies in so advanced a state of decomposition to require to be raised from the battlefield with cotton hooks. B. Wheatley, Undertaker, Alexandria, will testify this assertion.[40]

The cost of preparing and shipping remains home was a big factor, one of the reasons only a little over 5 percent of the 650,000 fatalities made it home. Lieutenant Chester K. Leach of the Second Vermont Infantry wrote to his wife early in the war from Camp Griffin about the cost of shipping a friend home: "The whole expense including the telegraph dispatch was $57.28." He goes on to add, "Was the Coffin a nice one? It was black walnut."[41] By the time his brother Corporal William Leach died of typhoid fever two years later in a hospital at Brady Station, Virginia, the price had gone up considerably.[42] Leach writes of the expense in an 1864 letter to his wife: "I learned there was an office for embalming at Brady Station so I got an ambulance & went there. . . . The expenses, including telegraph dispatch, were ninety-eight dollars & eighty cents ($98.80), 45 for coffin, 36 express charges, 15 for embalming & 2.80 telegraphing."[43]

A scathing editorial by H. W. Rivers, the medical director of the Ninth Army Corps, appeared the day after Christmas 1862 in the *New York Times*. Rivers wrote, "The expense of this process, in most cases, places its advantages beyond the reach of people of moderate means."[44] Rivers was absolutely correct. The cost of preparing and shipping a dead soldier home was a quarter of the yearly income of an average household in 1860, but the bottom line was it was necessary if a family wanted their soldier resting in home soil. The alternative was a cenotaph—a headstone over an empty grave that read "Buried on the Battlefield."[45]

Nearly two years prior to Albert Dwight's death, Rivers wrote in his hostile editorial, "Those who have adopted the business [of embalming] as a profession are, in some cases, extortionous in their charges, particularly where officers are the subjects."[46] Timothy Dwight wasn't the first or only citizen to run afoul with an embalming surgeon over price, despite Burr's justified costs of returning Dwight's son—an officer—to New York.

Dr. Franklin Augustus Hutton was arrested by Colonel Lafayette Baker, the provost marshal of Washington, DC, on charges of swindling. Hutton was a well-known embalmer in Washington, and perhaps Thomas Holmes's main competitor along with Brown & Alexander. Hutton ran a full-page advertisement in the Washington and Georgetown directory boldly proclaiming, "Bodies embalmed by me NEVER TURN BLACK." The ad modestly concludes, "I may embalm, at any expressed period of time, know that each and every body thus exhumed will prove an enduring monument of my skill."[47]

In early spring of 1863, Amos Hendrickson of Crosswicks, New Jersey, received a telegram that his son had died at White Oaks—a Baptist church that had been converted into a military hospital near Fredericksburg, Virginia.[48] It's unknown who sent the telegram, as the military did nothing—as protocol—to notify next of kin. Sometimes a sympathetic officer would contact family members. The Sanitary Commission and Christian Commission stepped in and tried to fill the void of notifying families, but they wrote letters.[49] The burden often fell on soldier-friends who might send a letter, because a telegram was an expensive endeavor.

Hendrickson rushed south to retrieve the body only to learn that citizens weren't allowed aboard the steamer to Virginia. Hendrickson contracted with Hutton to retrieve and embalm his son and ship him Philadelphia. The younger Hendrickson was a corporal, so Hutton quoted him $15 for his services, cheap by the war's standards.[50] Most embalmers had two prices: one for officers and one for the enlisted. At the beginning of the war, the average price was $60 for an officer and as low as $10 for an enlisted man. By war's end, the prices had crept up to the $160 and $80, though the price included a coffin, drayage, and railroad shipping costs.[51]

Hutton sent his partner, E. A. Williams, into the field to retrieve Corporal Edward Hendrickson. The only problem was Corporal Hendrickson wasn't at the hospital. According to the historian Steven Lee Carson, Hendrickson had been killed in a skirmish several miles north, near Aquia Creek.[52] It took several days to locate the body with the help of a fellow soldier and disinter it. The temporary interments done during the war actually helped stave off decomposition. Casper's law of decomposition states that a body will decompose twice as slow when immersed in water than left in air, and *eight* times as slow when buried. When Williams dug up Hendrickson, he discovered that field surgeons had mutilated him in an attempt to save his life, and despite the burial, decomposition was setting in.[53] Williams embalmed him there in the field.

When the body didn't arrive in Philadelphia as planned, Hendrickson telegraphed Hutton. Hutton understandably wanted remuneration for the additional work, but Hutton, either too harried or unsure how to explain the new situation, simply responded for Hendrickson to deposit one hundred dollars at the express office.[54] This would prove to be Hutton's downfall.

Hendrickson responded on April 20: "Send it according to contract or take consequences. Answer immediately."[55] The terms of the original contract had changed, but Hendrickson didn't know it. Nonetheless, Hutton ordered Williams to immediately ship the body.

It was too late. Hendrickson was on his way to Washington to complain to the military. Hendrickson's complaint put the embalmer directly in the crosshairs of Baker.

Baker's detectives arrested Hutton the next day on charges of attempted swindling. They seized the contents of his office and imprisoned him in the Old Capitol Prison, where the *Evening Star* commented, "An opportunity was afforded the embalmers for a review of their misdoings."[56] Hutton was released about ten days later after offering his version of events. It was too late. The court of public opinion rendered a verdict regarding Hutton's attempted swindling. His business never recovered.

Like the case of Timothy Dwight and Richard Burr, Hutton's was a misunderstanding fueled by emotion and poor communication that unfolded in the chaos of war. But the army was sick of the complaints rolling in, leaving a frustrated Lieutenant General Grant, who was devoting his energy to defeating Lee at Petersburg, with little choice other than to issue General Order 7 on January 9, 1865, ordering that "that all permits of Embalming Surgeons within the lines of the Armies operating against Richmond have been revoked and the Surgeons ordered with-out the lines."[57] Grant further tried to remove the teeth of the embalming surgeons by adding, "Friends and relatives of the officers and soldiers are hereby notified that hereafter the bodies of officers and soldiers who die in general or base hospitals can be embalmed without charge."[58]

The War Department, hedging its bets against a continued engagement, issued General Order 39 in March of 1865, which in part stated, "Hereafter no persons will be permitted to embalm or remove the bodies of deceased officers or soldiers, unless acting under the special license of the Provost Marshal of the Army."[59] It also stipulated that an embalmer had to demonstrate their skill and furnish a price list prior to being issued a license. These regulations were light-years ahead of their time. Virginia, the first state to issue embalmer's licenses, didn't do so until 1892, and the Federal Trade Commission didn't institute "The Funeral Rule," which mandated price disclosure, until 1984.

The order was too late to have any real bearing. The treaty at Appomattox Court House was signed a month later. Once peace was restored in the Union, the embalming surgeons disappeared from Washington as quickly as they appeared. Daniel Prunk and Charles Brown went back to practicing medicine in one form or another. Franklin Hutton died a year later. William Bunnell returned to New Jersey to continue undertaking. Joseph Alexander dropped off the pages of the history books, dying in 1871, and Richard Burr simply disappeared. The man who would gain the moniker "the Father of American Embalming" did the unthinkable—he gave up embalming. Sort of.

Thomas Holmes moved back to Brooklyn and opened an apothecary on the corner of Broadway and Marcy Avenue. In his store window hung a sign declaring "Revolution in Embalming." Displayed in a glass case was an embalmed dog to entice folks to come in and witness the revolution. The shop was filled with macabre specimens, the result of his ongoing embalming experiments. The *Brooklyn Daily*

Eagle described the glass jars lining the drugstore shelves as "many subjects for a nightmare."[60]

Holmes continued to sell Innominata in eleven-gallon kegs for thirty-three dollars or by the quart for fifty cents. That seems like a large volume of fluid, as modern fluids are sold in concentrated form and the embalmer dilutes to the desired strength, but in the late nineteenth century the fluids were sold premixed. Apparently, the quart volumes weren't necessarily for undertakers but could be purchased by the public for their own use as one sign in his shop window advertised: "Invalids traveling by sea or land can carry with them all that is necessary to insure [*sic*] the return of their bodies in a perfect state of preservation."[61] Which certainly begs the question: Who in the travel party would do the injection should the need arise to use the quart of Innominata?

Chronic arsenic exposure is correlated with cognitive dysfunction and has been linked to Alzheimer's disease.[62] It would be another twenty years before Holmes's dementia would manifest in an explosive event, but his decline seems to begin with the invention of his antiseptic chamber. By the time Holmes was arrested in 1896 in a state of raving lunacy, smashing his parlor furniture with an ax, he was penniless, having squandered his fortune.[63] The apothecary had been repossessed by the bank, the loan bought out by his brother-in-law, Theodore Dowd, so Holmes and his wife could remain living there.[64] It could be coincidental that Holmes suffered from dementia, but the fact can't be overlooked that he spent decades compounding Innominata, a fluid that in all probability contained arsenic. Holmes was committed to Flatbush Hospital, a lunatic asylum, and was, astonishingly, released into the care of his wife several weeks later.

Two things happened as a direct result of the war. It created a demand for this new, almost miraculous scientific advancement as families were amazed at how well the soldiers being shipped home looked weeks or *months* after death. Given their frame of reference, it's understandable how embalming seemed almost magic. Until this point in American history, when someone died, they were buried within a day or two because there was no proven method for preventing decomposition. When the martyred President Lincoln's family chose embalming for him, and the media ballyhooed his appearance, it bolstered the legitimacy of embalming.

The other result was, for the first time in history, the secret knowledge of human preservation jumped from medical men to laypeople. Embalmers such as Henry Cattell (Lincoln's embalmer) and William Bunnell (Richard Burr's nemesis) who weren't physicians were embalming during the war, but they were the exception and learned the trade through familial connections. Almost all of the other embalming surgeons were trained medical doctors. A few, such as Richard Burr, who was an assistant surgeon with the Seventy-Second Pennsylvania Volunteers, and Daniel Prunk, who was the assistant surgeon at the Second Division Hospital in Nashville, Tennessee, resigned their commissions to pursue the fortune to be made as a private embalmer. The war began the transfer of embalming knowledge from the medical men to laypeople, as the medical men, overwhelmed with the volume of dead soldiers, trained their assistants in the sanitary science of embalming. Such was the case with the first documented African American embalmer.

Dr. E. C. Lewis moved to Washington, DC, after graduation from Philadelphia Medical College in 1862 and approached Holmes about learning his embalming methodology.[65] Holmes let Lewis take a shipment of Innominata with him west where he set up his embalming practice in W. R. Cornelius's undertaking establishment in Nashville. Cornelius, a carpenter by trade, was the foreman of McComb & Carson in 1849, when James K. Polk died suddenly of cholera* just a few months after leaving office at age fifty-three.[66] Cornelius was called upon to conduct the funeral. By the time the war broke out in 1861, Cornelius had assumed ownership of the business and completely divested himself of the furniture operation. He secured a contract from the Confederate army, and he handled two to three thousand cases before Union forces captured Nashville in February of 1862. This was before Lewis's arrival, meaning Confederate soldiers were shipped unembalmed in sealed zinc-lined coffins. The Southern Express, the counterpart to Adams Express

---

* Polk has had trouble resting in peace. Given state laws at the time to limit the spread of infectious disease, Polk was initially buried for a year in a mass grave in Nashville City Cemetery before being moved to the lawn of his estate, "Polk Place." He was moved for a third time in 1893 to the Tennessee State Capitol after his wife died and Polk Place was sold. The Tennessee legislature brought forth a resolution in 2017–2018 to move him yet again, to his childhood home. For now, he's staying put.

in the North, had similar regulations for shipping remains. If remains weren't embalmed, they had to be sealed in a zinc-lined coffin.

Cornelius, a Yank from Pennsylvania and a consummate business-man, had no qualms about conducting business with the opposing side. He immediately secured the federal contract from the Union Army, and during the remainder of the war Cornelius estimates he buried or shipped thirty-three thousand soldiers, soldiers' family members, and federal employees.[67] An advertisement in the *Nashville Daily Union* pro-claimed, "Government Undertaker . . . Having secured the services of Dr. E. H. [*sic*] Lewis, of New York (and more recently from the Army of the Potomac,) for embalming the dead, by Dr. Holmes' [*sic*] *American Process*, acknowledged to be the best . . ."[68] In an article in an 1892 issue of *The Casket*, Cornelius said of Lewis, "He was quite an expert, but like a great many men, he could not stand prosperity, and soon wanted to get into some other kind of business."[69]

It didn't matter that Lewis moved on; he'd already taught the Holmes method of embalming to Cornelius, who in turn taught it to Prince Greer after Lewis left. Greer was an enslaved person from Texas serving a cavalry officer who was killed. He brought the body of his master to Cornelius's establishment for shipment home and stayed with Cornelius, assisting with embalming in exchange for room and board. There were so many cases flooding into the practice on a daily basis—Cornelius's firm embalmed thirty-five hundred soldiers during the three-year Union occupation—Greer had plenty of opportunities to hone his skills and become a skilled embalmer.[70] Cornelius said of Greer, "[He] appeared to enjoy embalming so much that he became himself an expert, kept on at work embalming during the balance of the war, and was very successful."[71]

Cornelius, burned out by the pace of the war, closed his business in 1871 to pursue a quiet life of farming. Greer moved back to Texas where he operated a reputable undertaking establishment until his death in 1906.[72] Cornelius—bored with farming—resumed his undertaking business in 1879, and by the time of his death in 1910 his obituary stated that "he had buried more people than any other man in Tennessee and probably more than any man who is living today."[73] At sixty-five thousand people—the number stated in the obituary—he probably had.

Cornelius is a good example of the first incarnation of the funeral director created by the war. He was a tradesman undertaker who previously had dabbled in burying Nashville's dead as a result of his vocation as a carpenter. After the war, armed with the knowledge of embalming, he set out in pursuit of a new profession: the funeral director, someone whose sole purpose was attending to the dead and overseeing the obsequies. The rise of this new vocation fostered the creation of many ancillary industries: factory-made caskets, vaults, burial garments, and specialty chemical companies.

As the medical men bowed out of embalming, self-compounded embalming fluids disappeared. Not only did the new class of the undertakers lack the chemical and pharmacological background required to compound their own fluids but also the emergence of chemical companies helped to standardize quality and results—and the chemical companies promoted the skill of embalming.

Early embalming fluid companies such as Mills & Lacey and Champion sent lecturers to various cities where attendees received certification in embalming after a two-day demonstration. Of course, the goal wasn't solely to foster the dissemination of embalming knowledge but rather to create apostles of their particular chemical. Aside from the short courses offered by chemical-company demonstrators, the knowledge of undertaking was still passed on in a very guild-like manner—from craftsman to apprentice—until Auguste Renouard, the former assistant army surgeon and fluid salesman, published the first textbook, *The Undertaker's Manual,* in 1878. Now, certified embalmers could at least enrich their scant technical knowledge and have something to refer to for difficult cases.

In 1882 the first[*] embalming schools opened. The Clarke School of Embalming convened in March at the Pulte Medical College in Cincinnati for three weeks of instruction by Joseph Clarke. Shortly thereafter, and prior to the first meeting of the Funeral Directors' National Association of the United States (that would become the National Funeral Directors Association [NFDA]) in June, Auguste Renouard opened the Rochester

---

[*] Author Todd W. Van Beck asserts August Renouard's first school at J. J. Walley's Undertaker Shop in Denver, Colorado, in 1876 was the first. Renouard's was more of a correspondance course rather than organized instruction; hence the reason the author is choosing to recognize the Clarke School of Embalming as the first. In fairness, things have come full-circle with the acceptance of online mortuary programs.

School for Embalmers to give embalming demonstrations to the gathered undertakers. The convention demonstrations were a success, but the school flopped as Renouard couldn't attract enough students willing to make the time commitment of a six-week period of study.[74]

As the nineteenth century drew to a close, more textbooks were created and professional journals such as *The Casket*, *The Shroud*, and *The Western Undertaker* were published. The NFDA gained power and pushed state health boards to regulate, license, and standardize education. Clarke reorganized his school in 1899 as the Cincinnati College of Embalming, which remains the oldest mortuary institution in continuous operation.

The century that saw a profession emerge, congeal, and organize drew to a close in an abrupt and rather ironic flourish. In January of 1900, Thomas Holmes's obituary headline, which ran in the *New-York Tribune*, read "Dead Embalmer Wants No Embalming."[75] According to the obituary, it was the Father of Modern Embalming's last wish.

Gone to Their Sleep

Victorian Sensibilities

L ate in the evening on April 14, 1912, one of the wealthiest men in America, Colonel John Jacob Astor, and his wife were strolling the decks of the RMS *Titanic* when it plowed into an iceberg. A waiter approached the Astors holding life preservers, to which Astor replied, "Pooh, this is nothing! There is no need for life belts," dismissing him.[1] And why wouldn't he? Astor had nothing to fear. The *Titanic* had been billed as unsinkable.

Less than two hours later, Colonel Astor assisted his wife into a lifeboat.

Seven days later, Astor's body was fished out of the North Atlantic by the crew of the cable ship *MacKay-Bennett* that had been pressed into service as a funeral boat. Astor was embalmed onboard and returned to Halifax.

The nation was captivated. A dead mogul who died in a spectacular fashion leaves behind a young, pretty socialite less than half his age who's also pregnant with his heir: the newspapers fed the public's voracious appetite inking story after story on reams of pulp. And Madeleine Astor did what every respectable woman at that time did: she went into mourning.

The mourning period was rigidly prescribed in 1912, based on years of tradition. The Washington *Evening Star* published a piece on mourning attire shortly after the *Titanic* tragedy. The piece read, "There are certain conventions which much be observed, if one's mourning is to be correct . . . who accepting the fact that they must wear black for a certain time, settle down for a year or two of dull, uninteresting garb of somber hue."[2] Women were expected to enter a mourning period following the death of their husbands—or other close family members—and retire from society wearing black to signify their status.

Mourning was no small-time commitment. Emily Post suggested that a "young widow should wear deep crepe for a year, and then lighter mourning for six months and second mourning for six months longer."[3] Full mourning, or "deep crepe," is exactly that: the widow was expected to wear black outfits—costumes really, complete with a veil—made of wool or silk crepe, a dismal fabric that stained the skin black and was loaded with arsenic. In lighter mourning, sometimes called "half-mourning," the widow could wear dull silk—black, of course—trimmed with crepe, and in second mourning, often called the "lighter sorrows," the widow was allowed to wear grays and purples. Americans had been adhering to this tradition since Prince Albert died in 1861 and Queen Victoria donned black habiliments, never to take them off for the remainder of her days.

Black isn't the universal color of mourning but rather the accepted color in the American-European tradition. Yellow signified mourning in ancient Egypt, and the Persians used brown, the color of withered leaves.[4] Buddhists and Hindus signify mourning with white. The British scholar Bertram Puckle believes the American-European color choice of black to be connected with the ancient fear of returning spirits. He asserts, "It was believed that when cloaked or veiled in sable hue human beings were invisible to the spirits and thus free from any possibility of molestation."[5]

Today, black is still the "accepted" (i.e., default) color of mourning, though many families have chosen to cast it off in an effort to personalize the funeral. Many causes (e.g., AIDS, colorectal and breast cancer, mental illness, gun violence) are associated with an "awareness" color. It's common for the obituary to invite guests to sport the awareness color related to the cause of death to the funeral. This new take on the old custom of mourning colors is interesting because it promotes solidarity among a group of mourners, which is a key component—community support—to helping the grief process. Another tangential form of textile mourning display isn't limited to a specific color but rather an interest, like tie-dye for the Grateful Dead fan or Harley-Davidson gear for the Softail owner. Despite the lack of a static mourning color, the culture clearly still values a display of overt mourning.

Mrs. John Jacob Astor caused quite the stir when she decided to toss social mores out the window and mourn on her terms. A headline in the *Washington Herald* proclaimed "Astor's Widow Will Wear White."[6]

White? This maneuver was not only unheard of but also unfathomable. Especially in light of the fact that even the Astor household staff donned the requisite black armbands, following the lead of Colonel Astor's twenty-year-old son, Vincent. Men were expected to mourn too, though the period was much shorter,[*] as men couldn't be bothered with prolonged mourning machinations when they had to earn a living. Men signified mourning by an armband on their left sleeve or a band on their hat called a "weeper."[7] The origin of this custom dates back to the Plantagenet period in England when men (and women) wore long strips of fabric bound to their upper arms and necks called tippets. The tippet morphed to a band around the hat, or arm, as a sign of mourning.[8]

Madeleine Astor's scandalous decision to wear white was couched as a health decision. She was "with child" (or, what the paper euphemistically called "the most important time of her life"), and her mother, Katherine Talmage Force, insisted she not wear black as it would affect her health and the baby's as well.[9] In fact, Mrs. Force was made the scapegoat in this drama that played out across the newspaper headlines saying she "overruled" her daughter's wish to wear mourning because it would "depress her spirits."[10] But the Astors were quick to point out to the papers that decorum had been preserved because the white gowns were crepe and "cut on the simplest lines."[11]

In August, Madeleine Astor gave birth to a baby boy, who she named John Jacob.

In retrospect, it almost appears that the Victorians had a preoccupation with death because they mourned publicly. Perhaps it wasn't a preoccupation but a healthy embrace, something lacking in modern society. Dr. Timothy Blade, the former curator of decorative arts at the University of

---

[*] Three months total for a spouse. In comparison, women were expected to mourn for at least a year for a parent, longer for a spouse.

Minnesota, explained the value of mourning rituals in *Dodge Magazine*, saying, "[Victorian rituals] accomplished two important things: easing the bereaved through the mourning period by providing a series of pre-made decisions, and identifying to the rest of society a family who had suffered a loss, thus assuring that the members would be treated with extra consideration and kindness."[12] Dr. Irene Clepper, who authored the article on Dr. Blade's "Gone, But Not Forgotten: Designing for Death" display, added, "In the last century [nineteenth century] there was no attempt to look away from death, one of the realities of life. People were not urged to 'get on with their lives,' but rather to experience their grief."[13]

The act of defiance by Madeleine Astor signaled the beginning of the end of mourning clothing, and all the rigid mourning customs that marked the American funeral for much of the nineteenth century, a time when what is now considered the traditional funeral—embalming, viewing, a service, and final disposition—congealed.

When someone died, word was sent to the undertaker. The undertaker loaded his embalmer's buggy, a smaller carriage that carried his instruments, fluids, and a cooling board. At the house, the undertaker affixed a door badge to let the neighbors know it was a house of mourning. This tradition was a throwback to the Roman tradition of placing a cypress bough on the door, and it was a purposeful way of letting the community know this household was bereaved. The door badge was a simple piece of crepe or a more elaborate rosette with crepe streamers, and the neighbors immediately knew by the color if a child (white crepe), adult (black and white crepe), or elderly person (all black crepe) had died. The embalming textbook *The Art and Science of Embalming* from the turn of the century states the cutoff age between mounting black and white crepe or all black is age fifty. *The Sunnyside* had a different opinion, stating the cutoff age to be thirty, but was quick to add, "In every case, of course, the [funeral director] should consult the wishes of the family."[14] *The Art and Science of Embalming* also advised, "[A]lways take two crepes, a good one, or a medium or poor one," and "never charge for crepes," as it "causes dissatisfaction."[15] This custom was practiced well into the late twentieth century in some areas of the Deep South with mourning crepe mounted to a mailbox. The closest approximation in modern times to this symbolic community notification would be tying balloons to a mailbox to signify a celebration or a yellow ribbon around a tree to signify a family member serving overseas in the armed forces.

The decedent was embalmed in bed or on an aforementioned cooling board, which was almost like a hinged folding table that allowed the dead to be positioned in the Fowler position—a reclining position. Embalming fluid was injected either via gravity injection or by hand pump, and the blood was collected in empty glass jars for disposal. When the embalming procedure was complete, the undertaker dressed the decedent in night-clothes and left them in bed or on the cooling board, or moved them to a slumber couch. Some cooling-board manufacturers advertised elaborate canopies that could be erected to dress up the apparatus, such as the Alter Ego Manufacturing Company of Boston, Massachusetts, who advertised an "extension" cooling board, "complete with white muslin canopy" for twenty-three dollars in an 1894 issue of *The Casket*.[16]

Before leaving the house, *The Art and Science of Embalming* urges the practitioner to "abandon, if you have not heretofore, many of the old customs for which there is no necessity in this age of advance-ment. The first is the use of the cloth upon the face."[17] This advice strikes in the face of practicality not only for cosmetic but infestation reasons. Many undertakers were still embalming with heavy metals, the effects of which were harsh and desiccating, and it was common to powder the face post-embalming to give the skin a matte, more natural look. The handkerchief would've prevented further drying out and maggot infestations. Air conditioning wouldn't be common in homes for another half century; as such, windows were commonly open. Open windows invite flies that immediately lay eggs in the exposed nasal passages of a decedent—embalmed or not.

Despite the favorable press coverage that Lincoln's funeral gave to em-balming, many folks were fearful of the new sanitary science, afraid the undertaker was going to mutilate the dearly departed, and refused it. As such, the corpse cooler was a staple of the undertaker's repertoire as an alternative to embalming. There were many different variations of the contraption, which was exactly what its name suggests.

Robert Frederick, a Baltimore chairmaker-turned-undertaker, and the undertaker Granville A. Trump patented one of the first corpse coolers, called a "refrigerator for corpses" in 1846. Nine years later, John Good of Philadelphia patented his airtight "corpse preserver."

Residential refrigeration hadn't yet been invented, and these inventions relied on ice. It was the duty of the people doing the waking to empty the drip bucket, a busy job during the hot months when the coolers were needed the most. Frederick and Trump's invention remained a popular model for many years. The remains were laid on a cooling board and a concave metal reservoir was filled with ice and placed over the chest and abdomen.[18] Good's corpse preserver was a coffin in which one placed a layer of ice on the bottom and then placed a false bottom with ventilation holes in it—much like a pot with a steamer insert—before the remains were placed inside.

Good's unit likely kept the remains colder until burial, but it was large and unwieldy, not something undertakers relished wrestling into homes in the heat of summer. Frederick and Trump's invention had the advantage of being more portable and using less ice. The "refrigerator for corpses" also had the added benefit that the body could be dressed and then the reservoir could be laid upon the remains.

Funeral arrangements were made at the house and the family picked the casket out of a catalog; premanufactured caskets became the predominant burial vessel in the 1870s, replacing artisanal custom-made coffins, though undertakers often trimmed caskets by hand, meaning they installed the interior padding and fabric. Arrangements were made at the home because the paradigm shift to well-appointed funeral parlors hadn't yet occurred. Undertakers didn't even need a storefront to operate; they were doing all the things now done at the funeral home—preparing remains, hosting the viewing and funeral—in the decedent's home. The undertaker would arrive the day of the wake with everything needed for a home funeral: the casket, sawhorses on which to place the casket, flower pedestals, folding chairs, drapery hangings for behind the casket, a lectern, and mourning bands (weepers) for guests.

After the service the undertaker organized a procession of carriages to the local cemetery for burial—always burial. There wasn't a viable alternate form of disposition, the cremation rate being *well* under 1 percent. Until the end of 1900, only 13,281 cremations had been performed nationwide.[19]

The Victorian funeral experience is best summed up by Colonel John O'Brien of St. Louis, who wrote of a recent funeral experience to *The Casket* in 1894:

> Death [of a relative] came at midnight. The undertaker was notified by telephone. He arrived with his assistants within twenty minutes. The members of the family, worn out with watching, were induced to retire for much needed rest. When daylight came the body of the deceased had been embalmed, dressed and laid out in a handsome coffin and carried to the parlor. When the family entered the room candles were burning, the mirror had been covered, the furniture arranged, flowering plants bestowed about the room. . . . During the day a wagon load of camp chairs arrived for the accommodation of those who were to watch all night. Crepe hung from the door, cut flowers were sent in, the priest had been seen, the hour arranged for the funeral, a choir engaged, carriages ordered, the grave dug, gloves and crepe scarves sent in for the hands, arms, and hats of the pallbearers. . . . This was the very science of funeral direction.[20]

John Jacob Astor's funeral was a shining example of a Victorian-era funeral, albeit a largely private event. His burial at Trinity Cemetery (Upper Manhattan, New York City) didn't buck social norms like his wife wearing white in mourning, but it did fly in the face of current burial trends. The rural cemetery movement had exploded. Fewer and fewer Americans were choosing burial in an old moldering churchyard, instead favoring the idyllic scenes and carefully manicured suburban oasis of the newfangled rural cemetery.

Like many who are ahead of their time, James Hillhouse's idea of burying the dead of New Haven, Connecticut, on land at the edge of town wasn't well received. The majority of Americans lived in rural settings where churchyards (also called graveyards or burying grounds) or little plots in a designated area of a family's property were used. In more populous areas, such as New Haven, the dead were buried in churchyards, empty building lots, or the town square.

This would all change with Hillhouse, who conceptualized the idea of the modern burial ground—the cemetery.

Hillhouse attended Yale and served gallantly in the Continental army. After the war he practiced law and went on to serve as both a congressman and senator, a public service career that stretched almost two decades. Around the time he began his career in the Senate in 1796, Hillhouse spearheaded a group of citizens to organize a new type of burial ground north of the green, or the town square. Two yellow fever epidemics in 1794 and 1795 had caused the green to reach capacity.[21] New Haven desperately needed a place to put their dead.

Hillhouse realized the need for an extra-municipal solution that wasn't the plots families created on their own land. Appraising the situation with an attorney's eye, Hillhouse understood family land that was later sold would terminate future burial or visitation rights.[22] He proposed a corporate cemetery, something not owned by a church or municipality, something that was to be a "sacred and inviolable" tract.[23]

The cemetery was incorporated in 1797 as the New Burying Ground.* The cemetery was laid out in a grid formation much like the city of Philadelphia was, and each of the three churches located on the green was given a section in which to bury their parishioners. Despite the seemingly sublime concept and design, the New Burying Ground wasn't popular. Only thirty people initially bought lots.[24] Despite the idea's initial flop, Hillhouse never lost faith, and when he died in 1832, he was buried there.

Around the time Hillhouse died, his idea was appropriated to unwittingly create the biggest tourist attraction on the East Coast during the early Victorian era: Mount Auburn Cemetery.[25]

In 1849 the English poet and writer Lady Emmeline Stuart-Wortley traveled to the United States, documenting her journey. The three-volume travel memoir propelled her to fame.† While visiting the Everett family in Cambridge, Massachusetts, Stuart-Wortley writes, "[W]e went [to] . . . Mount Auburn, the spacious and beautiful cemetery."[26] Stuart-Wortley goes on to describe the sights she saw: "The finely diversified grounds" and "the tombs graced with charming flower beds"; and the wondrous sounds she experienced: "the birds were singing most mellifluously and merrily—it was quite the din."[27] She wraps up her summation with the statement, "It is, indeed, a beauteous city for the dead."[28]

---

* The cemetery is now called Grove Street Cemetery.
† The fame was short-lived. She succumbed to dysentery in Beirut four years after publication.

After leaving the cemetery, the Everetts took her to see "a little of the colleges."[29] The colleges Stuart-Wortley writes of is none other than the oldest university in the United States, Harvard. Mr. Edward Everett, in August of 1849 when this visit occurred, was the immediate past president of Harvard and still living in Wadsworth House, the president's house. Entertaining norms were such that the Everetts opted to take their esteemed literary guest on a carriage ride around a *cemetery* before taking her to visit an educational institution of national acclaim.

It's almost baffling in contemporary times to entertain guests in such a fashion, but this was a normal—even pleasurable—activity in Victorian Boston. So much so that James Russell Lowell, a romantic poet and contemporary of Stuart-Wortley, grumbled about the Bostonian's seemingly insular idea of hospitality as "[a] dinner with people you never saw before nor ever wish to see again, and a drive in Mount Auburn Cemetery."[30] Lowell must've not had too big a gripe with his post-dinner party jaunts on the grounds of Mount Auburn as he chose to spend eternity there in lot 323, Fountain Avenue.

Mount Auburn was so fashionable a destination that a local printer named Nathaniel Dearborn began printing a series of guidebooks. The first, *A Concise History of, and Guide Through Mount Auburn* in 1843, appeared about a decade after the cemetery opened. The guidebook contained maps, descriptions, and locations of notable burials and attractions around the cemetery. It also included helpful reminders of the regulations, such as "No person is admitted on horseback; all persons are prohibited from writing upon, defacing or injuring any monument," and for the gunslinger who might forget himself, "all persons are prohibited from discharging fire-arms in the cemetery."[31] When he died in 1852, after having printed many editions of his popular guidebook, his son Nathaniel S. Dearborn continued the cemetery guidebook dynasty. Apparently the Dearborns, father and son, weren't enamored enough with Mount Auburn to be buried there; they were both buried at Lakeside Cemetery in Wakefield, Massachusetts.

The appeal of the rural cemetery wasn't limited to New England. Philadelphia opened Laurel Hill in 1836, followed soon after by Green-Wood in Brooklyn in 1838. Within twenty years of Mount Auburn's creation, almost every major city boasted its very own rural cemetery, ranging all the way down the Eastern Seaboard to Bonaventure Cemetery in Savannah, Georgia, and Magnolia Cemetery in Charleston, South Carolina. Each cemetery became a local attraction of sorts, Mount Auburn, Green-Wood, and Laurel Hill each receiving more than thirty thousand visitors annually.[32] Green-Wood in Brooklyn was so popular that the undertaking firm of Fritschler & Selle organized a line of twelve passenger carriages to run from Manhattan to Green-Wood every fifteen minutes from 8:00 a.m. to 6:00 p.m., charging twenty-five cents for the trip.[33]

Mount Auburn was the brainchild of Dr. Jacob Bigelow, a physician and botanist. Bigelow had serious sanitary concerns regarding burials. One was the colonial predilection for burial under churches[*]—a custom brought across the Atlantic. A contributor to the *Cincinnati Miscellany* wrote, "They [the dead] were crowded in so revolting a manner as to render the air in the churches unwholesome."[34] Bigelow's other concern was running out of space. It had been about two hundred years since the Pilgrims landed in nearby Plymouth, and some Massachusetts churchyards were bursting at the seams, especially after a particularly bad epidemic of yellow fever terrorized the port city during the years ending the eighteenth century and into the nineteenth. Boston responded by opening South End Burying Ground in a marshy area of Roxbury Neck to handle the poor and working class. The problem was, at the time before the marshes were filled in, Roxbury Neck was just that: a neck. Travelers had to use the thin strip of land to enter Boston, bringing them close to the burying ground. Bigelow dreamed up a place *outside* the city limits (unlike the New Burying Ground that was just a few blocks from the green in New Haven, Connecticut, and still very much in town) to bury the dead, a botanical retreat that also solved the sanitary quandary. A rural burial ground was the answer.

Eight men[†] convened in 1825 at Bigelow's home. They agreed to try to find a space for their burying ground, but their plans fizzled. Nothing was done until, five years later, George Brimmer offered the Horticultural Society of Massachusetts seventy-two acres of land west of the Charles

---

[*] Two American presidents and their wives are buried under a church. John and Abigail Adams, and his son John Quincy Adams and his wife, Louisa, are buried under the vestibule of United First Parish Church in Quincy, Massachusetts.

[†] One of the men was Judge John Lowell. His grandson was James Russell Lowell, the poet who griped about dinner parties and sightseeing trips to Mount Auburn.

River for $6,000.[35] A public meeting was called and it was unanimously agreed upon to accept Brimmer's offer. The cemetery was incorporated June 23, 1831, and consecrated on September 24 before a crowd of two thousand people.[36] Supreme Court Justice Joseph Story, who was reeling from the recent death of his ten-year-old daughter from scarlet fever, delivered an evocative dedication address:[37]

> It is to the living mourner—to the parent, weeping over his
> dear dead child—to the husband, dwelling in his own solitary
> desolation—to the widow, whose heart is broken by untimely
> sorrow—to the friend, who misses at every turn the presence of
> some kindred spirit. It is to these, that the repositories of the dead
> bring home thoughts of admonition, of instruction, and, slowly
> but surely of consolation also. They admonish us, by their very
> silence, of our own frail and transitory being. They instruct us
> in the true value of life, and in its noble purposes, its duties, its
> destination. They spread around us in the reminiscences of the past,
> sources of pleasing, though melancholy reflection.[38]

Story's dedication strikes at the changing relationship between Americans and their dead. No longer were crowded churchyards, the town commons, or vacant city lots desirable—or even acceptable. A place of rest and tranquility, but at an arm's length, is where Americans wanted their dead to repose. The quiet away from city noise, the meandering paths through every conceivable kind of flora and fauna, appealed to Victorian romantic sensibilities. Even the avenues and paths were meant to elicit a sense of peace: the avenues were given arbor-themed names such as Cedar, Chestnut, Laurel, and Magnolia; the walking paths were named for ornamental shrubs and flowers, such as Alder, Clematis, Hazel, Lilac, and Sweetbriar. Even the name Mount Auburn was evocative of the color of turning leaves in autumn, nothing so grim as "New Burying Ground." The president of the Ohio Horticultural Society, Dr. John A. Warder, wrote of rural cemetery planning, "[I]t is most important that we should be right, and so execute our plans as to keep within the pale of strict good taste. . . . These should be judiciously located, carefully planned and laid out in good taste . . . these grounds are intended to be quiet resting places."[39]

The bucolic setting of Mount Auburn—about four miles from Boston proper—echoed the emerging new living patterns. Prior to the Industrial Revolution, people typically worked where they lived—and buried their dead close by. Things were rapidly changing, due in part to changes in the ways people could move greater distances thanks to the introduction of the train and streetcar, and Americans were starting to live apart from their place of business. In *Inventing the American Way of Death*, the author James Farrell likens the rural cemetery to "an analogue to the suburb."[40]

While rural, sometimes called "garden," cemeteries remained immensely popular, American tastes shifted again with the advent of the "park" or "lawn" cemetery. Adolph Strauch, a Prussian-born landscape architect, was hired by Spring Grove Cemetery in Cincinnati in 1855 to redesign the ailing cemetery.[41] Strauch had a vision for a different kind of burial ground unlike the busy motif of rural cemeteries. His groundbreaking design focused on open space: wide expanses of lawn punctuated by clusters of trees and bushes, and selectively placed monuments. Flush markers achieve the openness of lawn cemeteries, so to the casual observer standing back, the markers can't be seen and the area appears as an expansive lawn.

There hasn't been a "new" cemetery design since Bigelow and Strauch introduced the rural and lawn cemeteries. Green cemeteries are gaining popularity in contemporary America, but they aren't a new type of cemetery, really the opposite. They're a throwback to the early American burial practices: hand-dug grave and no vault. Rural and lawn cemeteries remain popular burial destinations, and churchyard burials have regained favor after falling by the wayside, overshadowed by the rural cemetery. While the taste in cemetery architecture and design moved from elaborate (rural cemeteries) to simple (lawn cemeteries), a hallmark of the American funeral—floral tributes—didn't. In fact, it went the opposite. In the typical ostentatious fashion of the time, the "more is more" theme prevailed.

The practice of offering floral tributes was nothing new in the mid-nineteenth century. Which begs the question: Why flowers? When kin or friends die, it's an automatic reaction to call the florist. What, exactly, drives that impulse?

Puckle offers the pat explanation of "the half sovereign he [the mourner] paid for it saved him from the mental exercise of composing a suitable letter of condolence."[42] But is sending flowers merely that transactional? Hardly. Puckle quickly walks his glib answer back to amend, "The funeral wreath is a survival of the belief that it is necessary to provide comforts for the use or delectation of the departed spirit."[43] *Belief* is the operative word for the explanation offered by Puckle. In short, the impulse to offer floral tributes is something that predates the Victorian era by many years. It's written in our DNA.

Offering flowers is one of the oldest known mourning practices, dating back to Neanderthals. Dr. Ralph Solecki excavated flower spores of grape hyacinth, bachelor's button, hollyhock, and others in a grave in a cave in northern Iraq, proving prehistoric people gathered flowers to surround death with beauty.[44] There are many reasons people send flowers. One is the creation of a soothing atmosphere, something to soften the harsh visage of death—the dead body. It provides a comforting juxtaposition. The other is expression. It's often hard to find the right words to offer. An arrangement of flowers expresses the perfect sentiment without having to say a word.

As we've seen over the previous chapters, the early American version of a funeral morphed from a semiprivate family-centered affair into the public realm, incorporating more elements, flowers being one of them. This was coupled with the fact that mourning was not only socially acceptable in the nineteenth century but also *fashionable*. Americans were looking for an immediate outlet to express their grief and funeral flowers provided that.

Henry George, who wrote the bestseller *Progress and Poverty*, died in 1897 and his funeral was held at Grand Central Palace in New York City, where an estimated fifty thousand people viewed his body on Halloween day.[45] The *Waterbury (CT) Democrat* reported the following day on the floral tributes, as was the custom of newspapers to report not only what the arrangements were but also who offered them, which in itself appealed to people's narcissistic side and fed into the tradition.

"Floral tributes were profuse," the newspaper reported. "A mass of wreathed flowers from the Chicago Single Tax Club, a wreath of white roses and immortelles from the proprietor of the Union Square hotel and another wreath from Mr. and Mrs. Edward Maxham. These tributes were grouped around the casket . . . a wreath of immortelles and pink orchids from Joseph Pulitzer."[46]

The immortelles mentioned above are dried or artificial flowers, and were a popular floral offering, not only because they were cheaper than fresh flowers (due to the fact that logistics and transportation at the time made the ability to get certain fresh flowers inconsistent . . . and more expensive) but also they could be left on the grave for some time and still maintain their appearance, whereas the life of fresh flowers on a grave is measured in days.

Set pieces, or flowers arranged to look like an object or a scene, became the rage during the Victorian era. The broken pillar, gates ajar, crosses, doves, the broken wheel, and the unstrung harp became standard pieces that could be ordered from any florist. Gates ajar was literally two pieces of fencing set apart from one another—an unusual symbol to the uninitiated. The concept is based on the 1868 novel *The Gates Ajar* by Elizabeth Stuart Phelps. The novel hit a nerve with the public as the protagonist struggles with the death of her brother killed in the Civil War, until her aunt offers the explanation that the gates of heaven do not close but remain ajar to allow the dead to come and go and be near the living. Victorians liked the sentiment the allegory offered, that the departed were near, and it was a wildly popular floral arrangement.

Set pieces could also be custom-made. A police badge, a fireman's helmet, a horse for a breeder or riding enthusiast wouldn't be uncommon set pieces, but sometimes people got creative, such as the case of a dead California brewer whose employees created a beer wagon.

It was fitting then that Henry George's friends and family created a set piece of his bestselling book that was displayed at the funeral and paraded to the cemetery in grand fashion. The *Waterbury Democrat* described the scene: "When Colonel Waring* arrived, he gave orders that the floral tributes to the dead should be placed upon the catafalque. There was a score of beautiful emblems tacked to the sides of the catafalque, the most prominent of which was an emblem an exact counterpart of the dead man's book 'Progress and Poverty.'"[47]

George's remains were buried in one of the new, fashionable rural cemeteries, Green-Wood in Brooklyn.

Frederic T. Greenhalge died suddenly at age fifty-three, shortly into his third term as governor of Massachusetts. Being relatively young and

---

* Colonel George E. Waring, Jr., a sanitation engineer who cleaned up New York City streets, and the grand marshal of events.

a prominent figure, the floral tributes poured in from all quarters. It took a team of decorators three days to arrange the floral tributes in the First Congregational Church in Lowell. Among the hundreds of floral displays was the requisite broken column made of carnations from Highland Grammar School, and a towering eight-foot cross made of lilies, violets, and maiden hair from the city of Boston, as well as the city seal of Cambridge made from white carnations and immortelles.[48] The *Boston Globe* felt compelled to point out, "[T]here had been no attempt at extravagant display."[49] Apparently, extravagance just happened. Greenhalge was buried in Lowell Cemetery, a rural cemetery.

Like Greenhalge, General John Logan, a prominent public figure being a former congressman and sitting senator, died at age sixty the day after Christmas, 1886. Logan fought in the Civil and Mexican-American Wars, and he had a long distinguished public service career spanning twenty-five years. Because of this, Congress issued a resolution that Logan would lie in state in the Capitol Rotunda December 30–31—the seventh American to hold that honor. Though Logan's floral tribute display wasn't as many in number as Greenhalge's, the Washington *Evening Star* reported on a few of the more intricate set pieces, including two crossed cannons made of yellow flowers capped by a white dove from G.A.R., U.S. Grant Post 327, and a "huge" faux pillow with an American flag in the middle made of violets and immortelles.[50] Logan wasn't buried in a rural or park cemetery; because of his service, he was buried in the US Soldiers' and Airmen's Home National Cemetery,* a cemetery that holds predominantly Civil War veterans.

Elaborate and copious floral displays weren't reserved for celebrities and statesmen. At the funeral of Mrs. Edward Cooper, a New York socialite on "The Four Hundred," a prestigious society list, the "top of the coffin was completely hidden beneath a mass of white and purple violets."[51] Jessie Boies died at twenty-nine of "organic heart disease" (no specific cause was given), according to the Davenport, Iowa, *Morning Democrat*. Among the twenty or so arrangements at her funeral listed in the newspaper were three P.E.O. (Philanthropic Educational Organization) stars made from differing floral material and a harp with a broken string.[52]

---

* It is one of only two cemeteries maintained by the Department of the Army. The other cemetery is Arlington National.

Jessie Boies, being the daughter of the governor of Iowa, and Mrs. Cooper, being a prominent and wealthy New Yorker, got press coverage of their final farewell. The average citizen didn't get the same press coverage, but the practice of sending flowers or floral creations was *de rigueur*.

Not everyone bought into the extravagance of funeral flowers. Cornelius "Commodore" Vanderbilt, perhaps the wealthiest man in America when he died, requested that there be no pomp, eulogy, or flowers upon his death. The *New-York Tribune* reported, "He always looked upon floral displays at funerals as wasteful," and went further to say, "W. H. Vanderbilt has requested the railway employees not to send any flowers."[53]

Vanderbilt may have been a curmudgeon to deny a single stem at his obsequies, but he wasn't alone in opposition to floral extravagance. An editorial in the *San Francisco Chronicle* called floral designs "vulgar ostentation," though they didn't disagree with funeral flowers in general, saying, "It is a beautiful custom—one most certainly founded upon the purest and holiest instincts of human nature, one to which even the most degraded of our species must surely respond—to deck our dead and adorn their last resting place with flowers."[54] The writer of the article was railing against the perceived profligacy in set pieces, saying, "They send a floral piece to a friend's funeral because they're afraid they'll be thought mean if they don't. . . . To my mind the floral pieces are more funereal, more suggestive of death than death itself."[55] It isn't mentioned what the aforementioned brewer's cause of death was, but the editorial couldn't help but to include, "One might think that, in the presence of death, the brewer's friends would want to forget that he had ever had anything to do with beer." Perhaps the writer of the piece wasn't aware of the American tradition of funeral lyqr.

While there were no floral tributes at the funeral ceremony at Church of the Strangers Episcopal for Vanderbilt, his loved ones couldn't bear with the austerity of a flowerless event. This is further proof that offering beauty in the face of death is an ingrained impulse, humanity in the face of uncertainty. The *New-York Tribune* reported on the floral displays—some of them set pieces, no less—for the Commodore: "A simple laurel cross lay on the coffin. On the stand at the head was Mrs. Vanderbilt's floral tribute, a large crown of camellias and roses, surmounted by a small cross of violets. At the foot of the coffin was a large anchor of camellias and Marshal Neil roses."[56]

Flowers weren't *always* expressions of sympathy. Sometimes they served a practical purpose. Historically, mourners held rosemary and box sprigs because rosemary is for remembrance, but the fragrant shrub and herb probably had the more practical use of masking the odors coming from the coffin.[57] This was case with President Andrew Johnson. Johnson died of a stroke in July of 1875, and his wife, Eliza Johnson, chose not to have him embalmed. The four intervening days between his death and funeral in the middle of summer caused nature to take its course. The undertaker, Lazarus C. Shepard, "heaped loads of fragrant flowers on top and around the burial receptacle [casket]. The fragrance of the flowers hid the odor long enough for the funeral to take place."[58]

By the time Johnson died in 1875, his role as president meant he had been photographed many times during his lifetime. The first president photographed while in office was the eleventh president, James Polk, in 1849.[59] Sixteen years later, when Johnson took office, emulsion plates had replaced the expensive and time-consuming daguerreotype, and photography was becoming more accessible. Emulsion plates, or wet plates, were the common form of photography used during the Civil War, and this would've been what was used when the newly promoted Major General James A. Garfield hurried home to Hiram, Ohio, to be photographed with his dead toddler, Eliza, in his arms.[60] His civilian suit wasn't yet ready, so he had no other choice than to be photographed in his army uniform.[61] Eliza, named after Garfield's mother and whom he and his wife called "Little Trot," was their oldest child. She died December 3, 1863, at age three of diphtheria. As was the custom at the time, the Garfields chose to have a postmortem photograph taken. Many children didn't have their photograph taken while they were alive, and this was the only photograph the parents would have of their child—a token of remembrance.

General and Mrs. Garfield buried their daughter on December 5 in Fairview Cemetery. The stone, a simple vertical upright, has the words "Our Little Girl" etched into it. Garfield, heart-sore, resigned his military commission that day and boarded a train bound for Washington, DC. The 38th Congress convened two days later, to which Garfield had been elected a representative for Ohio. Hundreds of miles from his grieving wife and infant son, Garfield was able to keep a piece of Little Trot with him in the form of the treasured photograph.

The token of remembrance, or *memento mori*—a Latin phrase that translates to "remember you must die"—was nothing new to the colonial and antebellum Americans who remembered their dead with jewelry, paintings, and textiles. The postmortem photograph added something new to the *memento mori* repertoire. Previously, only the ultrarich could speedily commission a painting of a dead child. Photography offered the opportunity for people of more modest means to have a keepsake image of their child and be able to send reprints to far-off relatives who had never met the child. The postmortem photograph would often be sent out as a mourning card; a strong correlation to the trend of Americans favoring photo memorial cards in contemporary times. The only difference being the modern card typically features a photo of the person while they were alive. Americans in the mid-nineteenth century often didn't have that luxury. As such, the postmortem photograph quickly became a favored *memento mori*.

The window of the postmortem photograph was a relatively short one, less than eighty years, lasting about the length of the Victorian era. Prior to Louis Daguerre's invention in 1839 (the first successful photography process, a.k.a. the daguerreotype, which involved exposing chemically treated silver-plated copper plates to light), death masks and paintings were the only avenues for likenesses of the dead. But why do humans have the urge to capture the likeness of their dead? Aristotle explained that humans want and need to study likenesses because it gives pleasure and aids in reconciling securities and insecurities; it's the concept of "self-possibility."[62] Joe Smoke, a contributor to *Beyond the Dark Veil*, a book on postmortem photography, expounds on this self-possibility saying, "The possibility of our own death makes images into experiences of reconciliation."[63]

And there was a demand for it. In the 1840s, deaths and marriages were documented by photographers by an unthinkable ratio to the contemporary American of three to one.[64] The photographs run the gambit of the elderly to young men and women appearing to sleep in their bed or surrounded by flowers, to harsher images of emaciated bodies wracked with consumption or trauma and decay that no effort was made to cover, though the majority of subjects seem to be the innocents, the children such as Little Trot. Children are the favored subjects because of the unrealized expectations—their parents' hopes and dreams—they contained. These photographs played to the Victorian sense of death as a euphemism, or "The Last Sleep," the children posed as if sleeping on their journey to a benevolent afterlife.[65] Sometimes, the little figure is surrounded by flowers or in the embrace of a parent. If the child was a bit older, sometimes he or she would be propped in a favorite chair with the photographer's assistant valiantly hiding behind a drape holding the little form up, toys neatly posed, too, as if making them immemorial would carry them with the child to the afterlife, a photographic version of grave goods.

In other compositions, siblings surround the deceased. Those photos are often the most disconcerting. They must be studied carefully to determine who is the actual subject. Photographers were known—at the insistence of family members—to prop the eyes open with pins or mucilage (a gum or glue), or for an additional fee the eyes would be painted in later.[66] At the turn of the century a postmortem photograph could fetch as high as $100—about $3,000 in today's dollars—in New York City, with $10 prints for family members.[67]

By the Roaring Twenties, the practice of photographing the dead had been made obsolete. Modern medicine pecked away at the infant mortality rate and the personal camera meant there were more opportunities to photograph a child while alive.

The practice of postmortem photography is making a comeback due to access. Now that virtually every person has a camera in the form of a phone, funeral photography is undergoing a resurgence.

At no other time during America's history was the American funeral service more shaped and cast than the Victorian era. Sure, mourning rituals came and went, as did the popularity of postmortem photography, but certain tenets are still seen in contemporary funerals. Embalming was introduced and embraced by a public wishing to see their dead preserved long enough to be viewed. Certain facets of the ceremony itself morphed. Whereas in colonial times friends and family offered written elegies, the sympathy offering moved to grand floral arrangements. The funeral changed from a public event in colonial times to a private by-invite-only affair in Victorian times, later reverting back to a publicly announced event (via the newspaper obituary) in the twentieth century.

Coffin manufacturing moved from the dusty woodshops of trades-men to caskets, less anthropomorphic in shape than coffins, being mass-produced in factories. And Americans decided they liked the idea of burying that casket in the idyllic setting of a rural or park cemetery, not some overcrowded churchyard or town square. Despite remaining very popular, burial wasn't the only choice of disposition. The modern method of cremation was invented.

The master of the death rite—the undertaker—emerged from myriad tradesmen dabbling in the dismal arts. This new occupational specialist formed in the 1870s as the tradesmen embraced and learned the new sanitary science of embalming and legitimized themselves by beginning to set educational and licensing standards, as well as forming state and national trade organizations. In 1882 the Funeral Directors' National Association of the United States* met for the first time in Rochester, New York, in effect dropping the old term *undertaker* in favor of the new, progressive title of funeral director. An unnamed funeral director neatly summed up the emerging professional ethos at the sixth annual Northwest Funeral Directors Association meeting, saying, "The days of the old coffin-seller have passed into history . . . and instead we have, as a rule, the modern gentlemanly funeral director . . . [who has] familiarized himself with all the latest and best methods of scientific sanitation . . . taking charge of every detail, releasing family and friends of every care."[68]

---

* Now the National Funeral Directors Association (NFDA).

CHAPTER 8

Resurrectionists

Advent of the Burial Vault

L ong before undertakers organized themselves into the professional
group of funeral directors, tradesmen undertakers and families bat-
tled a group of ghoulish men called resurrectionists who operated
by the light of moon. The resurrectionists were body snatchers, yanking
freshly buried remains from the earth and selling them to medical men.
Body snatching was such an uncontrolled problem that it led to the invention of the burial vault, a device still used today.

It works like this: The casket fits in the burial vault much like a pair of
shoes nests in a shoebox. And though no state has a current law requiring the purchase of a burial vault, many cemeteries require one as a rule.
Body snatching went the way of the horse and buggy, but cemeteries
found the burial vault useful in maintaining the structural integrity* of
the cemetery grounds. Vaults prevent graves from collapsing with the
heavy machinery used in modern cemetery operations and thus keep
overall maintenance costs lower.

The scourge of body snatching rose in conjunction with medical
advances. The Christian dogma of the time was focused on the literal

---

* The topography of old burying grounds is uneven because graves collapsed when the wooden coffins rotted,
leaving depressions in the soil, causing monuments to topple, and leading to twisted ankles.

resurrection of the body. A Christian had to be buried "whole" in order to rise again for the second coming. One who had been dissected couldn't be raised in glory. During the Middle Ages, medical men were educated by reading the works of the Greek physician Galen, who had learned anatomy by dissecting monkeys, pigs, dogs, and oxen . . . but not humans.[1] Western physicians used Galen's flawed text, accepted by the church, for well over a thousand years, with anatomical knowledge perhaps better suited for a veterinarian. It wasn't until the sixteenth century, when the Flemish anatomist Andreas Vesalius disproved Galen, much to the consternation of the church, that it became clear to the medical community that the best way to learn and study human anatomy was to do what Vesalius was doing: study actual humans.

Since Christians didn't want to damn themselves for eternity at the hands of the medical men, the government came up with a solution to supply cadavers the burgeoning practice of medicine needed. Dissection became a form of punishment—one more severe than the actual execution as the criminal not only lost their life, but a chance at eternal life too.

In 1540 King Henry VIII passed an act that allowed the Barber-Surgeons the bodies of four executed criminals yearly for study. The company's beadle, akin to a porter, was tasked with the unpleasant job of retrieving the hanged criminals. The families of the executed, who knew what the beadle's presence represented, would fight violently to claim the remains. The beadle was often beaten in the melee to claim a body. The company had to pay the coachman to fix damages sustained to his vehicle, "as well as to give special gratuities to their Beadles by way of solatium for the beatings which they underwent."[2]

Rembrandt's 1632 painting *The Anatomy Lesson of Dr. Nicolaes Tulp*, which hangs in The Hague, depicts the doctor giving an anatomy lesson on the cadaver's left arm. The cadaver is an executed criminal named Aris Kindt. Similarly, the last engraving in a series titled *The Four Stages of Cruelty* by the English painter and engraver William Hogarth a century later depicts the body of a hanged criminal being dissected in an English surgeon's guild hall. The lecturer sits on a throne with a pointer as three surgeons labor away on the criminal. Hanging on the wall are two articulated skeletons labeled James Field, a famed pugilist and criminal, and James Maclaine, a highway robber, both of whom met with the end of a rope and were given over to the surgeons.[3]

The fledgling American jurisprudence system fashioned many of their laws after English common law. Modeling the English Murder Act of 1751, which aimed at "better preventing the horrid crime of murder," Massachusetts passed a punitive anatomy act in 1784, An Act Against Duelling [sic], allowing the courts to not only turn over for dissection the bodies of executed criminals but also those who died while dueling. The first medical school had been organized in America some two decades prior and already trouble was brewing.

American physicians encountered the same issue as their English cohorts of procuring a steady supply of cadavers for study. They resorted to questionable acquisition practices, and when their methodology was exposed, there was invariably violence. The first recorded instance involved Dr. William Shippen, Jr., who taught the first private course in anatomical dissection in 1762 in Philadelphia.[4] Three years later he founded the College of Philadelphia's medical school with Dr. John Morgan. When the public became aware of what was happening in the building that housed the dissecting theater, it was attacked several times; Dr. Shippen's carriage was attacked by an angry mob, and someone fired a pistol at it.[5] Shippen survived the attack and continued to practice medicine, later becoming the director general of hospitals* for the Continental army. Shippen tried to appease the public by publishing announcements in the paper, "to assure them [the public], that the Bodies he dissected, were either of Persons who had willfully murdered themselves, or were publickly [sic] executed, except now and then one from Potters Field" (a public burial place for paupers, unknown persons, and criminals).[6] Shippen went on to assure Philadelphians that "he never had one body from the Church, or any other private Burial Place."[7] Shippen's sentiment echoes the larger public one: they didn't care so much that doctors were cutting up the dead; they just didn't want them cutting up *their* dead. It was okay to fillet criminals and the poor, but the reaction was violent when the doctors dipped into the graves of the "worthy" dead.

---

* This is the precursor to the surgeon general of the army.

That's exactly what happened during the Doctors' Riot two decades later in New York—when doctors were suspected of snatching the "worthy" dead—this time with deadly results.

In the winter of 1788, the students at New York Hospital were busy pilfering Potter's Field and the Black burying ground outside the city limits. Public outrage simmered, but it didn't begin to boil until a newspaper article in February claimed a grave in Trinity churchyard had been disturbed.[8] All hell broke loose in April.

It was the Sabbath, a day of rest in puritanical America. But not for a group of physicians laboring in the anatomical theater. A group of boys was playing in the grassy area near the rear of the hospital located at Broadway and Duane Streets when curiosity got the best of them. There were whispers about what went on in the imposing brick structure, and the boys decided to investigate. Dr. Richard Bayley, seeing the boys peering in through the leaded glass, waved a severed limb* at the group.[9] The boys, terrified, scampered off to sound the alarm. In no time an angry mob assembled. The mob entered the hospital, and finding "some mangled bodies of the dead," it tore through the hospital destroying all anatomical specimens.[10] Mayor James Duane and Sheriff Robert Boyd arrived and escorted the medical men to the jail for their own safekeeping, but not before they suffered injuries at the hands of the mob. Duane and Boyd got things calmed down and hoped that was the end of it.

It wasn't. The mob returned the next morning.

This time Governor George Clinton, along with Mayor Duane, tried to assuage the mob, promising legal satisfaction. But the agitators within the crowd fanned indignation: *these ghouls were desecrating their friends and family.* By the afternoon their number swelled to five thousand, and they were armed and itching for confrontation.

Governor Clinton, sensing blood in the water, summoned the militia. The first group of eighteen was allowed to pass by the mob.[11] When the second group of twenty-two arrived an hour later, the crowd had worked themselves into such a lather that the militia was surrounded and disarmed.[12] The emboldened mob attacked the fortified jail with rocks and brickbats. The militia, under strict orders not to fire, had no other choice

---

* Some sources say there was a limb hanging out the window, for drying, that the boys spied. It seems unlikely, given the scrutiny the physicians were under for grave robbing, that they'd risk displaying limbs for all to see.

after two members* of Clinton and Duane's entourage were smashed in the head with flying rocks, leaving them bloodied and dazed.[13] The militiamen fired several volleys until the mob dispersed, leaving at least three dead and many seriously wounded. The actual death toll is likely several times higher as the wounded succumbed to their injuries at home in desperate need—ironically—of doctors' care.

An artillery regiment later joined the militia to maintain the peace. This wouldn't be the last time the military was called in to quell anatomy-related violence. In 1852, two infantry companies with fixed bayonets were called to the Western Homeopathic College in Cleveland to restore order.

Reports of body parts in the outhouses of the college caused the citizens of Cleveland to demand a search party be allowed to search the premises.[14] Mr. Johnson of Ohio City, one of the five searchers, made a grisly discovery. His daughter, or what was left of her, was discovered in the dissecting room. She had recently been laid to rest, or so the Johnson family thought. Johnson claimed to recognize his daughter's hands by their uniquely distinguishing marks.[15] When Johnson reported his outrageous findings to the hundreds gathered outside the college on the blistering cold February night, the crowd, many drunk and belligerent, stormed the building. The mob smashed all the windows of the building and emptied the contents of the building, including the beds and personal effects from the student apartments, onto the streets. A skeleton was "lashed to a barbor's [sic] pole and carried through the streets."[16] Twice the rioters tried to set fire to the building, but firemen were able to get it under control and save the building. So out of control was the mob that the sheriff deputized any able-bodied, sober citizens to help aid the military in quelling the unrest.

The professors of the college tried to justify the "evidence" found on the premises as a terrible misunderstanding. The faculty claimed they thought they were purchasing cadavers from hundreds of miles away, completely ignorant to the fact they were tacitly admitting to dealing with resurrectionists regardless if the bodies were local or not. "If any [bodies] have been [disinterred] here it has been without their knowledge," the

---

* John Jay, for whom the college is named and who would later become the second governor of New York; and Baron Friedrich von Steuben, Revolutionary War hero.

Detroit Free Press reported, further stating the faculty wanted the matter investigated thoroughly.[17]

Published affidavits from students and faculty later revealed the hand found by Mr. Johnson was in fact the hand of a male.[18]

The year after the bloody Doctors' Riot of 1788, New York passed a law "to prevent the odious practice of digging up and removing for the purpose of dissection dead bodies interred in cemeteries or burial places," essentially formalizing the illegality of grave robbing.[19] Lawmakers, however, realized that anatomical specimens were necessary for research and educational purposes, so the act allowed for judges to designate the bodies of executed criminals (much like in England) to be offered up for dissection.

Massachusetts followed its 1784 dueling anatomy act a half century later with a more liberal and sweeping anatomy act that allowed for unclaimed bodies to be turned over to medical schools for dissection. Despite grave robbing being made illegal in some states, it was still a lucrative endeavor, worth the risk. A body could fetch anywhere between two to thirty-five dollars depending on the condition.[20]

The Massachusetts Anatomy Act of 1831 was partially in response to an international scandal from Scotland where a pair of men, William Hare and William Burke, found dealing in corpses to be quite profitable. Burke and Hare weren't resurrectionists but murderers. By the time the authorities caught up with the pair, they had murdered sixteen people, including children, suffocating them after getting them drunk so their crime wouldn't be obvious to Dr. Robert Knox at Surgeon's Square in Edinburgh. To save his own skin, Hare turned King's evidence and testified against Burke. Burke was publicly executed in front of a crowd of twenty-five thousand hecklers. Then, perhaps in the greatest irony of this tragedy, Burke was dissected by Knox's rival, Dr. Alexander Monro, at Edinburgh Medical College and then put on public display where twenty-four thousand people pushed through the anatomy theater to gawk at his filleted remains.[21]

Despite the fact that Burke and Hare weren't technically resurrectionists, their heinous crimes shined a very bright light on the fact that if medical science were to advance, cadavers were in desperate need. The new anatomy acts helped some, but the proliferation of medical schools meant the demand still far outstripped the legal supply. Grave robbing continued to be a problem. New York followed Massachusetts's lead and passed what was colloquially called the "Bone Bill" in 1854, which allowed the unclaimed bodies of criminals and the homeless to be claimed by medical institutions.

The tipping point in the ghoulish behavior was a sensational body snatching splashed across the front pages of every major newspaper. The incident involved a president's son and a future president, and it uncovered an organized network of people working in the illegal trade of cadavers. The public was outraged. As a result, the next year the burial safe was invented, and the year after, the burial vault.

John Scott Harrison died of suspected apoplexy—a stroke—at his farm on May 25, 1878.[22] The former representative for the state of Ohio was seventy-three and the last surviving child of ninth president William Henry Harrison. Funeral services were held four days later at Cleves Presbyterian, a modest whitewashed structure, with burial afterward at Congress Green Cemetery about a mile from the church. The grave, next to that of his parent's tomb, had been prepared. The grave was dug extra deep—eight feet—and a brick vault constructed at the bottom.[23]

The funeral party—consisting of Scott Harrison's six children, extended family, and community members, as well as local politicians given the Harrisons' political ties; not only had the deceased been a major political figure but two of his sons were connected—arrived at the cemetery. Carter Harrison was a US representative for Illinois, and Benjamin Harrison was a prominent Republican Party member who'd conducted an unsuccessful bid for the governorship of Indiana two years prior. It was immediately apparent that the grave of Samuel Augustus Devin, who died the week prior and was buried near the Harrison family plot, had been "despoiled."[24] The thought that went through the brothers' minds was *Body snatchers are afoot*, but not wanting to upset Devin's mother, they passed the disturbed earth off to rooting hogs.[25]

To prevent the same suspected fate as the Devin boy, the Harrisons ordered a large rock lowered on top of the vault that took the strength of sixteen men* to lift into the hole, and the whole affair was covered in concrete. The concrete was given time to partially dry and the extra-deep

---

* Some accounts say eighteen men. Bottom line: the stone was pretty damn heavy.

grave was filled in. As an added protection, a guard was hired stand watch for the next thirty days.[26]

Once the funeral party left the cemetery, John Scott Harrison Jr. and his nephew George Eaton opened Devin's grave and made the startling, if not unsurprising, discovery. His coffin was smashed open and his body gone. Resurrectionists never went to the trouble to open the entire grave. Rather, they dug a small vertical hole at the top of the grave near the head end of the coffin. Digging was easy, as the earth had been freshly turned, and gravediggers at the time didn't have plate compactors used in modern cemeteries to tamp the earth. Once at the level of the coffin, the resurrectionist cracked open a small section at the head end of the coffin and dragged the remains out by the shoulders. Skilled resurrectionists bragged they could have the deed done and the body secreted in their wagon in twenty minutes time, with the grave filled back in and nobody the wiser.

The trade of the resurrectionists helped increase the popularity of rural cemeteries with the public. Rural cemeteries were "a distance" from the urban center, fenced and gated, and typically employed night watchmen. These seemingly appealing security features actually made the rural cemeteries more tempting to the resurrectionists. The distance from town meant they could work in relative peace and privacy, the fences being no matter to scale. And a medium-sized cemetery such as Laurel Hill in Philadelphia, covering seventy-eight acres, meant it was difficult for two or three watchmen* to make a regular, thorough inspection of the grounds in the middle of the night with nothing more than a lantern.

Poor Augustus Devin never stood a chance. Congress Green was little more than a private family burial ground. There was no fence, much less a night watchman. He'd been snatched for medical science.

Harrison and Eaton had a good lead. Thursday morning, the *Cincinnati Enquirer* reported a suspicious buggy had pulled into an alley off Vine Street around 3:00 a.m. and had offloaded a cargo at the Medical College of Ohio—driving off before they could be accosted.[27] Along with Cincinnati Detective Thomas Snelbaker and two constables, and armed with a search

---

* Night watchmen were known to succumb to melancholia, or in the worst cases, suicide, named "Tombstone Madness" in a March 29, 1883, article in *The Times* (Philadelphia, PA). Given that this was less than twenty years removed from the Civil War, and ex-soldiers were often hired as night watchmen, there's a strong argument to be made that their new vocation didn't cause depression. They were suffering from "soldier's heart," or what would be called post-traumatic stress disorder (PTSD) today.

warrant, Harrison and Eaton began a thorough search of the medical college. Led by the janitor, A. Q. Marshall, the group began scouring the five-story building, tearing apart piles of lumber and stone in the cellar in search of Devin's body. They found nothing. As they worked their way to the top floor, Marshall, growing visibly nervous, announced it proper that college officials be present for the search and disappeared.

Snelbaker, not trusting Marshall, sent one of the constables to follow him.

Instead of heading for the administration offices, the constable watched Marshall scamper upstairs to a deserted dissecting room in the southeast corner of the building. Lit by gaslight, the room contained four empty porcelain tables, a stove in the corner, an overhead rainwater tank, and two slop sinks.[28] There, the constable found Marshall hacking at the rope of the windlass, essentially a block-and-tackle system for hoisting things into the dissecting room.

"Stop!" the constable commanded, rushing into the room.

He quickly alerted the others and they hurried upstairs where Snelbaker began cranking the handle of the windlass.

Out of the gaping abyss emerged the nude form of a "heavy and large . . . old man," the rope looped under one arm and around the neck, his face hooded by a cloth—certainly not young Devin, who died frail, his body wracked with consumption.[29] Snelbaker urged Harrison to look at the body, so there'd never be any doubt that it wasn't Devin. They moved the trapdoor into place and lowered the nude form onto the floor. Harrison removed the hood and recoiled with horror, crying, "It's Father!"[30]

It was almost inconceivable that this was how John Harrison's search for Augustus Devin ended. It had been less than twenty-four hours since the Harrison brothers watched their father lowered into the ground and to now find him hanging from a rope—and mutilated. Scott Harrison's beard, which reached nearly to his waist, had been shorn, his hair too, and blood leaked from a cut on his neck where embalming fluid had been injected to preserve him for the students.[31] Additionally, Harrison's face was cut and discolored from being dragged from his coffin and then suspended from a rope.

The firm of Estep & Meyer—sworn to secrecy—was summoned to bring a coffin and take the remains away. The Harrisons attempted to keep the whole affair a secret. The story leaked immediately, and news of the grave robbing was splashed across Friday's papers. The public was beyond outraged. The son of a US president and a two-term member of Congress had been snatched for scalpel fodder. Citizens called for vigilante action against the doctors who created the demand for this ghoulish supply. Their rage reached a fever pitch when bail—$5,000, a hefty sum at the time—for Marshall, the janitor, was posted by Dr. Whitaker on behalf of the medical community.[32] The bail posting solidified a clear link between resurrectionists and medical men in the public's mind. Benjamin Harrison called for cooler heads and *legal* action. The *Boston Post* best summed up public sentiment, writing, "No one but a beast, even though in man's shape, could perpetrate such an outrage, which at once grieves, shocks, disgusts and terrifies society."[33]

How had Scott Harrison been taken from an all but burglarproof grave? The Harrisons had exercised an abundance of caution, even hiring a watchman. Surely he'd been bought off. While bribery can't be ruled out entirely, the fact is the watchman had been hired to check the grave every *hour*, not stand constant vigil.[34] An hour was more than ample time for an experienced resurrectionist to open a grave—even with the additional precautions. The large stone that took sixteen men to lift had only been big enough to cover the top portion of the vault. Two smaller stones covered the foot end.[35] The men opening the grave had dug down at the foot end of the grave, opposite the normal procedure, drilled through the smaller slabs enough to lift them, smashed the glass (inner liner) of the metallic coffin, and dragged Harrison out by his feet. The hole was filled in and the body snatchers long gone before the watchman's next round. The chilling fact remains that the men knew to dig at the opposite end of the grave, almost guaranteeing that someone present at the graveside sold the information.

Detective Snelbaker, spurred on by intense public scrutiny and political pressure, managed to shine a light on the larger network that Scott Harrison's remains had become ensnared in and bring the whole unsavory saga to a rather unsatisfying conclusion.

After an exhaustive investigation, Devin's body was found June 14 at the medical college in Ann Arbor, Michigan. Based upon information from the janitor of Miami Medical College, Snelbaker learned the resurrectionist Charles Morton had been operating in the area. Morton's notoriety was so well known the one newspaper simply referred to him as the "famous ghoul."[36] By bribing the janitor, Morton had been using Miami Medical College as a base of operations in the spring of 1878. Morton shipped the subjects to medical schools in barrels bearing a false company name: Quimby & Co.[37] Under Snelbaker's interrogation, the janitor gave it up that Morton had shipped a lot of barrels via American Express to the University of Michigan Medical College.[38]

Devin was found jammed in one of three vats of brine, along with forty-eight other cadavers in various states of decomposition, in the basement of the college. In an exchange at which the *Detroit Free Press* was present, an administrator at the college tried to explain to B. J. Devin, Augustus's brother, and Eaton that "their endeavor here was to get bodies of paupers . . . and of persons who had no friends. But they had to rely on their agents to obtain these bodies, and it was of course impossible to know exactly where they [sourced] each body."[39]

Augustus Devin was laid to rest a second time on June 17, but not before the coffin was opened at the train depot and an estimated 150 citizens, including the future president Benjamin Harrison, filed by to view.[40] Scott Harrison was kept for a year and a half in a secret location—the Jacob Strader family vault in Spring Grove Cemetery—until being quietly reinterred at Congress Green in December of 1879.[41]

The same year Harrison was reinterred, Indiana and Ohio hastily adopted laws that allowed for citizens who would be buried at public expense to be turned over to medical schools. Indiana's and Ohio's acts were steps in the right direction, but the reality was that at the turn of the nineteenth century, the Medical College of Indiana had a student body of four hundred with only six cadavers.[42] How was the college going to reconcile the shortfall? Probably in the local cemetery.

Despite the medical men trying to get their subjects "responsibly" sourced from the poor and destitute, the public had had enough of their cemeteries being emptied. It was time to stop relying on the lawmakers to protect their dead. Men such as Philip Clover decided to not simply passively defend against their kin's bodies being snatched but to mount a vigorous, active defense. The same year as the Harrison debacle, Clover was issued a patent for a "coffin-torpedo." The objective of his patent application was to "successfully prevent the unauthorized resurrection of dead bodies," which was achieved with deadly force.[43] Clover's invention worked like a shotgun. A barrel packed with gunpowder and metal balls was secreted in the trimming (i.e., lining) of the casket by the undertaker and a series of wires were attached to the arms and legs, so that any disruption of the remains tripped the trigger and set off the shotgun-like device. Clover went as far as to stipulate the barrel should be secreted in the head area of the casket, the area typically broken open by the resurrectionists, to maximize its effectiveness.

Several years later, a former probate judge from Ohio, Thomas N. Howell, filed a patent for a "grave-torpedo" that operated like the recent wartime invention called "land torpedoes," now known as land mines. Howell's invention operated when a contact point disturbed by "the slightest movement" exploded the shell.[44]

The *Norfolk Virginian*, in commenting on the recent sensational body snatching of Alexander T. Stewart,* one of the wealthiest men in America, pointed out the major drawback to such lethal devices: "This invention is intended to have a moral, rather than a practical effect, for it is difficult to see how it can explode without demolishing the dead body."[45] For many families, the choice of having their dead pulverized by a bomb blast was a more dignified fate than the scalpel of the medical men. Though Howell's invention stipulates to bury the charge "several inches" of earth above the casket to "prevent injury to the coffin."[46] Howell may have been an expert in the law but not in explosives. There was a good chance the charge—as his design appears more akin to a grenade exploding than a directional blasting device—would radiate downward with enough force to pulverize (or, at the very least disturb) the contents of the coffin.

It's unknown how many of these deadly inventions were deployed, but enough were used that it worked—at least once. Three men attempting to rob the fresh grave of Russell O'Harrel's daughter near Gann, Ohio, met with a torpedo.[47] The blast killed the ringleader; a

---

* Stewart's body was stolen from its mausoleum at St. Mark's on the Bowery over two years after his death. The purpose wasn't for medical science study but rather a ransom scheme because of the family's wealth. The ransom was paid, and the remains were returned. The event was so sensational that almost fifteen years later, when Charlotte Gibbes Astor (wife of John J. Astor III, and aunt of the John Astor who died on the *Titanic*) was entombed in Trinity Cemetery, guards were posted to prevent a repetition of the Stewart robbery. "Straws," *Sunnyside* 4, no. 30, (January 1, 1888).

man named Dipper, and severely wounded another—as evidenced by the blood in the snow. The lookout was able to get the wounded man into their sleigh and get away. They were never caught. The event was widely published, not only because it was a sensational bit of news but to serve as a warning to body snatchers.[48]

It's likely Dipper was killed by Clover's device as the thwarted body snatching happened in January 1881 and Howell's invention wasn't patented for almost another year. And while well intended, these devices were more or less permanent, despite the fact they were only really needed for a week or so until decomposition set in. They were more likely to kill an unsuspecting gravedigger opening the grave next to the booby-trapped grave or during a legitimate disinterment years later. Which begs the question: How many booby-trapped graves are still out there and functional?

Andrew Van Bibber of Ohio came up with a safe alternative the same year Clover unveiled his deadly grave sentinel. His "burial safe" was a cage made of a latticework of welded iron bars. The casket was placed in the cage, the cage locked, and then the earth filled in. The door on his burial safe was secured with padlocks on the side of the cage, which theoretically *could* be picked, but they weren't readily accessible on the top of the cage. The thought was the resurrectionists would target the low-hanging fruit—the unprotected caskets.

Van Bibber's invention was similar to the mortsafe, a popular device in Scotland where body snatching was rampant. The mortsafe was a cage made of iron bars (sometimes weighted with a ledger stone) placed on top of the freshly filled-in grave. The idea was that the mortsafe could be moved off the grave once enough time had passed and reused, whereas Van Bibber's burial safe was designed to be completely subterranean and permanent.

The following year, George W. Boyd, another Ohioan obsessed with grave security, patented his grave vault advertised in trade magazines as "burglarproof." In an 1882 advertisement in the Columbus Coffin Company's catalog, Boyd employs a none-too-subtle tactic, reminding undertakers of "the almost daily reports of the devastation of grave robbers."[49] Boyd's vault was made with steel plates riveted together to form a vaulted cover that snapped into a bottom metal plate.

Once snapped together, the two pieces couldn't be undone without a torch. *The Sunnyside* clarified exactly how secure: "Even if the ghouls succeeded in excavating the earth and reaching this vault . . . it cannot be opened, excepting by cutting the top casing entirely open which would take a skilled mechanic at least twenty-four hours."[50] Boyd's invention operated on the principle of an air seal,* making it waterproof as well as burglarproof. His invention was relatively light, and the arched dome lid made the vault incredibly strong and prevented grave collapse over time, something cemeterians took notice of.

One of the first instances of a burial vault in the style such as Boyd's being put into practical use was the vault for President Ulysses S. Grant who died in 1885. Undertaker of the rich and famous, Rev. Stephen Merritt of New York City ordered an arch-top metal vault from Franklin Iron Works in Troy, New York. Made from half-inch tempered steel, the entire contraption weighed seven hundred pounds, and ensured the former president's grave couldn't be burglarized.[51] Unlike Scott Harrison who was stolen for anatomical study, there was concern that there could be a politically motivated body snatching of the ex-president. A few years prior, the Secret Service had foiled a plot to steal Lincoln's body† and hold it for ransom.

Shortly after metal vaults entered the marketplace, Leo Haase, a German immigrant, began manufacturing concrete vaults. Made of two pieces, much like a shoebox, the bottom gets placed in the hole to receive the casket and then a lid is lowered on top. The whole unit, empty, weighs about a ton, a formidable obstacle for a resurrectionist. The demand for Haase's concrete vaults took off during the Spanish flu pandemic, and the company, Wilbert Funeral Services, is now the US's largest provider of burial vaults.[52]

In 1883 the Pennsylvania Legislature passed Senate Bill 117 enacting an anatomy act that was unlike any before it. This act, in response to yet another grave robbing scandal involving Jefferson Medical College and its chief anatomist, Dr. William Forbes, was different in that physicians drafted it. And instead of allowing the state to turn over unclaimed bodies, the law required the state to turn over unclaimed

---

* Think of inverting an empty glass into a sink full of water.
† The gang in the 1876 attempt got as far as prying off the sarcophagus's lid, revealing the coffin.

bodies to a newly created anatomy board, which would equitably distribute the cadavers. The act would solve a multitude of problems by relieving the public of the cost of burying indigents, keeping a supply of research material flowing to Pennsylvania medical schools, and most importantly to the public, keeping the graveyards filled. Over the next few decades, other states adopted anatomy acts similar to Pennsylvania's, and coupled with the newly invented burial vault, instances of grave robbing began to disappear from newspaper headlines.

Despite the newly adopted laws, there was a lingering fear with the public of having their corporeal remains misappropriated by ghouls. When George Pullman died in 1897, he was buried in an eight-foot-deep grave covered with asphalt, concrete, and steel bars. Once it was filled in with earth, another twelve-inch layer of asphalt was placed on top of the grave, making it "impossible for any earthly power to remove the casket."[53]

If the anatomy acts of the late nineteenth century had fixed the problem of grave robbing, the burial vault might be a curiosity of a bygone era. But the fact remained that the demand for legal corpses still far outstripped the legal supply—into the twentieth century—and George Pullman was cognizant that a problem still existed. Six years after Pullman died, the nation was scandalized when the self-proclaimed King of Grave Robbers went on trial in perhaps one of the most widespread and egregious body-snatching rings ever uncovered. Rufus Cantrell boasted he'd snatched an astounding twelve hundred bodies in six years. There was a very public trial that captured the attention of the nation in the winter of 1903. Cantrell was sentenced to ten years, but amazingly, the man who'd allegedly commissioned Cantrell's crimes, Dr. Joseph Alexander, went scot-free.

In response to the outcome of Alexander's trial,* a group of farmers gathered at a sleepy crossroads called Fishers Station to burn in effigy Alexander and Judge John Bailey, the judge who presided over Alexander's trial. A scaffold was erected near the train station amid shouts of "Death to the grave robbers!" The angry mob strung the dummies up with signs reading "Justice to Alexander [and] Bailey."[54] Joseph Alexander had been raised in this tiny community fourteen miles north of Indianapolis and

---

* Alexander wasn't acquitted. He was released after a mistrial due to a hung jury.

had made good in the big city as a prominent physician and an esteemed demonstrator at the medical college. Alexander grew up with many of the rioters, attending school and church with them. He was one of them. But the irate mob of farmers was past caring about community ties. They tried setting the dummies on fire but nearly set the train depot on fire, so they cut down and torched them on the ground, shouting, "We did 'em right. The courts didn't do it, but we did."[55]

This seems like an extreme reaction given Alexander's local connection, but he'd betrayed them by emptying their graveyards.

Dr. Alexander was the anatomy demonstrator for the Central College of Physicians and Surgeons at the recently completed facility at 212 N. Senate Avenue in Indianapolis. The prosecuting attorney John Ruckelshaus described him during the trial as a "Dr. Jekyl [*sic*] and Mr. Hyde . . . socially, professionally and commercially believed to be a good fellow." But Ruckelshaus said privately, "[He was engaged] in the desecration of human graves."[56] Alexander had been supplying the college with cadavers using the services of Rufus Cantrell, a young itinerant Baptist minister who found the trade of grave robbing to be much more lucrative than preaching the Word. Their association had been going quite well, with Alexander paying Cantrell fifty dollars for each body he brought him, until he sent him to empty the wrong grave.

There had been issues with bodies—who were supposed to be buried— turning up at the college in the past, but the faculty had been able to explain these "mistakes" away. All of this changed when Alexander sent Cantrell and his gang to pilfer the grave of Stella Middleton. It was dark in the cemetery, and it wasn't until Cantrell lighted a gas lamp in the college's basement did he realize he'd dug up the woman he was eyeing to offer a marriage proposal to. Horrified, Cantrell told Middleton's relatives the location of her body. The ensuing investigation forced Cantrell to turn state's evidence against his employer.[57]

In a panic, the medical college staff yanked six people out of barrels, tied them up in sacks, and deposited them in an alley.[58] But they overlooked one. The police found the body of Rosielee Neidlinger in a vat of brine in the college basement. She'd died July 17, 1902, at the age of twenty-two and was buried in Pleasant Hill Cemetery, a frequent harvesting ground of Cantrell's gang. It's suspected she'd been disinterred

August 21, which, if true, meant she'd been embalmed, otherwise her remains would've been in an advanced state of decomposition by the time of her exhumation and useless for medical dissection.[59]

Alexander was indicted in December on four counts: taking the body from the grave, concealing a dead body, buying a dead body, and having in his possession for dissection purposes an unlawfully obtained body.[60]

Ruckelshaus paraded a stream of citizens in front of the jury that clearly established Alexander funded Cantrell's gang and furnished them with tools such as shovels, pickaxes, rope, and drill bits; weapons such as shotguns and revolvers; and livery rental of buggies and wagons to haul their gruesome harvest. Some witnesses attested to the fact that they had seen Alexander and Cantrell together driving through cemeteries—a chilling thought in hindsight, as the witnesses now realized they were out shopping.

However, the most damning (and entertaining) testimony came from Cantrell himself. Cantrell told the jury that Alexander would visit the Board of Health and obtain a list of recent burials and send Cantrell out to retrieve them.[61] Alexander wasn't just sending Cantrell out into the night to do his ghoulish work; no, he was targeting specific people. Henry Spaan, Alexander's defense attorney, attempted to discredit Cantrell's testimony as that coming from someone who was insane, citing his medical discharge from the army. Spaan probably wasn't far off the mark that Cantrell wasn't of sound mind. This was a man who'd bragged of robbing thirteen graves of funerals he'd attended, as well as robbing the graves of people he'd preached the funeral service for.[62]

Spaan's defense of Alexander was that his client believed he was only getting bodies from Cantrell who were obtained by legal means— unclaimed bodies. Spaan created enough doubt to result in a hung jury and Alexander being set free.

Cantrell mounted a defense of insanity at his trial, but the jury didn't buy it. Cantrell was found guilty of grave robbing and, in perhaps the greatest injustice, conspiracy with Dr. Alexander. He was sentenced to ten years.

The public was outraged, and the "Farmers' Riot" resulted. Manson Neidlinger, Rosielee's husband, had vowed at Alexander's trial, "If this court fails to punish him I will seek just vengeance for his terrible desecration myself."[63]

Neidlinger didn't follow through.

Alexander continued to practice medicine, and he died in December of 1925 at the age of sixty-six. The greatest irony of the Cantrell and Alexander travesty is that Alexander is buried in an unmarked grave in Crown Hill Cemetery in Indianapolis, a place he was never able to pilfer the graves of because of the cemetery's formidable fencing and vigilant armed guards.

The Cantrell and Alexander scandal underscored the need for a "burglarproof" burial vault, even in the modern times of the early twentieth century. If the resurrectionists came across a ton of concrete or a seven-gauge* steel shell, they were going to move on to easier pickings. With a burial vault, the public was buying peace of mind that their loved one would lie undisturbed.

But the winds were beginning to shift. Not only were medical schools getting fed a steady stream of legally procured cadavers from unclaimed bodies but also people were starting to do something unthinkable—will their bodies to science. As early as 1896, Dr. Sherman Foote of Kansas City, Kansas, stipulated in his will—which he published with great fanfare—that his body be donated to science because of his "disgust at the sickly sentimentalism," and "the only source of obtaining such [surgical] skill [is dissection]."[64] Foote, an early proponent of cremation, called burial "[a] relic of an ignorant semi-barbarous past," but instead of cremation, Foot decided he wanted his body to be laid on the altar of science because he believed it would yield "scientific secrets."[65] Foote died alone in 1902 and fell victim to an ignorant semibarbarous past. His remains were buried in Maple Hill Cemetery.[66] Foote may have been a bit eccentric, but his unselfish, scientific-pioneering spirit was ahead of its time. It would only take a few generations for the culture to no longer view anatomical donation as subjecting oneself to butchery and desecration but as committing a philanthropic act—perhaps the *ultimate* philanthropic act.

In 1968 the Uniform Anatomical Gift Act (UAGA) was adopted by all fifty states in response to the first successful heart transplant the year before in South Africa. The purposes of the UAGA donations are for transplantation, therapy, research, or education.[67] Now, people can

---

* To put it in perspective: a modern car skin (ones that still have metal) is going to be made of twenty- to twenty-two-gauge steel, or three times thinner.

donate all or part—selected organs and/or tissues—of their body to science. What set this apart from previous anatomy acts was the donated organ or body was a *gift*, not an appropriation of an unclaimed body. The UAGA prevails upon ideals such as altruism, generosity, and progress, principles that are uniquely part of the American ethos. It's the same spirit the government tapped during the world wars with victory gardens, gasoline rationing, scrap drives, and the purchase of war bonds: sacrifice for the greater good. Americans now willingly turn over their corporeal remains to medical students in the name of scientific advancement, a far cry from the fear and anger that ruled during the Doctors' Riot of 1788 or more recently the Farmers' Riot of 1903.

As the fear of body snatching lessened, undertakers began to shift the focus of burial vaults from protecting the body from grave robbers to protection from the elements. Not that this was a new marketing push. From the get-go, the Boyd metal vault was advertised as being waterproof. As the twentieth century progressed, weatherproofing became the primary focus of why a consumer should purchase a burial vault, and cemeteries began to see the benefits of steel and concrete vaults. In the nineteenth century (and before), if a family had a burial vault, it was usually an outer wooden box. Sometimes, if it were a person of wealth, a mason would brick out a vault. But this was rare. Typically the decedent was buried in the ground in only their wooden coffin. Over time, the wood rotted and the grave collapsed, leaving a depression on the surface of the cemetery, which made it difficult for mourners to navigate and led to toppling headstones. And this was when graves were dug by hand and grass was maintained (if, at all) by grazing animals. By the mid-twentieth century, cemeteries found burial vaults* necessary for maintaining the integrity of the grounds, as industrial lawn mowers, backhoes, and stake body trucks regularly traversed the grounds. Of course, some cemeteries still don't require a vault, but by and large it's become a fixture of the modern American funeral, though most consumers don't think burial vault when they hear the word *funeral*. The piece of merchandise that has come to symbolize the funeral is much older than the vault. It's the vessel the body reposes in—the casket.

---

* The Federal Trade Commission requires funeral homes to use the catchall, roll-off-the-tongue term *outer burial container*.

CHAPTER 9

Vessels of the Dead

Coffins, Caskets, and the Hysteria Surrounding Grave Alarms

D r. Henry Hiller died November 7, 1888, of internal injuries sustained in a carriage wreck. His newly purchased colts bolted, tossing him from the vehicle; he clung to life for about six weeks.[1] The *Boston Globe*, reporting on Hiller's death, offered a rather odd note of sympathy: "Coffin and man are ready for each other."[2] But nothing could be truer. This—his coffin*—was what he'd be remembered for, his crowning achievement, his pièce de résistance. Hiller, a millionaire who made his fortune selling a cure-all elixir, had commissioned his casket construction to begin three years prior, when he was forty years old.

The masterpiece, unveiled to the press on November 10, 1888, had to be finished in a rush job by J. W. MacGregor. At a cost of $50,000† and weighing a ton, it was quite unlike any coffin America had ever seen.

The outer sarcophagus—there were actually two pieces to this ornate vessel of repose—wasn't finished by the time of his untimely death, so

---

* Hiller was buried in an octagonal-shaped vessel that was briefly popular in the late nineteenth century— Ulysses S. Grant was buried in a vessel with such a shape. Coffins have a hexagonal shape and caskets a rectangular shape; the octagonal-shaped burial vessel could arguably be called a casket *or* coffin.

† The cost of the casket varies from $17,500 to $50,000 depending on the article. The $50,000 price tag is quoted by the *Boston Globe* in the feature they did on Mrs. Hiller's Horticulture Hall display. On the low end, $17,500 in today's dollars is just over $500,000.

Mrs. Dr. France Hiller pressed on with funeral plans with just the inner coffin. It's little wonder the Cambridge cabinetmaker MacGregor, along with four assistants, took this long to make Hiller's coffin. It was no single-break plank coffin nailed together in a dusty workshop. No, this was a magnum opus—his *Sgt. Pepper*. Made of Spanish mahogany, it was adorned with a multitude of grim carvings in relief too numerous to list, though the *Boston Globe* tried, saying, "Dragons, dragons everywhere, they grin at you and glare at you with their hideous eyes."[3]

The funeral service began at 2:00 p.m. and continued until well after dark. To convey the massive casket to the temporary holding vault (as the Hiller's six-*thousand*-square-foot, seven-story mausoleum wasn't yet completed), William Lockhart, an undertaker from Boston, was commissioned to build a custom catafalque.[4] This "car of death," as the newspapers described it, cost $2,000* to construct and used an astounding 140 yards of black broadcloth. Four draft horses struggled to pull the monstrosity and its payload.

After the funeral, MacGregor resumed his work in the converted workhouse on the back of the property, this time at a frantic pace. MacGregor now had a deadline—Mrs. Dr. Hiller wanted to display the masterpieces for all to see.

The year after her husband's death, Mrs. Dr. Hiller put her sarcophagus and coffin as well as her husband's sarcophagus on display at the Boston Horticulture Show. To complete the peculiar exhibit was a wax figure modeling her burial gown. The gown was on par with the ostentation of the coffins. It was made from five hundred yards of handmade silk and had five thousand English daisies sewn into it for a cost of $20,000.[5] A skilled laborer would've made about three dollars a day the year Mrs. Dr. Hiller put her burial gown on display.

The papers gleefully went into great detail describing the display. Of note for her husband's sarcophagus was the carved foot panel featuring twenty-three cherubs, what Mrs. Dr. Hiller told the newspapers represented the children they had that died.[6] The sarcophagus lid was topped by a twelve-inch figure of France Hiller, recumbent on a bed of flowers, with Henry Hiller kneeling at her side, his right arm cradling her head.[7]

---

* The value changes depending on the news source, and ranges from $1,000 to $2,000. The author is using the value quoted by the *Boston Globe* the day after the obsequies.

"We are such stuff as dreams are made," read one of the many inscriptions on the lid.[8]

Surprisingly, or not surprisingly, the exhibit wasn't well attended.

In the years leading up to her death, the Lady of Caskets, as she became known, enjoyed passing the time by donning her lavish burial gown and climbing into the ornate vessel to admire herself in a mirror mounted on the ceiling. Select friends were invited over to preview events to come.[9] That event took place in 1900 when Mrs. Dr. Hiller died.

The grand mausoleum was never built.

In disrepair and voted to be an eyesore by Wildwood Cemetery in 1935, the temporary mausoleum was razed and the Hillers in their price-less coffins were buried.

The Hillers are an extreme, some might argue vulgar, example of ex-cess. The famous coffins took on a life of their own, gaining almost a celebrity status. The coffins garnered so much press they caught the at-tention of the Queen Mother. Mrs. Dr. Hiller was quick to tell the press she received a complimentary note from Queen Victoria for being the only woman to surpass her majesty in paying honor to a dead consort.[10]

The casket has become a focus of the American funeral—a symbol to the layperson not only of the profession but also seemingly of death itself. It makes sense; the casket is the eternal place of repose and there-fore makes it a tangible representation of death. Like many pieces of the American death rite, the casket was brought over with English settlers in the form of the coffin.

Vessels for the dead date to Egyptian times when the dead were en-cased in coffins made of acacia or sycamore fig, or cedar imported from Syria for royalty.[11] The Romans buried children in stone coffins, or sar-cophagi, which translates "flesh eater" as they discovered that nothing but teeth remained after a time in these stone containers.[12] Burial vessels constructed of stone, wood, and sometimes lead were used for thousands of years—for royalty. Occasionally they had to improvise. The legendary King Arthur, who died in the sixth century, was buried in a hollowed-out log.[13] The best common folk at this time could expect was to be buried in a shroud or winding sheet, which was often given as a wedding gift because cloth was so expensive and early death was probable. In fact, "chested burial" was reserved for persons of a certain social or economic status, and citizens in medieval England needed municipal permission to be buried encoffined. Carpenters and joiners could be fined for making an unlicensed coffin.[14]

The Christians co-opted the use of coffins from the Egyptians and Romans because of Joseph, the son of Jacob, who in the Old Testament was embalmed,* "and he was put in a coffin in Egypt."[15] Though common folk were buried enshrouded, their trip to the grave was in a coffin. The parish coffin was a communal container the body was placed in for transport only. The remains were removed graveside, and the parish coffin was used for the next decedent. This all changed in the late seventeenth century when the bubonic plague broke out. Tens of thousands of Englishmen and women perished in agony as their skin turned black and buboes, massive lumps, formed in their groin area. The victims were buried en masse in trenches. The practice of the communal coffin either fell away as multitudes of victims were dragged into the streets at night to be unceremoniously carted away to plague pits, or empirical evidence hinted to some bright clergymen that communal coffins might somehow spread the disease. The plague brought an abrupt end to the parish coffin.[16]

The word *coffin* is derived from the Greek *kofinos* which means basket.[17] The single-break hexagonal style didn't appear until the late sixteenth century in England. Previously, coffins were four sided, with the top wider and the sides tapering to the bottom like a keystone. This anthropomorphic "basket" design was brought from England to America and used until the late nineteenth century as carpenters, joiners, and cabinetmakers churned out made-to-order pieces.

From the days of the first settlers, coffined burial—as opposed to shrouded burial (without a coffin)—was the norm in the American colonies. The history professor and museum director Dr. Brent Tharp attributes the high rate of coffined burials to the "vast resources of wood available."[18] Unlike England, which had finite natural resources for an established population, the New World offered seemingly unlimited resources for the fledgling population. Thus, even the poor were buried in a coffin.

---

* Embalmed in this context likely approximated to the standards the Romans were practicing at this time: washing and anointing.

Well-to-do families differentiated their social status with embellishments such as fabric and metal ornamentation called coffin furniture. Prior to the Industrial Revolution, cloth was expensive due its labor-intensive production. Only the wealthiest individuals could afford the ultimate luxury of covering the vessel for the dead in fabric: George Washington's outer burial case was covered in cloth, Abraham Lincoln's coffin was covered in black broadcloth as was James K. Polk's, and Ulysses S. Grant's coffin was covered in purple velvet.

Coffin furniture—hinges, handles, escutcheons, plates, tacks, and the like—was imported from England before the Revolutionary War. It was constructed of silver, tin, or iron. The tradesman making the coffin bought coffin furniture from a furnishing undertaker or a jobber who sold funeral goods. After the war, American manufacturing took off, and Americans began decorating their coffins with American-produced hardware. Tharp asserts that no longer was a decorated coffin a status symbol—almost everyone decorated their coffin in some manner—but the "amount and quality of the hardware indicated status."[19]

Today, with so many choices available to the consumer, the material from which the casket is made, not the hardware, establishes the status of the casket buyer. Bronze and copper metal caskets, and rarer hardwoods such as mahogany, cherry, and maple are going to cost far more than a carbon steel, pine, or cloth-covered casket. The same goes for the interior. An expensive casket will likely have a velvet or silk interior, while a less expensive casket could have a crepe, satin, taffeta, or chiffon interior.

One of the biggest shifts in the way Americans encapsulated their dead came about when a New York stove manufacturer's brother died in the sweltering Mississippi heat in 1844. Of course, given the logistics of the time, he was unable to be brought home for burial. Embalming wouldn't even gain the tiniest of toeholds in America for another year, when Dr. Sucquet's method would be sold to Drs. Brown and Alexander, and common carriers refused to handle foul-smelling, decomposing remains. Almond D. Fisk used this family tragedy to almost single-handedly revolutionize the coffin. In 1848 Fisk patented his "air-tight coffin of cast or raised metal." Fisk wasn't the first to create a metal coffin. James A. Gray of Richmond, Virginia, received the first patent for a metallic coffin in 1836. But Fisk was the first to get it right. Perhaps Gray's was too heavy, or not economical to manufacture, but no records of Gray's coffin being manufactured or distributed have been located.

Fisk's creation was made of two shells of cast iron, and was mummi-form in shape, meaning it resembled a mummy (or shrouded person). The reason for the shape was twofold. The form-fitting cast cut down on excess material and kept the weight low, and it kept the air volume minimal "as entirely to prevent the decay of the contained body."[20] Cement was placed in the flange between the two shells and then they were tightened together with screws or rivets, creating an airtight seal. The tight seal also allowed for the coffin to be filled with preservative gas or fluid. A piece of plate glass* over the face allowed for viewing.

The genius of Fisk's invention was it could be customized to suit the decorative tastes of the public. In his patent application, Fisk presents a shrouded shape clutching a cross and states, "In the draw-ings I have represented a cross B [referring to the patent sketch] on the breast of the coffin . . . [that] have not anything to do with the construction of my coffin, and may be used or omitted at pleasure."[21] Later models were cast such that the iron resembled bunted and flut-ed cloth, flowers, and other emblems the public desired. There was a bronze-finished model, a cloth-covered model, and wood-finished model where rosewood veneer was glued to the iron.

Fisk debuted his invention at the New York State Agricultural Society Fair in Syracuse and the American Institute Exhibit in New York City in 1849. He also exhibited in the Rotunda at the Capitol in Washington, DC, where the newspapers said it was "worth an exam-ination."[22] Fisk's marketing ebullience quickly caught the right kind of attention. When the former senator and two-time vice president John C. Calhoun died in 1850, he was buried in a Fisk patent burial case. Fisk somehow managed to secure an open letter from Henry Clay, Daniel Webster, and Jefferson Davis, among other senators, stat-ing, "[It] impressed us with the belief that it is the best article known to use for transporting the dead to their final resting place."[23] The endorsement was reprinted in newspapers across the United States.

---

* A swivel, cast-iron cover protected the glass. When closed, the coffin was virtually indestructible.

With the advent of the Fisk coffin, not only could unembalmed bodies be held indefinitely and shipped anywhere—and *still viewed*—the public actually desired the intricate design casting allowed for. The only drawback was price. Tradesman undertakers were charging an average of six to seven dollars for an adult casket in 1850; an adult-sized Fisk was quadruple: twenty-five dollars.[24] If one could afford it, the price was worth it. Fisk cases actually worked.

In the fall of 2011, construction crews excavating a lot in the Elmhurst neighborhood of Queens, New York, stopped work and called the police when they uncovered a body. Homicide called in Scott Warnasch from the city's Forensic Anthropology Unit, whose job was documentation of the scene and recovery of the remains. Warnasch had prior experience with Fisk iron coffins, and upon seeing a piece of the coffin, "immediately knew we were dealing with a body from the mid-nineteenth century."[25]

The police had been called because this woman's features were still identifiable, as was her white nightgown and knee-high socks. She didn't *look* like a century-and-a-half-old burial. Warnasch has excavated many mid-nineteenth-century burials and may only find "hair, scraps of clothing and sometimes boots or shoes."[26] He attributes the level of preservation* to the Fisk metallic coffin.

This certainly wasn't the first time a Fisk coffin had been uncovered with the remains intact. In the 1920s, New York City officials uncovered a Fisk when excavating an old Fifth Ward cemetery in Kingsford Park in preparation to build a school. The cemetery was thought to have been completely moved in the late 1880s. The remains in the surprise discovery were described as "her hair was as natural as ever and the only change seemed to be that the eyes were sunken."[27]

The "Woman in the Iron Coffin," as the media dubbed the remains in Elmhurst, looked like she'd been buried weeks prior. Using data from x-ray and CT scans, and old maps and census information for Newtown,† Warnasch narrowed it down to thirty-six candidates. When he saw Martha Peterson, an African American woman who worked as a

---

* Martha Peterson, as she was identified, was so well preserved that the smallpox lesions covering her body were still visible. This was another reason the Fisk was so popular: it could contain contagious diseases.
† Renamed Elmhurst.

domestic servant for William Raymond, Almond Fisk's brother-in-law and a partner in the business, he knew he'd put a name to the "Woman in the Iron Coffin."[28] Warnasch attributes a servant being buried in an expensive coffin to the fact that Peterson likely died in Raymond's home. "[I]f you died in a coffin maker's house, you probably left the property in one of his coffins."[29]

By the time Peterson died sometime in 1851 or 1852, Almond Fisk was already dead, having succumbed to injuries sustained in a fire at his foundry. Fisk had licensed his patent to W.C. Davis & Co. in Cincinnati, Ohio, and A.C. Barstow & Co. in Providence, Rhode Island. The Fisk & Raymond Company was reorganized several times before folding several decades after Fisk's death. W.C. Davis & Co. also underwent several name changes before they reorganized into Crane & Breed Manufacturing Company and diversified into hearses and ambulances, but they continued building Fisk cases.

Fisk cases soon fell out of favor, but Almond Fisk had whet the public's appetite for something new: metallic burial cases. Tharp attributes this newly created consumer appetite to a connection with modernity: the railroad.[30] And what's more American than iron horses running down miles of track to fulfill Manifest Destiny? Metallic burial cases were "tied into the connotations and emotions . . . of the emerging middle class" in a "newly industrialized society."[31] It was patriotic; it was *American* to be buried in a modern metallic case. The demand existed, and manufacturers responded on the supply side with some key changes that changed metallic burial cases.

In 1859 A.C. Barstow patented the ogee, a curved "lip-like" shape on the metallic burial case that changed the way coffins—and later, caskets—were made. The ogee streamlined the shape, saving overall space and material, reducing the weight of metallic cases by 25 percent.[32] The ogee reduced the boxy shape, giving it a more pleasing form, and it is still used in the majority of caskets made today. Shortly after Barstow's patent, (what was then called) Crane, Breed & Co. began producing the first caskets made of rolled iron. In this method the iron is pressed into sheets and then molded into the casket shape, as opposed to a cast product where molten iron is poured into a mold. The rolled product provided a cheaper, lighter product, making caskets more accessible to consumers and more practical in the sense that pallbearers could carry the casket without the possibility that special equipment such as a block and tackle was needed. An empty cast-iron burial case could weigh three hundred pounds or much more.

The shift in the public's taste in coffin material was accompanied by a simultaneous shift in the shape. Americans cast off the old single-break hexagonal shape in favor of more modern look. Crane, Breed & Co. introduced the metallic burial "casket"—a rectangular burial case—in 1858, its advertising boasting that "[i]t will not promote, even if it does not check, disagreeable sensations."[33]

Demand for caskets took off after the Civil War. Americans, fatigued by four years of death and pestilence, favored the softening of the funeral rite by the new shape. And this may have been one of the first steps the culture took to disembrace itself from the familiarity with the ugliness of death. By the turn of the century, Americans had begun to give up their dying to hospitals and their dead to the newly formed cadre of funeral directors to bury in a streamlined *casket*.

The shape of the casket didn't resemble a dead body, like the anthropomorphic coffins. Even the name was more pleasing, coming from the Old French word *casset*, a small box for holding valuables or jewels. This renaming, or rebranding, of the burial case is a function of Victorian sentiment creeping in. For no longer were the dead put in a harsh-sounding coffin but placed in a box meant for something valuable. Habenstein and Lamers sum up that attitude in *The History of American Funeral Directing*: "The *encasing* of the body, the primary idea expressed in earlier receptacles [i.e., coffins], is modified toward the *presentation* of the dead in a receptacle designed to provide an aesthetically pleasing setting for its visually prominent and dramatically centered object of attention."[34] It's a strange duality; while Americans moved away from personally handling death, they simultaneously embraced mourning—embalming their dead and placing them on display in a casket to prolong the final goodbye.

Over the next four decades the rectangular-shaped casket completely usurped the coffin as the choice of burial receptacle, despite not everyone embracing the newfangled burial vessel. Nathaniel Hawthorne lamented in *Our Old Home*, "'Caskets!'—a vile modern phrase, which compels a person of sense and good taste to shrink more disgustfully than ever before from the idea of being buried at all."[35] Hawthorne died a year after publication, and he was thankfully buried in a *coffin* in Sleepy Hollow Cemetery* in Concord, Massachusetts.

Hexagonal coffins haven't been the standard offering of undertakers for over a century, but the word *coffin* is still used as a colloquialism for a burial receptacle. Around the time that the American consumer was replacing the coffin with the casket, there was a curious and short-lived departure from standard coffins and caskets into a specialty burial case that had incorporated into its design an alarm. The purpose of the grave alarm (or life signal, as it was sometimes called) was to alert the living that a premature burial had occurred. For the briefest of moments in time, burial technology, and the ability of the undead (or never-were-dead) to signal the living outstripped medical technology's ability to determine if a person was dead.

The fear of premature burial was nothing new. Civilizations had been employing preventative methods for thousands of years, usually waiting periods to ensure putrefaction, sometimes draconian quasi-medical tests. However, the fear reached a fever pitch led by organizations such as the London Society for the Prevention of Premature Burial and fueled by the emergence of widely available mass media. The cultural response to the scourge of premature burial was the invention of the grave alarm.

In 1804, Anne Hill Carter Lee, the wife of Henry Lee III, the former governor of Virginia, was declared dead by a doctor. While the sexton was filling the grave, he heard knocking and rescued Lee from a horrible fate, at least according to William Tebb and Edward Perry Vollum's sweeping treatise *Premature Burial and How It May Be Prevented*.[36] Three years later, Mrs. Lee gave birth to Robert Edward (named after her two brothers) whose military career almost changed the course of a nation. And while Mrs. Lee's health was poor for most of her life, and she was prone to cataleptic spells, the story is likely a myth. Robert E. Lee never mentions his mother's premature burial in his memoirs, nor is the incident recorded in any known family papers.

Mrs. Lee's supposed burial event is eerily reminiscent of an 1844 short story by Edgar Allen Poe, "The Premature Burial," where the unnamed

---

* Different from Ichabod Crane's Sleepy Hollow. That cemetery is in New York, and Washington Irving, the author of "The Legend of Sleepy Hollow," reposes there.

narrator relates the tale of the wife of a member of Congress and law-yer who is thought dead, and after three days is placed in the family vault. The gruesome fate of the congressman's wife is discovered years later when the vault is opened to receive another decedent. "Light Horse Harry" Lee (who delivered the eulogy at George Washington's funeral), Anne Lee's husband, had been a member of the House of Representatives, and he studied law prior to the American Revolution.

The mythologized story of Anne Lee is similar to that of Julia Legare. In 1852, Legare was a child who was visiting relatives on Edisto Island, South Carolina, when she was struck with diphtheria, a killer in the mid-nineteenth century that suffocated its victims to death as the bac-terial toxins create a "pseudomembrane" of dead tissue in the throat. It's a horrible, choking death as the victim struggles for breath. Legare's tiny remains were placed in the family mausoleum at the Edisto Island Presbyterian Church Cemetery. A decade later, when placing a Legare killed in the Civil War in the family vault, the bones of Julia draped in her tattered burial dress were discovered in a corner of the tomb. Claw marks crisscrossed the inside of the tomb's door.

The tomb door never stayed shut after the discovery.

The child's horrific saga harkens to Poe's "The Premature Burial," and like Poe's story, it's complete fiction.

Julia Legare did die in Charleston, South Carolina, on April 16, 1852, of unknown causes (it very well could've been diphtheria, but her death notice in the *Charleston Courier* didn't list a cause), and she was entombed in the Legare family mausoleum.[37] She was twenty-two. Depending on which legend one consults, Legare's age varies between that of a child and a young woman. Many versions favor a young Julia, probably because it's a bit more sinister to think of a young girl clawing at a marble slab than a grown woman.[38] Two years later—not ten—Legare's son, Hugh, was entombed in the family crypt. Two years after that, 1856, Legare's husband, John, was entombed in the family crypt. Neither time did the newspapers report a newsworthy find. Aside from the above glaring inconsistencies, there's the logical issue of Legare hav-ing to first break out of the coffin and then break out of the crypt space itself—a formidable task that would involve smashing marble—to even get inside the main chamber of the mausoleum.

Like many premature burial stories, it's just that—a story (albeit a juicy one) that's been repeated enough times that it's become legend. The legend has gained credibility by the fact that the Legare mausoleum no longer has a door.

Fanciful stories like Lee's and Legare's were often repeated as fact, and they kept the public fearful of the possibility of premature burial and spawned the London Society for the Prevention of Premature Burial,* pamphlets and articles on the topic, and the wildly successful book *Premature Burial and How It May Be Prevented*. Authors Tebb and Vollum were an unlikely pair. William Tebb was something of a rabble-rousing reformer who had earlier hitched his wagon to the cause of anti-vaccination before setting his sights on premature burial reform. Conversely, Edward Perry Vollum had almost forty years of practical medical experience as a respected army physician. However, it wasn't only Vollum's medical degree that lent credence to their book; Vollum knew the horrors of premature burial in his bones. As a boy, he'd been declared dead after a near drowning and revived in a New York City morgue.[39] Because of his brush with a premature grave, it was easy for Tebb to recruit Vollum for his project.

It's unknown where Tebb, who did most of the writing for *Premature Burial*, dug up the story about Mrs. Lee. He scoured newspapers for stories (unverified stories) on premature burial and cherry-picked facts from medical articles to put together his book.[40] There was a story about Mrs. Lee's burial place at Ravensworth† appearing in an 1895 *Washington Post* article (Tebb wrote the book in 1895) that Tebb may have conflated with Poe's horror story. But the book isn't all myth and innuendo; Tebb injected it with enough scientific knowledge of the time that legitimate medical publications endorsed *Premature Burial*.

The *Medical Times and Hospital Gazette* (of London) said, "This book is essentially practical . . ." and the *Medical Record* (of New York) said, "The pages are replete with instructive though at times gruesome details . . ."[41] *Premature Burial* covers the causes of mistaken death,

---

* Articles of incorporation for an American Society for the Prevention of Premature Burial were filed in New York In July of 1900, but this society was never as active as its London counterpart, perhaps in part because medical science had advanced to such a point by 1900 that the public's fear of premature burial had waned.
† Her remains were later moved to the Lee crypt at Washington and Lee University in Lexington, Virginia.

trance and catalepsy,* the causes and conditions of "death counter-feits," the signs of death, and other helpful subjects for preventing premature burial.[42]

For centuries, the only sure sign of death was decomposition, which is marked by five signs: color, odor, gas, purge, and skin slip. Typically the first sign to appear is a green streak (color) on the lower right quadrant of the abdomen followed by a combination of any of the other four signs. The waking of the dead was created as a practical mechanism to prevent prema-ture burial as families waited for the signs of decomposition. Sometimes the vigils worked with surprising results. In Decatur, Illinois, in the summer of 1882, Charles Athens, age thirty-three, suffered six paralytic strokes and died. His family laid him out in his burial clothes and began a vigil. Upon going into the room at 2:00 a.m., they found his eyes open and he was breathing. Athens had no recollection of "dying," but the waking may have saved his life from a hasty burial.[43] In ancient Rome, the waking period lasted three to seven days. In other cultures and at other times in history, the family, once satisfied the decedent was in fact dead, would shroud them and proceed with the funeral rites. There was simply no alternative to prove death.

It wasn't until the 1846 Prix Manni, a contest put on by the French Academy of Sciences, that the French physician Eugène Bouchut put forth the idea of using the invention of René Laënnec—the stethoscope—to determine "the cessation of heartbeat."[44] Despite support from notable clinicians, Bouchut's idea was widely criticized, and it would take several decades to gain traction as a proof-positive test that life had ceased.

Germans began erecting *leichenhäuser*, or waiting mortuaries, in the late eighteenth century where the dead were taken to lay in repose until signs of putrefaction began to show. The dead—surrounded by mounds of fresh flowers to control the odor—were supervised by around-the-clock watchmen ready to provide aid at a moment's notice. The dead lay with their fingers and toes rigged to elaborate warning systems of strings, pulleys, and bells.[45] It stands to reason that the watchmen were plagued with false alarms as the decaying remains stiffened and relaxed from rigor mortis and swelled with putrefactive gases.

---

* Trance is defined in *Premature Burial* as "abnormal sleep, which is produced by no known external agency" and catalepsy as "an obstruction in the organic mechanism of the body, on account of its exhausted nervous power."

A handful of European countries followed Germany's lead in the construction of waiting mortuaries but the idea was mostly scrapped by the middle of the nineteenth century, though some German towns would hold on to their *leichenhäuser* for another half century. No waiting mortuaries were ever constructed in America. The hysteria behind the waiting mortuary was the (supposed) number of citizens being buried alive. Tebb and Vollum put forth a couple of different statistics posited by "experts" that range from 0.1 percent to 0.5 percent of the population being buried prematurely.[46] These shockingly high estimates were for industrialized nations with access to technology and the most recent medical and scientific advances. By that logic, in 1900, around the time they published their book, taking the lowest premature burial rate of 0.1 percent, Americans were burying alive three to four people *every single day.*

The actual number of premature burials, though speculated by a great many, will never be truly known. Dr. Séverin Icard of Marseilles, who was fascinated by apparent death, wrote an article in the journal *La Presse Medicale* where he chillingly stated, "The only witnesses of which are the boards of the coffin."[47]

The medical advances of the nineteenth century did little to quell the fears of some famous taphephobes.* Frédéric Chopin was one of the most accomplished pianists and composers of the century, but he was terrified of live burial, as was Hans Christian Andersen. Andersen's stories are known by children all over world, having created such classic fairy tales as "The Emperor's New Clothes" and "The Little Mermaid." But the man who wove such fantastical tales was also plagued by neurosis. According to Jackie Wullschlager's biography *Hans Christian Andersen: The Life of a Storyteller*, when Andersen traveled, he left a note on the bedside table that read "I only appear dead."[48] As Andersen lay dying of liver cancer in the Copenhagen home of his friends Dorothea and Moritz Melchior, he made Mrs. Melchior swear she'd open his veins before they put him in the ground.[49]

The Melchiors didn't.

Philosopher Herbert Spencer, novelist Edmund Yates, and scientist Alfred Nobel were all reputed taphephobes, but the fear wasn't

---

* Taphephobia is the fear of being buried alive.

limited to men and women of fame. Dr. Charles F. Heuser, a south Baltimore physician and druggist, was terrified of premature burial and stipulated in his will that his heart be cut out.* When he died in 1891, his friend Dr. Benson refused, and the executors secured Dr. Adolph Boehm to perform the task. As an added precaution, Dr. Heuser was cremated at Louden Park following the postmortem procedure.[50] Despite the rapid advances in medical science, taphephobia continued well into the twentieth century. When Albert H. Olmsted died in 1929, his will set forth that his jugular veins be opened to ensure death. Then, to be triply sure he wasn't buried alive, he further stipulated he be embalmed and then cremated.[51]

In the twenty-first century, it's almost laughable to think that a stethoscope *wouldn't* be the way to determine death. It's what is taught in mortuary schools as an "expert" test of death, meaning it has to be conducted by someone with training (e.g., a physician or nurse), and the results (i.e., for the stethoscope: no heartbeat) are accepted as definitive proof of death. Other expert tests include the ophthalmoscope to look for blood circulation in the retina, EEG to test brain activity, or ECG to test heart activity.[52] There are also "inexpert" tests when expertise or equipment isn't available. Inexpert tests have been used for centuries to try to determine if death has actually occurred or if the person is in a state of catalepsy or trance. They include checking for a pulse, holding a mirror to the mouth to determine if there's fogging, or conducting the "ligature test," where a piece of string is tied around the finger to check for swelling.[53] Of course, other, more barbaric inexpert tests were also used, such as the application of highly irritating mustard plasters, the dripping of hot wax on exposed skin, and even the downright bizarre suggestion floated by Jean-Baptiste Vincent Laborde, a well-respected French physiologist, who recommended "rhythmical tractions" of the decedent's tongue.[54]

The Massachusetts legislature proposed a premature burial bill in which no person was to be placed in a casket or "other receptacle by which air or light is excluded," embalmed, buried, or cremated until a death certificate had been issued. The catch: for the death

---

* When Dr. Heuser's wife, Susan, died circa 1883, the good doctor assumed the task of piercing her heart with a knife to ensure death.

certificate to be issued, the tests for death—eleven of them!—had to be performed by no less than two doctors. *The Casket* dryly stated in May of 1906 that the bill has "no reasonable prospect of passing."[55] Thankfully it didn't, for some of the proposed tests* were rather severe.

The same year Tebb and Vollum published *Premature Burial*, Carl Lewis Barnes published *The Art and Science of Embalming*, in which Barnes scoffs indirectly at Tebb and Vollum's fear mongering, saying, "Premature burial is such an exaggerated theory that I feel as though it deserves only a passing notice in this book . . . our complete mastery of the phenomena [of circulation and respiration] makes such a thing as premature burial absolutely impossible."[56] It's interesting that Barnes even mentions the subject, much less devotes a section to it in a scientific text, unless his aim was to give students answers to something that was the subject of much media attention. Despite the alarmism by anti-premature burial advocates and calls for reform from organizations such as the London Society for the Prevention of Premature Burial, almost every media story about premature burial didn't hold up under scrutiny and turned out to be journalistic sensationalism. The media's tall tales didn't stop the undercurrent of public fear; there's something primal about the terror of live burial. And embalming didn't help things either.

Embalmers in the late nineteenth century had some issues convincing customers to practice the new science on family members because it made the dead look too good—undead. Families were unsure of burying someone who didn't look 100 percent dead, because that person might still be alive. There was a case in 1905 in Ballard, Washington, of an unnamed person embalmed by Addie L. Williams. The family refused to allow the dead woman to be buried because she didn't look dead. They were convinced she had lapsed into a long sleep (what Tebb and Vollum would call a "trance") because "so life-like was the appearance of the body."[57]

When the New Jersey embalmer George Bunnell† invited a *New York World* reporter to witness an embalming procedure in 1888, the reporter wrote, "The embalmer's art produced such a change that one of

---

* One of the tests, clearly inexpert, was "a bright needle plunged into the body of the biceps muscle, left there, shows no oxidation."
† Son of William Bunnell, who allegedly had his embalming tent burned by Richard Burr and nephew of Thomas Holmes.

the relatives of the deceased woman after viewing the embalmed body declared the body had so much the appearance of life, it was difficult to realize the fact of death."[58] Until this point in history, Americans had been caring for their dead at home and preparing them for burial. They were familiar with the unpleasant sights, sounds, and smells that accompany death. They had closed eyes, tied handkerchiefs around jaws, and lovingly bathed remains ravaged by disease while confronted face to face with decomposition.

And then embalming stood death on its head.

Suddenly there was a man who, as if by magic, could arrest decomposition—seemingly death itself—and with his fluids, ligatures, and powders, he could restore the dead to a vibrant lifelike appearance. It's no wonder embalmers faced an uphill battle promoting the new methodology. Embalming flew in the face of thousands of years of visual cultural mechanisms that ensured the dead were really, well, dead. Thomas Holmes mentioned this issue in an 1877 letter to Hudson Samson, an undertaker in Pittsburgh: "I embalmed some bodies with a fluid that made them as if they were not dead all the people objected to it saying a body ought to look like death not like life . . ."[59]

So, how did the people of the nineteenth century (and early twentieth century) reconcile their fear of premature burial until medical science was able to provide indisputable proof of death? Some enterprising engineers modified the standard burial receptacle—the casket (or coffin)—to stave off disaster.

The first patent issued in the United States was to Christian Eisenbrandt of Baltimore in 1843 for a "life-preserving coffin in doubtful cases of death."[60] The coffin was spring-loaded with a "strong spring." A ring attached to a chain was placed around the decedent's finger, and there was a plate over the head so "the slightest motion of either the head, or the hand, acting on the spring catch, will cause the lid to fly open."[61] What a surprise that would be in the middle of a funeral, especially in a case of false alarm due to rigor mortis.

The only flaw in Eisenbrandt's design was it was only effective if the decedent was above ground. Franz Vester, a diesinker* from Newark,

---

* Someone who engraves the dies (or plates) used in stamping out coins, etc.

New Jersey, fixed that flaw. Vester's invention, the "improved burial case," featured a square tube affixed to the head end of the coffin. A cord was placed in the hand of the decedent that was attached to a little bell mounted to the top of the tube *super terram* (above ground). Mounted on one wall of the tube was a ladder. The top of the square tube, which resembles a submarine hatch, featured a glass door for viewing the body. After several days passed, and the family was fully satisfied the decedent was in fact dead, the tube was removed.

Vester's patent application states, "Now, should the person laid in the coffin, on returning to life, desire to ascend from the coffin and the grave to the surface, he can do so by means of the ladder H [a reference to the accompanying diagram]; but, if too weak to ascend by the ladder, he can pull the cord in his hand, and ring the bell."[62] Vester's invention was certainly an improvement on Eisenbrandt's in terms of practical use *if* someone was indeed buried alive, but it still had serious shortcomings. Vester assumed that the newly revived decedent would be small enough to slither through a shaft about eighteen inches wide and have enough strength after prolonged recumbency to pull themselves up out of the shaft, which seems unlikely. The backup—the bell—is a great idea if there's someone around to hear it ringing. Granted, cemeteries during the time of Vester's invention employed night watchmen to keep the resurrectionists at bay, but a cemetery such as Mount Auburn in Boston is well over a hundred acres. The tinkling of a small bell would easily be swallowed by the sounds of nature unless one was pretty close. But if all else failed, Vester's invention proposed including refreshments so one wouldn't die of starvation while they waited for help to arrive.[63]

Both inventions, well intentioned, failed to account for air supply. The dimensions of a modern casket allow for about an hour and twenty minutes' time of breathable air. That's assuming a person is breathing a normal amount of roughly ten liters per minute. If a person was in such a trance that their breathing was so shallow it couldn't be detected, the volume of breathable air could stretch for three, four, or even five times that. Even at eight hours, a person in a trance would have to revive not long after the last shovelful of earth thumped upon the coffin lid and shimmy up the ladder in Vester's improved burial case before their air supply ran out.

Later inventors addressed the air supply issue. Hubert Deveau's 1894 "grave-signal," like Vester's, had a tube protruding out of the earth, though the tube was much smaller in diameter. At one end, a push rod was positioned above the decedent's forehead and a breathing tube that looked like a periscope was placed over the nose and mouth, "so that in case there is any tendency to revive, the air may be applied where it will do the most good."[64] Above ground, at the other end of the tube, was mounted a brass and glass housing that looked like a lantern. If the decedent struggled, the push rod would move a bright red cylinder up in the tube, exposing air inlets and allowing the person below fresh air, and alerting passersby to the horrific struggle taking place six feet under.

The grave alarm that garnered the most publicity—international publicity—was invented by Count Michel de Karnice Karnicki. Count Karnicki was a Russian noble inspired to engineer a grave alarm after witnessing the funeral of a Belgian* girl "who was awakened out of her lethargy by the first shovelfuls of earth thrown upon her coffin."[65] Karnicki's invention, humbly named "Le Karnice," consisted of an iron box sitting on top of the earth and connected to a tube three and a half inches in diameter running into the coffin. A glass sphere sat on the chest of the decedent, and if disturbed, a spring action tripped, opening the lid of the iron box and allowing fresh air to flood the prematurely interred victim. Attached to the lid of the box was a flag, looking much like a bicycle flag, on a four-foot pole. When the lid opened, it raised the flag in the air signaling for help. Karnicki gave some thought to the vastness of some cemeteries, and in addition to the visual signal of the flag, the opening of the box triggered a siren that would wail for a half hour. It also triggered a lantern in the box, that was to provide some light to the poor soul trapped underground and presumably provide a beacon if the system were triggered at night.[66]

After a failed demonstration at the Sorbonne in Paris in 1897, where Karnicki nearly buried an assistant alive, demand never materialized. The French press lambasted Count Karnicki, though the American press was

---

* In some accounts, the girl is Polish. This may be due to translation errors, or it may speak to the questionable validity of the story.

a bit subtler, with one newspaper commenting, "There is no indication that his hope of seeing it introduced into actual use in the cemeteries of the French capital will ever be realized; but the newspapers have found a fresh, though ghastly, bit of news in the incident."[67] Count Karnicki was undeterred, sending his French attorney, Emile Camis, to America to promote it. Considering Camis didn't speak *any* English, why Karnicki thought this would be the best way to endorse his product still stands to reason. Camis presented Le Karnice to the New York Academy of Medicine on December 20, 1899, and then left the contraption on display at 835 Broadway in Greenwich Village.[68] Tebb and Vollum reported the price of the potentially lifesaving device to be "exceedingly reasonable" at twelve shillings, or a little under a hundred dollars today.[69] Notwithstanding the cheap burial insurance, medical experts and funeral directors showed only a passing interest, if any.

It's unknown how many life-signal coffins were sold and put into use, but the number likely isn't high. The hysteria of anti-premature burial that swept continental Europe never reached American shores. Americans viewed the life-signal coffins as mere curiosities, despite the fact that patents for these devices were issued well into the twentieth century.[*]

Despite life-signal coffins being something of an oddity, it's worth noting their creation was a technological response to a problem. For generations, the only way to ensure death were the signs of decomposition, and suddenly men such as Eisenbrandt and Vester offered a "practical" solution for people who wanted to hedge their bets. This idea of using technology to hedge a bet against death still exists today in the form of cryogenic preservation. People choosing cryogenics[†] are cooled to an ultra-low temperature immediately after death and remain in a state of suspended animation while they await the scientific and technological advances to be brought back to life.

While the life-signal coffin may be a curious historical aside, the fear of premature burial isn't. It shaped the modern tradition of the wake, or viewing, as families sat vigil looking for signs of life until the signs of

---

[*] As recently as 1983, a Frenchman named Fernand Gauchard was granted a US patent 4,367,461 (January 4, 1983) for a "coffin alarm system" comprised of circuitry that sent out alerts when someone awoke from a semilethargic state (i.e., it detected movement), and not due to movement resulting from putrefactive changes.

[†] There are currently two facilities in the US that offer cryogenic preservation.

death were certain. The Romans established their waking period in part to prevent what Pliny the Elder relates in *Natural History*: Consul Acilius Aviola and Praetor Lucius Lamia, both accidentally burned alive, shrieking for assistance from their pyres.[70]

This need to ensure our dead are actually dead has intercalated itself into the human DNA, such that it is an important part of the grieving process: to confirm death. It's the first task outlined by the psychologist William Worden, who organizes healthy grieving into four such tasks. Worden's first task is to accept the reality of the loss. And there's nothing more realistic than seeing and confirming the decedent is dead. The parents of the Civil War fallen didn't have Worden's model, but they knew it on some level, proving it by spending 25 percent of the average household income to have their dead soldier embalmed and shipped home—those that had the wherewithal and the money to hire an agent to track down a missing soldier. Some were simply too poor to afford the "luxury" of having their dead shipped home. And for what? Some would argue there's no value in human remains, saying, "It's just a body." True, there's no extrinsic value in the dead human body, but we as a species prove its intrinsic worth by the way we care for it: washing and anointing, dressing and casketing, waking it, funeralizing, eulogizing, elegizing, and gathering to commune with a post-funeral meal.

The casket and coffin are therefore not wanton expenditures of funerary extravagance but symbols of intrinsic worth. And the display of the remains in the casket to friends, family, and the community isn't some bizarre peep show invented by the funeral profession but rather a ritual started long before the creation of the profession that satisfies the innate need to confirm death.

CHAPTER 10

The Temple of Honor

Vehicles of the Dead

T he World's Columbian Exposition in 1893 was just two days from closing on October 28 when a man knocked on the front door of the stately mansion located at 231 S. Ashland Avenue near Union Park in Chicago. Mary Hanson, a servant, answered the door and was greeted by a young man with clean-cut features and dark eyes.[1]

"Is Mr. Harrison in?" the man politely asked.

"He is." Hanson stepped aside. "Please, come in."

Carter H. Harrison, the mayor of Chicago, was in the dining room at the rear of the house after a long day of official events related to the fair. A great hulking man with a flowing white beard and waxed mustache, Harrison ambled into the center hall at the sound of the caller's voice.

"Sir?" Harrison inquired.

Patrick Eugene Prendergast pulled a revolver and wordlessly commenced firing. The first bullet shattered Harrison's left pinkie finger. Harrison reeled backward and shouted, "Murder!"[2]

Prendergast continued the barrage of bullets. The second shot caught Harrison in the gut. The mayor turned and tried to flee to the dining room. Prendergast shot him in the back, the bullet plowing through his liver and coming to rest behind his right nipple. The fourth and final shot caught Harrison in the right shoulder.[3]

Prendergast tucked the revolver under his coat and hurried out of the house.

Harrison collapsed in the butler's pantry off the dining room.[4]

The screams of Mary Hanson brought Harrison's son, William, tearing down the stairs and the coachman from the backyard. William found his father with blood pumping out of his wounds, the pantry looking like the bloody stockyards Chicago was famous for, and urgently called for Hanson to summon a doctor. The coachman, armed, fired two shots at the retreating Prendergast without hitting him.[5] Prendergast boarded a passing streetcar and escaped.* Harrison exsanguinated in less than twenty minutes.

Prendergast later told police in an interview he'd murdered Mayor Harrison because he wasn't made "corporation counsel" in the mayor's cabinet.[6]

The city, coming off of the heady excitement of hosting an international fair that drew a crowd in excess of twenty-one million people, was shocked.[7] Carter H. Harrison was beloved by Chicagoans. In addition to being a five-time mayor, Harrison was a former Illinois congressman and he also owned the *Chicago Times* newspaper.

Condolences poured in from around the globe, including one from his second cousin and the former president Benjamin Harrison: "My daughter, Mrs. McKee, joins me in offering to you and to the family the fullest sympathy of our hearts in your appalling sorrow."[8]

Instead of the grand closing ceremonies planned for Monday, October 30, the city turned its attention to the slain mayor and planned a funeral. A statement released by George R. Davis, the director general for the fair, read, "In view of the assassination of the chief magistrate of the city of Chicago, the ceremonies which were announced to take place tomorrow—Monday, October 30—in connection with the World's Columbian Exposition will be wholly dispensed with."[9]

Thankfully, the most magnificent hearse the world had ever seen was on hand to properly funeralize the mayor as the nation had its attention

---

* Prendergast was apprehended later that day. After a failed insanity defense, Prendergast was hanged for his crime.

on the fair in the White City and the unfolding tragedy. Crane & Breed Manufacturing Company of Cincinnati unveiled their Processional Hearse for the fair, displayed in the Transportation Building alongside casket displays. As one newspaper described, "A more magnificent death car can scarcely be imagined."[10] The hearse, made of eight carved columns separated by thick French plate glass, featured gold-plated lanterns and gold ornamentation inside and out. The interior was richly draped with gold-fringed and tasseled velvet as well as matching hammercloth covering the coach box—or driver's seat. An intricately carved processional scene over the center glass (also gilded) depicted Christ's Passion: the cross, the thieves, the Roman centurion, the two Marys, and the Pharisees in bold relief. Gold-plated carvings of the adoration of Christ graced the roof.[11] In a twist of fate almost too ironic to be true, Harrison stood in the Transportation Building one week before his assassination admiring the hearse, and he remarked, "It is beautiful enough to almost make a man wish to take a ride in it, even if he had to die."[12]

Collins H. Jordan, who founded one of the oldest undertaking establishments in Chicago, located at 14 and 16 Madison Street, and who was charged with Harrison's funeral, telegraphed William James Breed, the president of Crane & Breed Manufacturing Company, on Tuesday, seeking permission to use the displayed hearse. Jordan was familiar with the company as it is where he got his start. He landed in Chicago in 1854 as the western agent for Crane & Breed, who at the time was manufacturing stoves, caskets, metallic burial cases, and other funerary products.[13] Jordan is a good example of a furnishing undertaker, or someone who joined the professional ranks through the function of supplying other undertakers with the supplies they couldn't make for themselves, such as "coffin furniture" (i.e., hinges, plates, cast handles, and escutcheons), candles, robes, drapes, door badges, and a myriad of other items. The furnishing undertaker opened the door to nonskilled tradesmen, as undertaking was previously dominated by tradesmen such as carpenters, upholsterers, chandlers, and the like.

According to the newspapers, "Permission to use the car was at once granted by the manufacturers."[14]

The same day that Jordan telegraphed Crane & Breed—Halloween— Harrison's body was taken from his home on Ashland Avenue to City

Hall using Jordan's regular livery. There were some wild claims that 150,000 people viewed his body; in actuality, it was likely closer to fifty thousand.[15] It was reported that "the late mayor appeared to be sleeping. Old city employees brushed away a tear as they went by."[16]

At 10:00 a.m. on Wednesday—fittingly All Saints Day, as Chicagoans had sainted their mayor in his martyrdom—the magnificent Crane & Breed hearse rumbled down La Salle Street driven by veteran whip Ben Ransom and pulled by four* silk-draped black horses.[17] The hearse was essentially a prototype, built for the fair, and as such only had temporary axles not designed to be used for a hearse 50 percent heavier than the others on the streets.[18] Jordan was either unaware of this or praying for the best. If an axle snapped, it would be no simple wheelwrighting job. It would spell disaster.

At 10:30 a.m., Jordan covered the casket and it was borne outside by eight police captains. The city's population had swelled from the fair, and an estimated half a million people clogged the city streets with "bared and bowed head" to watch the procession.[19] There were so many people that the police had to clear a path to the Protestant Episcopal Church of the Epiphany, and then to Graceland Cemetery located north of Lincoln Park. The journey of six miles to Graceland took almost four hours through the densely packed streets. An axle bent a few miles into the journey, causing the horses to strain to pull the load, but it miraculously held.

In a sense, Harrison's funeral was the grand finale—the closing ceremony—of the fair. The grand hearse† that conveyed the man who brought the prestige of the fair to Chicago reflected the city's love for Harrison.

Some argue the hearse is a useless trapping of the funeral profession—an extraneous piece of equipment pushed by profit-minded undertakers. Why use such an ornate vehicle when a much simpler one, such as a station wagon or pickup truck, would suffice? It's a perfectly valid argument in the same sense a dead body is worthless in the practical sense. The worth of the body comes from the sentiment wrapped

---

* This is astonishing, and seemingly reckless, as the hearse was designed to be pulled by eight horses.
† The February 1894 issue of *The Casket* announced the grand hearse used for Carter Harrison was sold to "Madam," the widow of John Bonnot, in New Orleans for a whopping $14,000.

around that body. The hearse, and all its ornamentation and trappings, is just another way to reinforce the value of a life well lived. Would a regular hearse have gotten the job done for Mayor Harrison? Without a doubt. At this time, the "mosque deck" hearse, a flat-roofed hearse with little ornamentation on top, supported by six or eight columns, was the predominant style, and Jordan undoubtedly had several in his livery that he could just have well used with little worry about the axles. But the passion Chicagoans had for their beloved mayor made it such that the last ride of his earthly remains *had* to be in the finest vehicle available. We saw this same phenomenon three decades prior with Lincoln's multicity funeral, when each city tried to outdo the other with the grandest hearse to move the slain president's remains.

Almost every city visited by the Lincoln Special train made a special hearse, usually described as a "catafalque" by the newspapers, a popular label—along with "temple of honor"—for hearses during the nineteenth century. *Catafalque* is a term that means a structure used to display a coffin or casket; it can be stationary or it can take the form of a hearse to be used for processional purposes. The cities on the Lincoln funeral route had roughly a week, some only days, to create the most elaborate cata-falques ever before seen. But they rose to the occasion. Peter Relyea, the sexton undertaker, created a monstrosity of a hearse for New York City in just three days for the cost of $150,000 in today's money. The grand vehicles, made with canopies supported by ornate columns, featured rich draperies, tassels, American flags, plumes, feathers, flowers, and other emblems and were drawn by six, eight, or in the case of New York, six-teen horses. The horses were draped in appropriate mourning—black mesh nets and headstalls of black feathers and crepe streamers—and led by individual grooms.

It was an honor for the city—really, a point of pride—to provide the best transportation for the martyred president. The ornate catafalque was the closest valuation they could provide for Lincoln's life and his sacri-fice. The *New York Herald* humbly stated of Relyea's creation, "This was, without doubt, one of the finest specimens of the upholsterer's art ever displayed in this or any other city."[20]

Lincoln's funeral didn't stand alone with respect to custom-built hearses, though it serves as the grandest example. The undertaker James

F. Harvey of Washington, DC, built a custom hearse for the occasion of the death of John Quincy Adams.* The hearse had a canopy upon which perched an eagle draped in crepe, and it was pulled by six white horses in "sable attire."[21]

The man whose military prowess saved the Union, and the former president, Ulysses S. Grant, was also borne to his tomb in a custom-built vehicle. Theodore Gunsel, the designer of the magnificent vehicle, had thirteen days from the time of Grant's death until his arrival in New York City, to pull off a miracle. Designed to highlight Grant's military career, Gunsel's creation was adorned with Maltese crosses, and clusters of American flags with spear points were attached to the columns.[22] Gunsel called the hearse "[a] perfect mass of draperies, tassels, and fringes."[23] So colossal a vehicle—144 square feet—it took twenty-four horses to pull. When Grant's body arrived in the city, a low-hanging telegraph wire sheared off the top plume.[24] One of the grooms leading the horses scurried to retrieve the top ornament before souvenir seekers could grab it.[25]

Chicago held a memorial service the same day as Grant's entombment in New York that featured a custom-built catafalque *larger* than New York's. Unlike the all-black New York hearse, the Chicago hearse featured silver symbols "of the hero's martial and Christian glory."[26] Despite pouring rain, Chicagoans clogged the streets to catch a glimpse of the empty casket borne by the hearse.

A monument erected where there's no body present—like the Lincoln Monument in Washington, DC—is called a cenotaph. The etymology of the word translates to "empty grave." The Grant hearse in Chicago could be called a cenomobile. Despite being "empty" it still served as a rallying point, or focal point, for the people of Chicago to direct their grief.

Harrison's, Lincoln's, and Grant's hearses are the pinnacles of the ornate, specialized vehicle used to convey the dead to their sepulcher. The origins of the hearse are much more modest. Early hearses were nothing more than litters, the coffin placed on a bier carried by hand. The word *hearse* comes from the Latin *hirpex* or the French *herse*, which mean "harrow" or "rake." The bier had grids of iron spikes—looking a lot like an

---

* Harvey, a carpenter by trade, was busy for the Adams obsequies for he also built the coffin. When Harvey died at age forty, his wife, Maria, ran the business until their son Richard was old enough to come into the business. Richard accompanied Lincoln back to Springfield on the train with Dr. Brown.

inverted rake—on which to impale candles. The practice of mounting candles on the *hirpex* originated with the Romans, who buried their dead at night. Burning tapers on the *hirpex* continued after the empire fell, not because Christians buried their dead at night but rather to symbolize eternal light.[27]

The men selected to carry the bier were called bearers. They were usually younger men as it was heavy, treacherous work navigating muddy, rutted roads. If the distance to the grave was far, a set of relief bearers called underbearers were employed as well. When the funeral rite included a pall, pallbearers held tassels sewn onto the corners of the cloth covering the bier. Pallbearers were older, less able-bodied men as they only had to carry a cloth, while the bearers did the real work.

In the Middle Ages, pallbearers carried cudgels to ward off highwaymen. The cudgel, similar to a police baton, became known as the undertaker's staff as the undertaker would inscribe his name or symbol into the cudgel. A vestige of the tradition persists as the undertaker's name mounted in the hearse window.[28]

Beginning in the seventeenth century, hearses were fitted with embellishments such as canopies and frameworks adorned draperies, fringes, tassels, and plumes—much like a miniature temple. Families tacked favorite Bible verses and elegies to the framework as a way of personalization; and in England, heraldic crests were displayed. The added weight meant that hearses shifted from people-carried litters to horse-drawn carts and a visage of the modern hearse was born.

Specialized vehicles didn't appear in America until the mid-to-late eighteenth century* for the reason that most burials were localized to where people lived. Families buried in their family plot on their land in rural settings, and in urban settings the distance from the house to the town green or churchyard was close enough for bearers to carry. When transportation was necessary, a wagon was used.

As early as 1753, an advertisement in the *Pennsylvania Gazette*, submitted by John DeNyce, joiner and undertaker, read, "Said undertaker has a very convenient carriage, or herse [*sic*]. That may be of great service to those that have a distance to carry."[29] Hearses from

---

* A hearse believed to be the oldest restored hearse in the country resides at the National Funeral History Museum in Houston, Texas. It's from Cambridge, Vermont, and was built in 1832.

this era were open-sided affairs with fringed draperies hanging from the canopy obscuring the coffin. Carved wooden urns were the common roof ornamentation, the cinerary urn being a Roman symbol of mortality.[30] Pre- and post-Revolution hearses were something of a rarity. Not only had coach builders not caught up to the skill of their English counterparts but also a vehicle used for such a specialized purpose was something of frivolity for a people trying to carve a life out of the harsh new landscape.

By the time the Civil War broke out, hearses were a common sight on the roads. The population had sprawled to the point where people were living farther and farther from the traditional burying grounds, and rural cemeteries located well outside the city limits were becoming popular. Carrying a bier by hand simply wasn't feasible anymore. And the number of Americans had swelled—well over 1,000 percent since the Revolution—such that livery owners in population centers could justify owning a hearse or two. The Civil War–era hearse was enclosed with glass sides, but the most remarkable feature was the plumage that had replaced the carved urns. Just as white hearses were used to denote a child's death during the Victorian era, the amount of plumage denoted a person's standing in society. The only surviving photograph of the Lincoln hearse used in Springfield, owned by the St. Louis liveryman Jesse Arnot, shows eight massive plumes sprouting from the roof. A passing citizen on the street could gauge the decedent's station in life by the number of plumes on the roof.

After the war, hearse styles changed regularly every fifteen years as coach builders dialed in on the fact that undertakers—and consumers—wanted the latest style to convey their dead. Automakers seized on and accelerated this trend during the next century, rolling out new model cars every year. Hearses during the 1870s were dainty and oval shaped with the driver sitting on a gooseneck seat separate from the hearse body, flanked by large brass lamps.[31] In the 1880s and 1890s, a boxier style of hearse emerged, with six or eight columns inset with carved wooden drapery panels—works of art themselves made by specialized woodcarvers.[32] Plumage on hearse roofs was short lived; during the last three decades of coach building, wooden urns reappeared as the predominant ornamentation and then disappeared altogether in favor of the smooth-topped mosque deck.[33] The age of horse-drawn hearses lasted only about a century before the automobile replaced them.

The first all-automobile funeral was for the taxicab chauffer Wilbur Pruyn in 1909.[34] As Pruyn lay dying with pneumonia, he summoned his union buddies. "Boys," Pruyn said, pausing to struggle for breath, fluid filling his lungs, "I'm almost gone. I want to have an automobile funeral. When you're on the way to the cemetery with me, just put on a little speed. It'll be quicker."[35] It was an apropos wish given that Pruyn was the first taxicab operator in Chicago. Due to a city ordinance that forbade the use of a private vehicle for funeral purposes, the Automobile Livery Chauffeurs Union had to act quickly. The first motorized hearse wouldn't be unveiled for another six months by the Crane & Breed Manufacturing Company. The union had planned on using an "auto ambulance" until they were informed that would be illegal.[36] They decided to Frankenstein one.

The union members took a seven-passenger touring car and dropped the coach of a horse-drawn hearse onto the tonneau, making a motorized hearse the city lawmakers couldn't argue with.[37] Despite adding a half ton of glass and carved wood to the touring car, the homemade hearse, powered by a beefy six-cylinder engine, was still capable of speeds approaching thirty miles per hour. The eighteen-vehicle procession breezed from undertaker Ludlow's chapel located on East Forty-Seventh to Oak Woods Cemetery,* a distance of three miles, in about twenty minutes. In a horse-drawn hearse it would've easily taken an hour. The *Inter Ocean* described Pruyn's funeral procession as "unique, ultra modern," and that it "will travel at high speed."[38] The mode of transporting the dead was forever changed with Pruyn's ultra-modern cortege.

Like Pruyn's dying wish, the hearse can be dependent on the decedent's vocation. Today, it's not uncommon in rural areas for the casket of a farmer to be driven to the cemetery by a tractor. Nor is it an uncommon sight for a fireman to be taken on a last ride on a piece of

---

* Some newspaper accounts put Pruyn into Oakland Cemetery, a distance of seventeen miles. It seems unlikely that Ludlow would be burying people that far from his neighborhood. That distance in those days would mean an all-day burial in a horse-drawn hearse.

fire equipment. Similarly, a fallen service member that qualifies for full honors at Arlington National Cemetery may receive a ride in a caisson, a type of artillery wagon used during the Civil War that served double duty to ferry the dead and wounded from the battlefield.

The value of that piece of the funeral rite, the last ride to the grave—the procession—isn't purely contingent upon the vehicle. The migration is just as important. Since humans first gathered around their dead and took them to the place where they burned them or buried them, there was *movement*. It's an act of mourners' solidarity to gather and take the dead to their place of disposition. The movement of the procession not only pays honor to the decedent but also aids in the grieving process. Lincoln's multiple funeral processions were a way Americans could participate in the obsequies and express their grief.

In addition to the hundreds of thousands of military personnel, dignitaries, civic leaders, and citizens who took part in the twelve-city processions, *millions* of Americans gathered to catch a glimpse of the Lincoln funeral processions, both streetside or trackside. Even if their corporal act of mercy was to merely watch the procession, it still felt participatory. They could be part of the movement; they could stand in solidarity with other citizens. A nation mourned as one.

Ulysses S. Grant, two decades later, was afforded the same honor, though he had only one grand procession, despite his funeral train stopping at the state capitol, Albany, for him to lie in repose, before continuing to New York City. On the morning of August 8, 1885, the procession of fifty thousand people left City Hall bound for Riverside Park where Grant was to be temporarily entombed. The procession line stretched for over five miles, and it took five hours for the cavalcade to pass any given point.[39] An estimated million people jammed the eight-mile stretch in the blistering August heat attempting to catch a glimpse of the casket.[40] So packed were city streets that ambulances tooled up and down the parade route rescuing people fainting from heat exhaustion and suffocation.[41]

Hearses, despite undergoing stylistic changes, have remained by and large the same for the past century. In the 1920s the body of the hearse became less boxy, more streamlined into what is called the "limousine"-style hearse and remained that way, and the landau (faux convertible) top that first appeared the late 1950s has remained the favorite style coach.

There have been variations on and some interesting departures from the automobile hearse. In the late nineteenth century, a few New York hospitals boasted side-loading electric ambulances. Side loading is easier to maneuver for patients in crowded city streets. Coach builders realized the benefit of loading a casket from the sidewalk in a crowded city. For a half century, many hearses were available with the side-loading option. According to the professional car author Walter McCall, vehicle downsizing killed this feature and the last side-loading hearse was produced in 1984.[42]

It's no surprise that hearse builders took design cues from the ambulance. Ambulance and hearse manufacturers were, for most of the century, one and the same, especially given that many funeral homes ran the local ambulance service in their town. These manufacturers—such as Superior, Eureka, Flxible, Sayers and Scovill, and others*—were able to sell multiple vehicles to the same customer. Some were built as combination vehicles, meaning they were marketed as a hearse *and* an ambulance. The 1959 Cadillac Futura coach built by Miller-Meteor featured in the *Ghostbusters* movies as Ecto-1 was a combination hearse/ambulance. Many funeral homes divested themselves of their ambulance business in the 1960s and 1970s when states began passing laws on training requirements and the amount of specialized equipment an ambulance needed to contain.

Undertakers haven't been limited to a hearse with four wheels. Some city undertakers opted to forgo the hassles of a horse (or horseless) hearse in city traffic and employed a trolley. The trolley hearse could conveniently take the casket, flowers, family, and mourners to the local rural cemetery, typically located at the end of the line. The press touted the trolley hearse "to effect economy in funeral expense" by eliminating the expense of a separate vehicle to carry the body and allowing everyone to ride together.[43] To provide more room for friends and family, and eliminate the need for additional trolleys,

---

* The number of coach builders and chassis used over the past century is staggering. Seems as if everyone tried their hand at coach building at one time or another. Today there are ten coach builders (Platinum, MK Coach, Eagle, Federal, Armbruster Stageway, S&S, Miller Meteor, Eureka, Superior, and Rosewood) building on two chassis, Cadillac and Lincoln (except for Rosewood who builds on their own chassis).

Reuben McCauley of Baltimore patented a trolley hearse where the casket was placed on top of the trolley—on display in a glass case—to allow more room in the trolley car.[44] McCauley's version of the trolley hearses had two separate compartments: one for the bereaved family members and one for everyone else. When arriving at the end of the line, the casket was removed from the roof by a chute and tackle.[45] Surely McCauley's method of casket transport never really caught on as the method of casket egress was less than graceful. The screeching, clanging trolley hearse never gained popularity in the States as it did in Mexico and South America. They enjoyed a brief time of popularity in urban centers from the turn of the century through the Roaring Twenties and then went the way of the horse-drawn hearse as automobiles took over and many municipalities abandoned their streetcars.

Similar to the trolley hearse, the funeral omnibus was meant to eliminate the multiple vehicles of the procession and condense the entire procession into one vehicle. Fred Hulberg of New York City, president of NFDA from 1901 to 1902, patented such a "combined hearse and passenger vehicle" in 1909.[46] Hulberg's invention could hold the casket, eight passengers, and the flowers. Others followed suit—such as L. Glesenkamp, Sons & Co. of Pittsburgh with their enlarged omnibus that held thirty-two people—but these multipurpose hearses never gained public fancy and disappeared before the trolley hearse.

Strictly speaking, hearses aren't limited to ground transportation, though without waterways as in Venice, hearse boats are rare. Frank E. Campbell, the pioneering undertaker of New York, owned a sixty-five-foot luxury yacht, the *Hourglass*, which he used for spreading cremains at sea. Campbell ran the carriage trade business of New York and, ever looking to promote his business in new and unique ways, he would also use his yacht to transport remains and mourners to cemeteries that were easier to access by water from Manhattan than by car or rail. He even had a pipe organ installed on the vessel to conduct floating funerals.[47] However, Campbell's waterborne hearse wasn't a purpose-built hearse boat but rather a pleasure craft pressed into funeral service. The Bradshaw family of Maryland built such a hearse boat. In the Chesapeake Bay there are two isolated, inhabited islands, Smith and Tangier, that sit miles off the mainland. In 1931, Harvey

Bradshaw commissioned the construction of a forty-two-foot boat, *King Tut*, to become known as the "hearse boat of the Chesapeake Bay," so he could service death calls on the islands.[48] The boat remained in service until the 1970s, eventually rendered obsolete as the dead were transported off the islands by local emergency services. Today, caskets are still floated to the islands for burial, though no longer on a hearse boat; they go on the mail boat.

Whether it be by water, road, or rail, the hearse is still the lynchpin in the American funeral rite, transporting the dead from the place of funeralization to that of final disposition.

So why the hearse—or "funeral coach," as some are wont to call it? A pickup truck will *function* to move the remains. A sedan or bicycle will do for a set of cremains.* But it's not often we see a pickup truck leading a funeral procession. Why? Doesn't that seem infinitely more practical? And isn't that what Americans pride themselves on—practicality? No, the hearse remains because it's more than just an engine, transmission, and four tires assembled over some burled wood and draperies and trimmed with a landau bar.

It's a symbol—merely one symbol in the complex array of symbols—co-opted from the English/European tradition of moving the dead on a specialty vehicle that Americans use to affirm they value their dead. The symbolism a hearse conveys is complex, but boiling it down to basic terms, it expresses an idea: this person was loved, they contributed to society, they were important in some way.

From the rude beginnings of the black-painted buckboard in colonial America, the flamboyance of the hearse rises and then falls, reaching its peak sometime in the late nineteenth century when hearses were sometimes mini "churches," adorned with plumes, carved urns, elaborately carved draperies, and gilded saints. Recently they have become somewhat less ostentatious, though that's not to say less important. There's little sign the pickup truck will replace the hearse in the near future. No, the de-ornamentation in coach building coincided with the enormous and swift changes affected by the Great War in how we bury our dead.

---

* Hearses now come with fancy decorated alcoves the undertaker screws in the back for transporting urns to the cemetery.

CHAPTER 11

Mourning the Great War

T he Great War was a marvel of killing. No longer did soldiers congregate at opposing sides on a field of battle to engage in tactics with weapons largely unchanged since Alexander the Great. No, this killing was scientific and technological. Men hunkered in hundreds of miles of muddy trenches while bombs rained from above and poisonous gas blew in the prevailing winds. And when the sergeant blew the whistle, it was up and over the top and into the maw of Lewis, Browning, and Bergmann machine guns spitting out five hundred rounds per minute, dodging grenades, land mines, and flamethrowers. Submarines prowled the high seas and tanks plowed across battlefields. It was slaughter perfected.

Twenty million soldiers and civilians perished in World War I. Of those dead, 106,000* were doughboys, soldiers of the American Expeditionary Forces.[1]

The war not only directly affected mourning customs and governmental policy on dead warriors but the industrial-economic apparatus that fed the war effort also had reverberating effects on the methods by which Americans buried their dead. This was the time that Americans gave up their dead, shifting their care from home funerals to the institution of funeral homes.

---

* Another eleven thousand sailors and marines died too.

In light of the staggering loss of life in the trenches, Americans cast off the overt symbols and rules of mourning almost overnight. Not that the public wasn't primed for it. Mrs. John Jacob Astor and her very public defiance of "proper" mourning was the first chink in the armor nearly five years before America entered the fray. The impetus to cast aside the rigors of public mourning had nothing to do with the war but rather embracing modernization. America was an economic powerhouse propelled by science, technology, and industry. There was less and less room in the evolving culture for the old, cumbersome ways of black crepe and retreating into woe. The Great War gave Americans an excuse to cast off the old ways of mourning.

Like so much of America's culture aped from England, the English were the first to discard the longstanding Victorian mourning customs. America soon followed suit. By the time Congress declared war on the Axis powers, British Tommies had been slogging it out in the trenches for almost three years. The geographic proximity of England to the front line meant that a British soldier could be huddled on muddy duckboards one evening and the next, eating bangers and mash in a public house in London. Mourning garb immediately became a morale issue, not only for the mothers, fathers, brothers, sisters, wives, and children with a male family member serving in France or Belgium but also for regular citizens. The death toll was such that it affected every citizen, and the entire country would've been clothed in black crepe. A Tommy home on a few days leave didn't want to walk around his hometown with the constant reminders of the death that awaited him back at the front.

The bloodshed was so great that it quickly became wholly impractical to keep track of proper mourning etiquette as women lost multiple kinships—for example, a husband *and* brother *and* cousin—in a short time span. This was now a country at war, worried more about pressing survival issues such as acute food and fuel shortages than what seemed almost frivolous—who was wearing proper mourning attire.

Congress officially declared war on April 6, 1917, but it would be months before the American war machine could be mobilized and take to the field. On November 3, Lance Corporal James Gresham was likely the first American killed, along with two others from the Sixteenth Infantry Regiment, in the trenches near Bathelémont. Two months later as the war machine continued to churn out a daily casualty list, an article appeared in the *Chattanooga Daily Times* suggesting "that the war widows of this country might adopt the sensible plan of refraining from mourning—or, at least heavy mourning."[2] Mourning garb quickly became a morale issue in the States, and one of practicality as women quietly assumed the job vacancies left by the nearly three million mobilized soldiers, sailors, and marines.[3] The answer was the resurgence of mourning jewelry: subtle so as not to be demoralizing, yet the bereaved could identify one another and have the benefit of solidarity. The abandonment of heavy mourning by war widows was seen as sensible.[4]

The Woman's Committee of the Council of National Defense organized women across the country to fill vacated jobs. In a letter to President Woodrow Wilson, Chairwoman Dr. Anna Howard Shaw recommended adopting a brassard to replace mourning garb. It simply wasn't practical for these women who were now working outside the home to be confined by the impractical old-fashioned mourning gowns. The suggested replacement armband—the brassard—was a three-inch strip of black broadcloth or silk worn on the left arm with a gilt star embroidered for each family member lost. Wilson responded in a letter to Shaw: "I do entirely approve of the action taken by the Women's [*sic*] Committee . . . I hope and believe that thoughtful people everywhere will approve of this action."[5] One could argue that casting off mourning garments was a tangible symbol of women moving outside of the home and a strictly domestic role, a move that culminated two years after the war ended with the passage of the Nineteenth Amendment and women gaining the right to vote.

With the disappearance of mourning garments, mourning jewelry once again became popular as a small way (aside from the brassard) to observe mourning. Rings and brooches were favorites, with the *Times* of Shreveport, Louisiana, proclaiming, "[M]ourning ring comes back into popular favor: Chicagoans with relatives sleeping on French battlefields revive ancient custom."[6] The new fashion of mourning rings was about simplicity; gone were the old images of coffins and skeletons. The Great War rings were often plain black enameled affairs with the fallen's initials and date of death inscribed in the circlet. Sometimes they were inset with amethyst, the mourning stone.[7] In another departure from the old custom, the bereaved were allowed brightly enameled (black, of course) or polished jet rather than matte rings, and they could be adorned with pearls. Hat pins, watch ribbons, simple necklaces, earrings, and bracelets were all permitted and even considered correct.[8] In essence, the old guard of austerity and asceticism was tossed out the window in the maelstrom of machine gun fire and choking clouds of mustard gas.

More recently, mourning jewelry has experienced a resurgence due to the exploding popularity of cremation. Whereas in the early mid-nineteenth century, jewelry made from the decedent in the form of hair jewelry was fashionable, now cremation jewelry is. Bracelets, rings, necklaces, and earrings can all be made to hold a bit of cremains. Mourning jewelry has also morphed into the more permanent medium of body art, or tattoos. Names and dates of remembrance are common memorialization motifs, as are portraits, but the options for body art memorialization are really only limited by the imagination.

It wasn't just abstract notions such as *morale* and *practicality* that were changing the death rite. The body, or lack thereof, was changing the way Americans mourned. On the western front, men were dying in great numbers by acts of war, but worldwide and stateside, staggering numbers would perish by an invisible enemy, a virus.

There's no way to accurately know exactly how many people worldwide were killed by the Spanish flu. Some estimates are as high as one hundred million people.[9] That means the H1N1 1918 flu potentially killed one out of every twenty people in the world. It was nothing short of devastating. Death lurked everywhere: churches, schools, markets, on the street, in one's own home. Hundreds of people were dying *each day* in metropolitan areas during the second wave surge in the fall of 1918. The victims completely overloaded the public health system, leading to mass burials as undertakers struggled to get the estimated half a million people buried.[10] In October, in an effort to get people in the ground, Philadelphia temporarily suspended burial permits. Across the river in Camden, New Jersey, police officers and firefighters were tasked with knocking together caskets, as people lay in their homes and piled in mortuaries for lack of burial vessels.[11] Grave diggers—graves were still exclusively dug by hand in 1918— were soon grossly overworked, that is, the ones that chose to stay and didn't flee in fear of catching the contagion from burying scores of infected caskets a week. In Philadelphia, the situation was so dire that Archbishop Dennis J. Dougherty called students from St. Charles Seminary to pitch in and dig graves.[12] Many family members simply picked up a shovel and got the job done, and there was even a report of a husband digging his wife's grave, though it probably occurred far more often than was reported.[13]

In an effort to control the spread of the flu, many states and municipalities banned public funerals. Funerals were limited to immediate family and pallbearers, and in some states, such as Iowa, open caskets weren't allowed,* even at private services. Suddenly Americans were faced with an impossible quandary: not only did the death rite not include community support—a vital benefit of a funeral service—but the guest of honor wasn't there either because the casket was closed, or the body had been whisked away for immediate burial, or the solider had died thousands of miles away. The death paradigm was challenged in a way that it hadn't been since the Civil War. Of course, there were other cultural and socioeconomic factors that contributed to the shifting manner in which Americans funeralize their dead. The presence (or lack thereof for many, many families) of the body during the Civil War pushed Americans to embrace the rigid and ritualized mourning customs of the late nineteenth century. It was almost as if the cultural conscience, the collective of those who lived through the war, wanted to mourn in extravagant fashion to honor all those boys in blue and gray who never made it off the battlefield. It's perverse, but it was something society *could* do in response to the frustration of the great national tragedy. A generation of young men left home never to been seen again, not even afforded the dignity of burial in home soil. It took another phantom body crisis—this time the confluence of two events, the war and the virus—to cause Americans to cast off Victorian-era mourning. And it *was* a crisis. Americans were missing the most important piece of the mourning puzzle: the body. The government

---

* If a soldier was shipped home from a domestic post (from the many cantonments slapped together to train the massive army the military was raising), the undertaker was allowed to let the parents identify the solider, but only after covering the face with gauze saturated with 40 percent formalin, and the parents had to cover their mouths and noses with gauze when in the room. "Epidemic in Iowa Is Under Control," *Des Moines (IA) Register*, October 12, 1918.

had made a promise. That promise was first glimpsed a half century prior, during the War Between the States.

Overwhelmed by casualties, the War Department was forced to issue General Order 33 on April 3, 1862, in which the commanding officer was responsible for laying out burial grounds and seeing to it that the dead were interred with a headboard erected, containing, "where practicable, the names of the persons."[14] General Order 33 expanded upon General Order 75, issued seven months earlier, that required the commanding officer to maintain a record of soldiers killed under their command and their place of burial. Despite the real-time difficulties of executing General Order 33 in combat situations, it helped provide a framework for disposition in the aftermath of a battle, but it did nothing to solve the issue of wounded and diseased dying in Washington, DC's general hospitals. After only a year at war, Washington's burial grounds were filling up fast. On July 17, 1862, Lincoln signed an omnibus bill authorizing him to "purchase cemetery grounds and cause them to be securely enclosed, to be used as a national cemetery for the soldiers who shall die in the service of the country."[15] Lincoln turned the power of national cemetery creation over to the quartermaster general of the army, Brigadier General Montgomery C. Meigs. Meigs, whose duties consisted of supplying men with food, clothing, and matériel, now included burying the dead. Meigs's responsibility to this point in the war, as directed by General Order 75, was to supply blank burial registers to officers and the "means for a registered head-board."[16] Meigs took his new charge seriously. By the end of the year, fourteen national cemeteries had been created as far west as Kansas.

Cemetery creation was more than duty for Meigs. He became emotionally invested.

Meigs's son, Lieutenant John R. Meigs, entered the war midway through, in 1863, after graduating from West Point with "the highest honors."[17] With a mop of blond hair swept up over almost delicate features that made women sneak a second glance at the dashing young soldier, Lieutenant Meigs stares intently past the camera lens in a portrait. The still frame of the camera doesn't contain his youthful vigor, his seriousness about soldiering. Meigs wasn't planning on riding through the war on his famous father's coattails, and immediately got to work making a name for himself as an engineer at major engagements such as Bull Run, Gettysburg, and New Market.

On a rainy day in early October, Meigs was completing a survey near Dayton, Virginia, returning to headquarters along Swift Run Gap Road accompanied by two orderlies when he was shot in the face at almost point-blank range.[18]

One of his orderlies was captured. The other escaped to tell the tale to General Philip Sheridan. The ambushers were suspected bushwhackers, or rebels engaging in guerilla warfare. The reason Meigs got so close to the rebels was that they weren't in uniform—a must according to the rules of engagement—and Meigs assumed since they were so far behind Union lines they were his men. There was much finger-pointing. The Confederates claimed the men were scouts in uniform wearing India rubber cloaks over their tunics because of the rain, and it was a fair fight, not an ambush. Enraged, Sheridan ordered everything burned within a five-mile radius. The fact remained that no amount of Sheridan's wrath would bring back Montgomery Meigs's only son.[19]

Meigs had his beloved son interred in Oak Hill Cemetery in Washington, DC, with a bronze statue* cast the way Lieutenant Meigs was found lying in the mud of Swift Run Gap Road serving as his monument.[20] The death of John was something from which Montgomery Meigs never recovered. What Montgomery Meigs was able to recover were the remains of his son. He buried them in the family plot, a luxury hundreds of thousands of other families weren't afforded.

The summer after hostilities ceased, Meigs ordered an accounting of interments and sent Captain James Moore, assistant quartermaster, into the field to report on the location and condition of battlefield cemeteries. The results were dismaying.

At Spotsylvania Court House and the site of the Battle of the Wilderness, Moore found hundreds of unmarked graves covered with underbrush and skeletons bleaching in the sun.[21] Moore got to work laying out proper cemeteries, disinterring the haphazard temporary burials, identifying the remains—a Herculean, often impossible task—and erecting wooden headboards. And the results from his quartermasters weren't any better. Only 116,148 (Union) soldiers were reported buried, a number well short of the 360,000 dead.[22] The reported numbers told

---

* General Meigs had his son and the bronze statue moved to Arlington National Cemetery in 1880.

Meigs that less than one in three dead soldiers were accounted for, and most of that one-third wasn't buried properly.

Meigs sent his men to scour the countryside and locate the fallen. As the interment records trickled in, Meigs published them in a twenty-seven-volume record, referred to as the "Roll of Honor." The roll lists the soldier's unit, rank, date of death, and burial location. By 1870 the Quartermaster Department had located 299,696 soldiers (and sailors)* who now lay in seventy-three newly established national cemeteries.[23] The paper slips pinned inside campaign tunics and metallic pins from *Harper's Weekly* and embalming surgeons may have helped in some instances, but clearly there was a better way—a staggering 42 percent of the dead remained unidentified, and forty-four thousand remain unlocated.[24] An entire generation of young men had marched off to war and simply vanished, their families forced to do the awful grief work with no remains and always left to wonder. The missing men forced a sort of mourning purgatory on a whole other generation. So awful was this purgatory that Americans tacitly decided this was culturally unacceptable.

The dead must be accounted for.

During the Spanish-American War in 1898, soldiers were carefully buried post-combat in marked graves. This was an abrupt departure from American war policy from just several decades prior in that not only was there a concerted effort to collate the dead, but also this conflict was fought on foreign soil and America was going to undertake the task of repatriating them. Quartermaster General Marshall Ludington said of the policy that his department was going to "disinter the remains of all its soldiers who, in defense of their country, had given up their lives on a foreign shore, and bring them . . . to their native land."[25] By the end of June 1899, a Quartermaster Burial Corps comprised of civilian morticians returned 1,222 soldiers.[26]

This promise would be put to the test in just a few short years during a war being fought with weapons and tactics that made recovery *and* identification a trickier prospect than anyone could've imagined.

---

* Another 13,575 were accounted for in post and private cemeteries.

One man—a civilian—wanted to tackle the recovery issue. Dr. Howard S. Eckels had seen the condition of the soldiers sent home from the Spanish-American War. And Eckels, who ran the Eckels College of Embalming located on Market Street in Philadelphia, decided he could do something about it. In the summer of 1917, long before the first American casualty of WWI, Eckels and Jay H. Mowbray formed the American Purple Cross Association. It was an unusual partnership, with Mowbray being a newspaper editor, for a membership "limited to those who have made care of bodies their life pursuit," but perhaps Eckels thought the bully pulpit of a newsman would further the cause.[27]

In addition to furnishing embalmers, the Purple Cross offered to equip and train the men, provide vehicles, and *fund* the entire operation.[28] House bill 5410—"a bill to render possible the return of the bodies of our soldier dead to their home burial grounds in a sanitary and recognizable condition"—was put forth in Congress.[29] Mowbray whipped up support through his media channels. Newspapers across the country carried headlines such as "The Purple Cross: Bill Before Congress May Soon Come a Law—Urge Our Congressman to Act" and "Seek Approval of Purple Cross: Urge People to Sign Petition to Congress."[30] Despite the widespread support of House Bill 5410 and the "enthusiastic" support of Quartermaster General Henry G. Sharp, the War Department declined Eckels's offer. A letter signed by the adjutant general of the army, Brigadier General H. P. McCain, stated, "The secretary of war directs me to inform you that the subject . . . has been given careful consideration. It has been decided that a suitable organization for this force shall be adopted for service in the quartermaster's corps. The department is deeply appreciative of your generous and patriotic interest."[31] On August 7, 1917, under General Order 104, the Graves Registration Service (GRS) under the Quartermaster Corps was formed.

It would be three more months before the whistles sounded for the doughboys to scramble over the earthen walls to meet withering machine gun fire in no-man's-land. James Gresham and the thousands of casualties that followed made one thing crystal clear to the government: the bodies of the soldier dead would have to wait. Despite having the newly formed GRS to focus solely on the fallen, like in the Civil War the army was almost immediately overwhelmed by the dead. On average, 143 men were dying per day in battle. An additional 168 men were dying per day from illness, accident, and all the other noncombat ways a soldier can die in the theater of war, meaning the GRS was wrestling with over three hundred deaths per day.

However, unlike the Civil War, there was a plan in place. The function of the GRS wasn't to preserve (i.e., embalm) the dead; no, they were charged with identifying the dead and marking graves as well as establishing permanent and semipermanent cemeteries.[32] Identification of the dead was much improved owing to the fact that the period between battles, recovery, and burial was considerably shorter than in the Civil War, and it was aided by the fact that the military introduced aluminum identification tags in 1913.

Back home there was a fight brewing over the martyrs.

General John "Black Jack" Pershing,[*] the commander of the American Expeditionary Forces, sent a widely publicized cablegram to the War Department regarding his thoughts on the American dead: "Have given the entire question of our dead men thought and my opinion is that we should leave our dead near where they fell . . . [I] [b]elieve that could these soldiers speak for themselves they would wish to be left undisturbed in the place where, with their comrades, they fought the last fight."[33] Black Jack was lauded as the savior, propelling America and its allies to victory, but the bodies of the soldiers weren't his to decide. Alice Gresham Dodd, the mother of Corporal James Gresham, said in a May 1919 interview, "I want my boy's body brought back. I want him near me, so I can go to his grave . . . I cannot go over to where they have lain him. And even if I could, just coming once to his grave and then going away forever, would break my heart."[34] Dodd was dubbed the "First Gold Star Mother," and as such her words carried weight, echoing the sentiment of many American mothers and wives that *we want our dead back.*

The government pushed ahead with its plan of overseas burial grounds. Assistant Secretary of War Ralph Hayes visited France and concluded that three "Fields of Honor" be erected at Romagne, Belleau, and Suresnes,[†] effectively condensing the 769 scattered burial grounds.[35]

---

[*] The riderless horse, Black Jack, in President John F. Kennedy's funeral was named for General Pershing.
[†] Eight Fields of Honor were ultimately created: one in Great Britain, one in Belgium, and six in France.

Not mere "cemeteries," the government was going to bury the fallen in "Fields of Honor." Some citizens supported the practicality of the Fields of Honor; Blanche K. Wheeler wondered in an editorial in the *New-York Tribune*, "How any parent can consider with equanimity the desecrating alternative of having the body moved about like a piece of cargo." Wheeler continued, writing that the proposed Fields of Honor were the "sane, logical solution." She concluded by saying, "A Gold Star mother whose love for her son could never be questioned."[36] It wasn't only average citizens like Ms. Wheeler advocating for the soldier dead to repose in France. Powerful men such as Theodore "Teddy" Roosevelt were in favor of America's martyrs staying put. And he had a dog in the fight.

On July 14, 1918, Lieutenant Quentin Roosevelt was patrolling the skies about ten miles behind the German line in the Chateau-Thierry sector when he was separated from his squadron. Roosevelt, who was last seen alive being pursued by two German airplanes, became an American martyr, falling on French soil on Bastille Day. The young ace was twenty years old and had just jumped into the fray, shooting down his first airplane only four days prior.

When the former President and Mrs. Roosevelt learned the fate of their youngest child, Teddy Roosevelt said sanguinely, "[We] are very glad that he got to the front and had the chance to render some service to his country."[37]

On August 11, the Allies were able to push the line back and take the ground where Lieutenant Roosevelt crashed. The Germans had buried him next to his downed airplane, northeast of a village called Chierges. They'd erected a crude wooden monument with his name and rank chiseled in it.[38] The Roosevelts wanted their son's remains to rest in peace, stating, "We greatly prefer that Quentin shall continue to lie on the spot where he fell in battle and where the foeman buried him."[39]

Coming from a former president, it was a powerful endorsement for the government-sponsored cemeteries. But there were still no clear lines on what to do with the dead, so the War Department sent out a survey to every family who'd lost someone. Only 26 percent of Gold Star American families felt the same way as the Roosevelts, General Pershing, and Colonel Charles Pierce, who headed the GRS. They wanted their sons, husbands, brothers, and fathers to lie undisturbed in meticulously planned military cemeteries with their brothers-in-arms. However, that sentiment was the minority. An overwhelming 59 percent* of respondents wanted their solider dead repatriated.[40]

Regardless of what the American citizens wanted, getting their soldier dead back looked like an impossibility. In spite of the agreements France made with the US prior to the war, the French government had dug in its heels after the war ended. The dead were staying put. France was in the process of rebuilding a decimated country and the last thing they needed were trains of bodies rumbling across the countryside. They cited their refusal on health reasons as well as morale.[41]

Theodore Boice, a Pittsburgh newspaper columnist, began a grassroots organization called "Bring Home the Soldier Dead League." Chapters sprang up almost overnight, urging citizens to contact their representatives to support funding for repatriation, and chapters sent delegates to petition Congress. During a convention of American War Mothers in October of 1919, one unnamed speaker summed up the general attitude of Gold Star families: "They are our boys; they belong to us, and we want them home. We sent them to France and they gave up their lives, and the least the government can do is to give us back their bodies."[42] The American Legion† threw its support behind the soldiers' families.

On January 14, 1920, Secretary of War Newton Baker, in response to mounting pressure, reiterated the War Department's position on the soldier dead, stating, "The bodies of all American soldiers who died of disease or wounds in France would be brought back. . . . That promise will be kept in letter and spirit."[43] The clock was ticking; it had been more than a year since the guns had fallen silent on the western front and nothing had been done to bring the dead home. Alice Dodd's words from a 1919 interview hung heavy in the minds of many families in limbo: "I hope they bring him back while I'm still alive."[44]

Congress, in response to the repeated calls to action by the Bring Home the Soldier Dead League, continued to pressure the French. By the end of 1920, France had capitulated, and a few months later on March 4, 1921, Congress passed the law earmarking repatriation funds.

---

* At the time the results of the survey were published, 15 percent hadn't responded.

† Ironically, the American Legion was founded (in part) by Lieutenant Colonel Theodore Roosevelt, Jr., son of T. R. and Edith Roosevelt, who wished their son to stay in France.

On July 10 the first wave—over seven thousand caskets—of doughboys lay in Hoboken, New Jersey. General Pershing, who had been against moving "his boys," embraced the sentiment of those who wanted their kin buried on home soil and addressed the crowd, saying, "It remains for us with fitting ceremonies, tenderly, with our flowers and our tears, to lay them to rest in the America for which they died."[45] Pershing then placed wreaths on Gresham's casket, along with the other two, Privates Thomas Enright and Merle Hay, who perished with him that day.

Gresham was buried five days later in Locust Hill Cemetery in his hometown of Evansville, Indiana. Dodd, who died six years after her son was returned home, is buried in the same cemetery.*

Interestingly, the government turned to the very people they'd refused at the outset of the war, civilian embalmers, to help disinter and identify the soldiers.[46] The Purple Cross didn't assist in the postwar recoveries, but it remained a self-financed disaster relief organization for several decades after the war, an indirect precursor to the modern-day federal organization Disaster Mortuary Operational Response Team (DMORT).[47] DMORT responds domestically to mass fatality incidents, and comprises, like the Purple Cross, funeral directors and embalmers, among other professionals.

A total of 46,300 soldiers would be brought home by the end of 1921.[48] Beginning in 1950, the military adopted the policy of concurrent return, meaning personnel dying in the battle theater are repatriated immediately. Transportation advances have rendered obsolete the old practice of temporary burials until hostilities have ceased. Modern forensic techniques have also rendered obsolete the problem that plagued the military for years—the unidentified.

Amazingly, given the incessant shelling that could literally blow a man to pieces, the GRS was able to identify all but 1,237 soldiers, or 1.1 percent.[49] That's an enormous improvement from the 42 percent left unidentified after the Civil War. The big question was, what to do with the unidentified? Of course, they were buried in the Fields of Honor, marked with "Here Rests in Honored Glory an American Soldier, Known But to God," but the political and social climate wasn't the same as fifty years prior. Those 1,237 families weren't going to go as quietly. They wanted answers. They wanted closure.

---

* Alice Dodd had two (adult) children succumb during the flu pandemic, dying within a week of each other in the fall surge of 1918.

They found closure in the form of a venerated tomb containing *one* unknown soldier who could be any one of the lost.

The idea of a tomb for an unknown soldier was proposed by Hamilton Fish III, the newly elected representative from New York. Fish, a highly decorated combat veteran, didn't dream up the idea on his own. France and Great Britain had each already buried an unknown solider—France's under the Arc de Triomphe, and Great Britain's in Westminster Abbey—on the two-year Armistice Day anniversary. Fish proposed America do the same at the amphitheater at Arlington National Cemetery. Army Chief of Staff Peyton March opposed Fish's proposal on the misguided grounds that the GRS would eventually identify all the unknowns.[50] But that wouldn't be a reality; the machinery of modern warfare coupled with the chaos that accompanied trench warfare meant some men would remain known only to God, despite the best efforts of the GRS.

Pershing, seen by Americans as the savior of the free world, endorsed Fish's proposal, despite March's opposition. That was the push Fish's resolution needed. Three short months later, on March 4, 1921, Congress approved the return of an unknown soldier as well as construction of a tomb at Arlington. Fish's original date of Memorial Day was deemed too soon, and Armistice Day was settled upon.

On October 22, four unknowns were dug up from French Fields of Honor at Aisne-Marne, Meuse-Argonne, Somme, and St. Mihiel. The remains were inspected to ensure they were members of the American Expeditionary Forces, they died as a result of wounds sustained in battle, and they were truly known only to God.* The remains were placed into identical caskets and transported to the town of Châlons-sur-Marne and placed in a makeshift chapel in city hall.

It was Pershing's wish that a regular doughboy—not an officer—make the selection. That honor fell to Edward F. Younger, a twenty-three-year-old sergeant from Chicago. Despite his youth, Younger—wounded twice, once severely—had seen more during a year in the sodden trenches than most men see in a lifetime, though one would be hard pressed to tell. Younger's eyes were clear and his posture ramrod straight. Outside city

---

* In addition to the soldier's name (or any other clues pointing to identity), rank and date of death were also unknown.

hall on October 24, an American officer handed Younger a bouquet of white and pink roses.[51]

In the background a French military band played the ominous notes of "Dead March"—the same dirge used in George Washington's public funeral in Philadelphia.[52] Younger smartly walked through a line of French Honor Guard into the makeshift chapel. The four identical caskets, draped with American flags, sat in the stillness of the chapel. Younger was completely alone in this momentous selection. The room was chilly and smelled vaguely of wood from the freshly hewn shipping cases the caskets sat upon as temporary biers. Younger slowly walked around the caskets three times, the only sound the creaking leather of his trench boots. Stopping, he placed the bouquet on the casket closest to the entrance, saluted, and left.[53]

The Unknown Soldier's remains were transferred out of the casket and placed in a "silver and ebony coffin sent from home" under the supervision of Colonel Harry F. Rethers, the head of GRS, and Major General Harry L. Rogers, quartermaster of the Army on the Rhine, and displayed in the rotunda of city hall for French citizens to pay their respects.[54] The remaining three unknowns were placed back in the transfer cases and buried at Meuse-Argonne.[55]

The *Olympia*—the ship bearing the Unknown Soldier—arrived at the navy yard in Washington, DC, on November 9 and the casket was transported to the Capitol with great military fanfare. The Unknown Soldier was placed on the Lincoln catafalque in the Rotunda and received by President and Mrs. Harding. The following day, the public was admitted. The Washington *Evening Star* estimated that during the course of sixteen hours, upward of 96,000 people paid homage to the American soldier known only to God.[56]

The Unknown Soldier was borne out of the Capitol at 8:30 a.m. on Armistice Day for a nearly three-hour procession through the packed streets of Washington, with the president following the caisson, a poppy pinned in his lapel, along with ranking members of all three branches of government and other dignitaries. After the processional crowd assembled in the amphitheater—all 5,200 seats filled—Bishop Charles H. Brent, senior chaplain of the American Expeditionary Forces, delivered an invocation, and at noon a two-minute silence was observed. Around the nation, cars and trains stopped. Men knelt on sidewalks and in the streets, heads uncovered, and factory machinery ground to a halt.[57] An entire nation paused in solidarity, in mourning. In the amphitheater, after the silence, President Harding addressed the crowd and the Unknown Soldier was bestowed with the highest military awards from seven countries, including Harding awarding the Congressional Medal of Honor and the Distinguished Service Cross.

The body was borne to the tomb* by the pallbearers while the band played the somber John Philip Sousa dirge "Our Honored Dead." As the casket was lowered into the crypt—which had already been layered with a measure of French soil—the band switched to the softer, more melodious "Lead Kindly Light." Bishop Brent read the committal service. Hamilton Fish, who championed the idea, had the honor of placing the first wreath at the tomb, followed by Mrs. R. Emmett Digney, president of National American War Mothers. The troops in attendance stood at "present arms" while three thunderous artillery volleys sounded. The mournful notes of taps floated through the air, and the artillery fired the national salute, twenty-one guns, to conclude the service for America's most venerated hero.[58]

The burial of a national hero was like a giant funeral for the entire nation, putting all the dead warriors to rest. The healing could begin, but Americans were forever changed. There would be no returning to Belle Époque mourning. The "practical" way of mourning—subtly—during wartime just made sense to continue into the Roaring Twenties. Prescribed mourning and all the accoutrements (e.g., crepe dresses, black-bordered stationary, weepers, black cigarettes) that accompanied it faded quickly from the national consciousness. Just as one war clothed Americans in set patterns of mourning, another as equally devastating cast them off.

Mourning rituals weren't the only things changing. Funerals were becoming institutionalized, giving rise to the "funeral home," a place of business for the purpose of conducting funerals that simulated the look of the home. In "If You Are Thinking of Building" in the August 1910

---

* Sergeant Edward Younger, who selected the unknown, died in 1942. He rests in section 18, about three hundred yards from the Tomb of the Unknown Soldier.

issue of *Ladies' Home Journal*, the featured home layouts showed a conspicuous absence of a parlor. Instead, a newly named room was featured for American readers: the living room. No longer was the social room of the house reserved for, and yoked to, the dead and their wakes and funerals. The main room of the home was claimed for the living.

Americans wanted their dead moved out of the home. This wasn't an isolated phenomenon. Americans also began outsourcing their sick to institutions and hospitals, and their elderly to care "homes." Before the twentieth century, the sick and dying were cared for at home. Before germ theory and anesthesia, the average citizen saw a trip to the hospital as a death sentence. That changed by the mid-twentieth century. It was normal—preferable—for institutions to handle births, sickness, dying, and the dead.

New York's Frank E. Campbell was one pioneering undertaker leading the charge promoting the use of the funeral home for the waking and service. Todd W. Van Beck writes in *The Genius of Frank E. Campbell* the issues Campbell faced when arriving in New York. "Since elevators were still rare, getting caskets and all necessary funeral equipment up flights of stairs to prepare and set up for an apartment funeral was an engineering feat," often requiring, as Van Beck points out, the services of a carpenter to remove windows or doors.[59] Around the turn of the century, Campbell, a visionary, introduced "slumber rooms" at his undertaking establishment on West Twenty-Third Street in the Chelsea District of Manhattan.[60] No longer did families need to worry about having an undertaker bring chairs up flights of stairs to entertain family and friends during the wake in their cramped cold-water flat. They could receive guests in the large and lavishly decorated Frank E. Campbell undertaking establishment. Shortly after introducing slumber rooms, Campbell built a grand chapel in 1905 that he named the "Funeral Church."[61] The bereaved now had a spacious alternative to their cramped apartment for a funeral service even if they weren't affiliated with a church. Funeral notices often proclaimed the location in all capitals—FUNERAL CHURCH—as Campbell's had become a destination of distinction.

A 1920 advertorial in the *Evening World* by Campbell's marketing man, Dr. Berthold A. Baer, asserted that if one were to ask fifty thousand

New Yorkers to name two city undertakers, "forty-nine thousand nine hundred and sixty would say: 'Frank E. Campbell and —' but they would hesitate to think of the 'and —.'"[62] And this is at a time when there were sixteen hundred undertakers operating in the city, according to Baer. And Baer wasn't making baseless claims. The name Frank E. Campbell was on the tip of every New Yorker's tongue when someone said the word *undertaker*. He positioned himself as the premier funeral director, spurred on by his relentless marketing campaigns. One popular ad simply stated, "The best costs no more."[63]

Across the country, progressive undertakers were building facilities to accommodate crowds larger than any regular house could contain, with lavish décor the average person couldn't afford, essentially enticing people into the funeral home and creating demand for the funeral-home funeral. J. William Lee, the carriage trade undertaker of Washington, erected a sixteen-thousand-square-foot building on Pennsylvania Avenue, a stone's throw from the Capitol, that boasted a chapel with stained glass, electric lighting and a seating capacity for 132 people.[64] Similarly, in Philadelphia, Oliver H. Bair began construction on a new building about the same time Campbell unveiled the Funeral Church that would feature many luxuriously appointed "parlors"—service rooms—spread over almost eighty thousand square feet.[65] Berthold A. Baer captured the essence of the sentiment (despite it being an advertorial) that funeral directors across the nation were attempting to convey with their new facilities as a place where "the dead are honored and the living find consolation."[66]

And they were getting their patrons by paid death notices. Gone were the days of death criers, and the Inviter to Funerals, and printed invitations. Newspapers were now dailies, many running morning and evening editions, and it made sense to publish the obsequies in the paper—another idea credited to Campbell. Prior to Campbell, only the rich and famous funerals were given news ink, but Campbell convinced the New York City newspaper editors to run paid death notices.[67] Not only did a death notice benefit the bereaved family by getting the word out to the public of the service details but it was also good for the newspaper's bottom line, and it gave a subtle marketing plug to the funeral establishment hosting the event.

But undertakers weren't just getting the living into funeral parlors for services. To do so, they also needed to get the dead into their newfangled operations called "funeral homes," "funeral chapels," or "mortuaries." They achieved this by installing "preparation rooms" or "morgues" to embalm the dead. No longer did the undertaker wish to engage in the messy business of embalming the decedent in bed or on a cooling board set up in a cramped bedroom, any more than a modern early-twentieth-century surgeon would want to conduct surgery in such conditions. Many funeral homes billed this new room at their facility—the prep room, as it was colloquially called—as an operating theater. Tiled, with indoor plumbing, gleaming white porcelain tables, incandescent lighting, and stocked with sparkling stainless instruments—that's exactly what it looked like.

Frank E. Campbell* was one of the first—if not the first—in New York to install such a specialized room in his facility for the preparation of the dead.[68] J. William Lee had done so when he built his facility in 1885 in Washington, DC, and Bair's new building that he moved into in late 1908 had what the *Philadelphia Inquirer* called a "large mortuary."[69] By the outbreak of the second great war, the dead were almost uniformly prepared, waked, and funeralized (the alternative being the church) at this new American institution.

Perhaps there was no greater change in America's funeral practices than the period prior to and following the Great War. Not only did the culture shift from a primarily home-based funeral model to embracing the institution of the funeral home, but the mourning culture changed drastically from the public grief that marked the rigid parameters of the Victorian era to the discreet, individual mourning that is still largely a hallmark of American bereavement.

Through this period of great change another revolution was slowly building, one that would change the trajectory of American death practices: cremation.†

---

* Frank E. Campbell, the archetypal funeral director, would not rest in peace himself for sixty-seven years. His massive bronze casket wouldn't fit in the crypt he selected at Bergen Crest Mausoleum, so it sat in a storeroom. In 2001, the then current president of the Frank E. Campbell firm ensured Campbell (and his mother) were properly buried at Woodlawn Cemetery in the Bronx.

† J. William Lee, a visionary, embraced cremation a full century before it became commonplace. In the new facility he built in 1885, he had a retort (a fancy name for a cremation machine) installed in 1895, one of the first to be installed in a funeral home.

CHAPTER 12

Flame Burial

C remation is now the preferred method of disposition in America. It's the eight-hundred-pound gorilla in the room of funeral service. Perhaps the biggest reason families choose cremation is the memorialization flexibility it offers. But cremation in America is new to the party as far as funeralization is concerned, having only been an option for about a hundred and fifty years and coming to the forefront of the public consciousness in the last fifty years. Prior to that, earth burial was the only disposition option—an option seen as so frightening to some it led to the rise of the safety caskets seen in chapter 9. This fear of premature burial was the root of the first documented cremation in America: a man terrified of being buried alive. And with good reason. He witnessed his infant daughter come within minutes of succumbing to the horrific fate.

Henry Laurens is a lesser-known patriot of the American Revolution. Described as "short, swarthy, and cocksure," Laurens prospered under British rule as a slaver and rice planter in South Carolina, and he rose to the rank of lieutenant colonel in the local militia.[1] But Laurens's ambitions didn't stop with commerce and military matters. He represented South Carolina during the Second Continental Congress, where he served as president from 1777 to 1778, and a year later Laurens was appointed as the Dutch ambassador tasked with treaty negotiations. Laurens was captured by a British frigate off Newfoundland and held in the Tower of London—the only American to hold that honor—for fifteen months.[2] The stint in prison ruined his health. After the war, he retired to Mepkin, his twenty-thousand-acre plantation located thirty miles from Charleston, where he died on December 8, 1792.[3]

Laurens and his wife, Eleanor Ball, had thirteen or fourteen children—the exact number blurred by time.[4] A staggering nine (or ten) died.

In 1759, baby Martha took ill during a smallpox outbreak brought in from recent slave ships originating in Jamaica and Calabar and she was given up for dead.[5] Her bed was set before an open window and Martha's tiny body lay in repose while the grave was prepared. An afternoon thunderstorm swept in and rain on her face revived her.[6] The screams of the infant brought servants and family members running, staring in abject horror at the little writhing form, very much alive.

The near grisly fate of baby Martha* coupled with the alarmingly high death rate of his offspring had an immense psychological impact on Laurens and he feared premature burial. Such was his fear that when he died his instructions in his will were as follows:

> I solemnly enjoin it on my son as an indispensable duty, that as
> soon as he conveniently can alter my decease [sic] to cause my body
> to be wrapped in twelve yards of tow cloth and burned until it be
> entirely consumed, and then collecting my bones, deposit them
> wherever he may think proper.[7]

The pyre was built on the hill opposite his house and his shrouded body was carried to the pile on the shoulders of four of his favorite enslaved people.[8] With the conflagration of Henry Laurens, cremation sparked to life in America.

Laurens certainly wasn't the first person in history to choose disposition by fire. The earliest known cremation took place about twenty-six thousand years prior in Australia.[9] Mungo Lady, as she became known because of the discovery of her charred remains near Lake Mungo in New South Wales, was cremated twice, the speculation being the first cremation had been botched, owing to a problem that would plague cremationists for years—achieving sustained high temperatures.[10]

---

* Martha went on to live a full life (considering life expectancy was around forty), dying at age fifty-one.

The Indo-Europeans adopted cremation during the Stone Age. This form of disposition had the practical advantage of protecting bodies from wild animals when the ground was too frozen to dig, but it also fed Indo-Europeans' spiritual side. Fire was life for hunter-gatherers (and later, farmers), and wood was a precious resource. It seems counterintuitive that they would "waste" resources that could sustain them. Burial by the "Sacred Fire" turned the body into light, and the light ascended into the sky to feed the stars.[11] In a sense, cremation transformed the dead into something divine.

The Greeks first brought the practice to "civilized" society. They adopted the practice around 700 BCE partly to solve the age-old problem of returning slain warriors home.[12] The Greeks erected great pyres on the battlefields, and they conveyed the ashes home to receive the honors due them. Denying glory to a fallen soldier was punishable by death. Mourning parents successfully petitioned the Council of Athens for the execution of a victorious general who hurried back too soon for his triumphal, leaving the bodies of their sons strewn on the battlefield.[13]

Cremation took root as the preferred method of disposition for civilians as well as soldiers, but not because it was a simpler method of removing the dead from society. In fact, the opposite was true. Cremation was the more labor- and resource-intensive method. Instead of digging a simple pit, great timbers needed to be felled and dragged. The cremation pyre was something *crafted* with the utmost care in selection of materials and ritual. The ancient Roman poet Virgil describes the process in the *Aeneid*: "They reared a vast pyre, rich with pine wood and cleft oak whose sides they interweave with dark leaves, and place funereal cypresses in front and deck it above . . ."[14]

As discussed in chapter 3, Roman citizens were given the pageantry of a *pompa* prior to placement on the elaborate pyre. Essential oils, spices, and herbs were typically added to the pyre as "gifts" with the practical attempt at odor control. "Gifts of frankincense, piled together are burnt, viands* and bowls of liquid oil," Virgil describes in the *Aeneid*.[15] In reality, the added aromatics would've done little to negate the smell. Modern retorts emit no smoke and are odorless, but the people participating in

---

* Archaic term for an item of food, typically a meat or seafood dish.

the ancient open-air pyres were used to being up close and personal with their dead, despite sights and smells that would likely make most contemporary Americans squeamish.

By the time Christianity gained a toehold, the practice of cremation had spread such that it was the norm, with three notable exceptions: mummification in Egypt, sepulcher entombment in Judea, and inhumation in China.[16] Early Christian doctrine didn't expressly forbid cremation, and some early Christians actually chose cremation because it was so ingrained in the culture. The practice of Christian inhumation has roots in the Jewish tradition. The Jews not only viewed cremation as the destruction of God's creation but associated the practice with paganism.[17] Some early Christians also viewed cremation as paganistic, but the main reason burial became the preferred mode of disposition was to follow Christ, who had been entombed.

Cremation has been co-opted throughout history and used as a form of humiliation, not as a valid form of disposition. Heretics burned at the stake during the Spanish Inquisition, for example, can't fairly be called cremated—a more accurate label would be corporeal burning, and negative connotation may be one of the reasons why cremation took so long to gain popularity.

The Romans used corporeal burning to punish Christians, beginning with Nero, who in July of 64 CE was suspected of ordering a fire set that consumed ten of Rome's fourteen districts and then justifying his persecution of Christians by blaming them. Cornelius Tacitus* documented the persecution in *The Annals*: "[Christians] covered with wild beasts' skins and torn to death by dogs; or they were fastened on crosses, and when daylight failed were burned to serve as lamps by night."[18] As an added indignity, the Romans often burned the bodies of martyrs and scattered the ashes to defy the notion of resurrection.[19] Eusebius described the desecration of forty-eight martyrs in Lyon, France, in 177 CE under Marcus Aurelius, "After six days of exposure to insults [the bodies were] burnt and swept into the nearby Rhône."[20] This practice drove Christians underground and was the impetus behind the creation of the catacombs around 200 CE.

---

* Tacitus's cremains were scattered in the Middle Ages by Pope Pius V as a punishment. Hugo Erichsen, *The Cremation of the Dead: Considered from an Aesthetic, Sanitary, Religious, Historical, Medico-Legal, and Economical Standpoint* (Detroit: D. O. Haynes, 1887), 16.

In an ironic turn of events, the Christians later co-opted the Roman practice of corporeal burning as a form of postmortem humiliation. The most famous case perhaps being John Wycliffe, a theological dissident who translated the Latin Vulgate into English and is credited with laying the groundwork for the Protestant Reformation. Wycliffe attacked Roman Catholicism by denying transubstantiation (turning the bread and wine into the body and blood of Christ during Communion), repudiating indulgences, and even suggesting the pope was the antichrist.[21] Wycliffe was declared a heretic* by the Council of Constance in 1415. In 1428, forty-four years after Wycliffe's death, Pope Martin V ordered his corpse exhumed, burned, and his ashes scattered into the River Swift.[22]

The persecution of Christians in the Roman Empire continued almost unabated until Constantine's reign. Constantine ascended the throne in 306 CE and converted to Christianity six years later. He immediately began to pass legislation banning the persecution of Christians that also restored confiscated privileges, titles, and lands. In 321 Constantine banned cremation, the preferred method of Roman disposition. There is some debate as to his motives. It's doubtful this ban was strictly a religious move but rather part of a larger military strategy. Widespread cremation in the empire was beginning to threaten wood supplies that might be needed for strategic military purposes.[23]

Earth burial remained the predominant method of disposition in Western civilization for fifteen hundred years, with exceptions made for public health crises. This cultural more was only reinforced during this time period by political and religious leaders. Charlemagne issued a proclamation in 789 CE making participation in a cremation a crime punishable by death. Half a millennium after that, Pope Boniface threatened excommunication to anyone facilitating a cremation. Of course, burning at the stake, including nineteen-year-old Joan of Arc, continued as a church- and government-sanctioned punishment.

Sir Thomas Browne, an English physician, was the first to offer, or suggest, an alternate form of disposition to earth burial. His book *Hydriotaphia, Urne-Buriall*, published in 1658, is his response to fifty Roman cinerary urns found in Norfolk, England. Browne presents

---

* His second time—a posthumous award to boot. Never excommunicated, he had been declared "heretical" by Pope Gregory XI in 1377.

cremation from a historic lens, and doesn't serve to promote it possibly so as not to antagonize church officials. *Hydriotaphia* is the first modern book on cremation, but for the time it served merely as a curiosity. The only way to cremate a body in the seventeenth century was an open-air pyre, an act still strongly associated with paganism and quite difficult to do with success.

The problem of sustained heat continued to plague cremationists, but there was a new, larger issue that had nothing to do with religion. An open-air pyre was becoming discordant* with the sensibilities of a more refined civilization as evidenced by the cremation of Percy Bysshe Shelley, the famed English romantic poet. Shelley drowned at the age of twenty-nine on July 8, 1822, in the Gulf of La Spezia in Sardinia (now Italy). His body washed ashore August 15 near Viareggio. Tuscan health laws at the time dictated drowning victims be cremated to prevent the spread of disease.[24] This was a sound policy as disease causation was unknown (germ theory wouldn't be widely adopted for about another half-century), and health officials were leery of plague outbreaks. After nearly five weeks in the ocean, Shelley's body was in an advanced state of decomposition, described by his friend Edward Trelawny as "staining [the body] a dark and ghastly indigo colour."[25]

Trelawny goes on to describe the grisly scene on the beach in his 1858 account *Trelawny's Recollections of the Last Days of Shelley and Byron*:

> More wine was poured over Shelley's dead body than he had consumed during his life . . . The heat from the sun and fire was so intense that the atmosphere was tremulous and wavy. The corpse fell open and the heart was laid bare. The frontal bone of the skull, where it had been struck with the mattock, fell off; and, as the back of the head rested on the red-hot bottom bars of the furnace, the brains literally seethed, bubbled, and boiled as in a cauldron, for a very long time. . . . but what surprised us all, was that the heart remained entire. In snatching this relic from the fiery furnace, my hand was severely burnt . . . [26]

---

* This is specific to the Christian European burial traditions that shaped America's. Open-air pyres are still common in India.

Lord George Byron, friend and fellow poet, was so dismayed by the sights and smells despite the salt, wine, and oil that had been added to the pyre, that he fled, swimming back to the *Bolivar*—his yacht—anchored offshore.[27]

Trelawny buried the cremated remains of his friend in the Protestant Cemetery* in Rome, near the grave of Shelley's contemporary John Keats. The fate of the unburned heart remained a mystery that wouldn't be solved for nearly three decades until his wife, Mary Shelley, died. Percy Shelley found the heart in his mother's desk drawer wrapped in a copy of "Adonais," a poem elegizing John Keats.[28] It seems downright bizarre for Trelawny to have sent such an item to a bereaved widow.† Given her authorship of *Frankenstein*, perhaps Trelawny thought it a fitting remembrance.

Despite Trelawny's graphic account of conflagration, there was something romantic in the *idea* of a poet's mortal remains reduced to ash in a roaring fire on sandy Italian shores. As a result, cremation experienced a minor renaissance as Shelley's followers copied the mode of the disposition, though cremationists would remain vexed by the heat issue for another half century.

Four years after Shelley's drowning, James Sharp, a British inventor, patented the gas oven. This was the first step toward the advent of the retort, a cremation chamber, but the gas oven still didn't produce enough heat to completely burn a human body, and the blast furnaces powering the industrial revolution were far too powerful—at temperatures reaching 4,000°F, they'd vaporize a human.

In the mid part of nineteenth century, Giovanni Polli proposed using illuminating gas as a fuel, but it was Lodovico Brunetti, the chair of the anatomical pathology at the University of Padua, who considered using a reverberating furnace. In the most basic sense, this type of furnace isolates the charge—or in the case of cremations, the body—from the fuel and relies on reflected heat and gases, not direct flame. Brunetti created a prototype of his oven, called a retort, and completed the first experiment with modern cremation in 1869.[29] Brunetti displayed his

---

* Trelawny, unhappy with Shelley's burial site, would later move Shelley's cremains to a spot under the shadow of a pyramid in the cemetery. And when he died in 1881, his cremains were buried next to his friend's. (Dale Bailey, "Cromwell's Head, Poe's Bones, and Other Grave Curiosities," *Dodge Magazine* 100, no. 4 [Fall 2008]: 31.)
† The heart was buried with Mary Shelley at St. Peter's Church in Dorset.

machine at the 1873 Vienna Exposition, as well as a glass box with four pounds of cremated remains and a neat little sign reading "Reject ignorance, strive for restored reason."[30] Cremationists now had the means for a modern, scientific way of disposition. They just needed an entrée. Sanitary reform was it.

The movement of public health reform began in Great Britain and Europe, the genesis being Edwin Chadwick, who published his famous report *Sanitary Condition of the Laboring Population of Great Britain* in England in 1842, that decried the unhealthy living and working conditions. Chadwick published a supplement a year later, *A Report on the Results of a Special Inquiry into the Practice of Interments in Towns*, which shined a light on unsanitary funeral customs—leaving the dead putrefying in crowded tenement houses for days, interments in overflowing churchyards tainting drinking water, among other public health atrocities. Chadwick quotes a Professor Brande on the diminished London water quality: "The water of which had not only acquired odour but colour from the soil . . . very many of these wells are adjacent to churchyards, the accumulating soil of which has been so heaped up by the succession of dead bodies and coffins, and the products of their decomposition, as to form a filtering apparatus."[31]

Chadwick also refers extensively to "miasmas"—what was believed to be the root of pestilence before microscopic organisms called germs were postulated—causing illness in medical students, undertakers, and members of the public. Where would be a more fecund source of miasmas than the overcrowded intramural graveyards? Something had to be done.

In light of Professor Brunetti's experiments across the English Channel, Sir Henry Thompson, Queen Victoria's personal surgeon, decided the time was right to put forth his radical ideas regarding sanitary reform. His paper "Cremation: The Treatment of the Body after Death" appeared in the London *Contemporary Review* in January 1874 and caused quite a stir. The American press immediately took notice. Chicago's *Sunday Times* reported, "The author [Thompson] argues that the system of burying the dead is full of danger to the living. . . . When the globe was thinly populated . . . the subject was an inconsiderable one; but the rapid increase of population, and especially man's tendency to live in crowded cities, forces it to notice." The *Times* went on to describe Thompson's radical pitch: "Sir Henry proposes that the bodies be burned in a properly constructed furnace. The gases can be driven off without offensive odor, and the mineral constituents will remain in a crucible. No scents or balsams are needed, as on Greek and Roman [funeral] piles to overcome the noxious effluvia."[32]

Thompson's paper exploded on American shores like a stick of dynamite, whipping the media and sanitarians into a frenzy. Dr. F. Julius LeMoyne, a liberal physician, immediately got to work erecting a crematory. LeMoyne was a colorful character, the type of person who would build a personal crematory. In addition to three failed bids in Pennsylvania's gubernatorial race in the 1840s, LeMoyne was outspoken about women's rights and an ardent abolitionist whose barn was a stop on the Underground Railroad.[33]

LeMoyne had long theorized that effluvia from putrefying bodies (and certainly toxic chemicals from the new science of embalming) were leaching into drinking water. Cremation was just the solution needed for a more sanitary alternative.

LeMoyne's hometown of Washington, Pennsylvania, is about thirty miles southwest of Pittsburgh, and was dubbed by the media as "Little Washington." When the trustees of a local cemetery refused to entertain LeMoyne's proposal to construct a crematorium on cemetery property— at LeMoyne's expense—he was undeterred.[34] LeMoyne decided to build it on his estate.

For all of his eccentricities, LeMoyne was a man ahead of his time. Decades later, when cemeteries realized the viability and profitability of cremation, they wholeheartedly embraced it, many building magnificent chapels on their properties. According to research by a cemetery operator in Chicago by 1938, just over sixty years after the cemetery in Little Washington snubbed LeMoyne, a whopping 60 percent of crematories were located in cemeteries and memorial parks.[35]

LeMoyne hired a local builder, John Dye, to erect a twenty-by-thirty-foot redbrick building containing a furnace of LeMoyne's design. To ensure the efficacy of the furnace, LeMoyne performed a "muttony experiment" by killing two sheep to conduct a test run, netting a gallon of "grayish powder."[36] LeMoyne's crematorium had two rooms—one for viewing, and the furnace room—on "Gallows

Hill," a knoll where county executions* had historically taken place.[37] The entire project cost $1,600, or $39,000 in today's dollars.[38]

LeMoyne built the retort for his own disposition, not as a commercial venture, but even as his crematorium was under construction, Colonel Henry Steel Olcott approached him. Olcott desperately wanted to use LeMoyne's facility for a member—a penniless Bavarian nobleman—of his Theosophical Society.

Joseph Henry Louis de Palm hailed from a Germanic baronial family whose lineage traced back a thousand years to the crusaders.[39] A former chamberlain† to King Ferdinand of Bavaria, de Palm immigrated to the United States in 1862. He joined the Theosophical Society when Olcott and famed occultist Helena Blavatsky formed it in 1875. Theosophy is an amalgamation of occult philosophies. The bylaws, as published in the *New York Herald*, state, "to obtain knowledge of the nature and attributes of the Supreme Power and of the higher spirits by the aid of physical processes."[40] The newspaper went on to clarify, "They hope that by going deeper than modern science has hitherto done into the esoteric philosophies of ancient times they may be enabled to proof of the existence of an 'unseen universe.'"[41]

De Palm, broke and sick, moved in with Olcott and died shortly thereafter on May 20, 1876. Despite de Palm's claim that he knew of a woman buried alive, that's not the sole reason he chose cremation.[42] Olcott, an early member of the New York Cremation Society, convinced his ward before he expired that cremation was a better alternative to burial and thus de Palm changed his will stipulating flame burial.[43] Olcott, the named executor (along with Henry J. Newton, another founder of the Theosophical Society) of de Palm's nonexistent estate, was set on seeing de Palm's wish for cremation carried out. From the beginning, Olcott stressed to the newspapers the first modern cremation "was a scientific experiment," and "there would be no ceremonies."[44] In fairness, perhaps Olcott was referring to not having ceremonies during the actual cremation, but that later turned out not to be completely true. Whatever the case, Olcott couldn't help himself but to debut Theosophy in grand style now that the world was watching.

---

* *The Times* (Philadelphia) reported that the old gallows poles were leaning against one side of the building during the de Palm cremation. "The Baron Burned," *The Times* (Philadelphia, PA), December 7, 1876.
† The king's spokesman in council and parliament.

Olcott knew there would be a significant interval between the obsequies and cremation because there wasn't a single working crematorium*
in America, so he went ahead and had de Palm embalmed. The honor fell
to the janitor† of Roosevelt Hospital, August Buckhorst, who injected de
Palm with arsenic, a highly toxic metallic salt but with excellent preservative properties.[45]

The funeral took place at the Masonic Temple on Twenty-Third Street
on May 28, with four thousand curious New Yorkers showing up to
experience a mystic funeral. Only thirteen hundred ticket holders were
admitted to the hall.[46] The coffin bearing de Palm was displayed on the
stage with seven candles burning on the lid in the shape of a triangle and
mysterious pendant seals displayed in front of the bier. This Theosophic
tradition was borrowed from Christianity, as lighted tapers were placed
around a body during the Middle Ages to "scare the evil spirits from an
attack on the now helpless 'sleeper.'"[47]

Next to the coffin was an urn from which smoke billowed—not
because de Palm was scheduled for cremation but as a symbol of first
worship. At the head of the coffin was the image of a serpent twisted
around a cross.[48] As the *New York Herald* reported, Olcott led the "coterie
of immature philosophers" dressed in long black robes. The funeral rite,
based heavily on Egyptian mystery rites, included orations; prepared
questions and answers from Egyptian liturgy on topics such as the
nature of God, human soul, and future state of existence; and Orphic
hymns from a mystery cult based on the mythical Greek hero Orpheus.[49]
The headline of the *New York Herald* the following day billed the odd
ceremony almost neutrally—despite the fact it was largely critical of
Theosophy and cremation—as "a queer funeral," and the ceremonies
were described as "an agreeable sort of entertainment," though many
attendees were left puzzled by what exactly they'd witnessed.[50]

After the funeral, the baron's remains were transported to a holding
vault at the Lutheran Cemetery.‡[51] Speed was of the essence, but not
because Olcott was anxious to carry out his grand science experiment.

---

* LeMoyne's crematory was still months away from completion.
† Like many tradesmen undertakers of the era, August Buckhorst likely took up embalming by mere virtue of
his access to Roosevelt Hospital's dead house.
‡ Though the author can't find a source with any more details than the "Lutheran Cemetery," he thinks it likely
that the referenced cemetery is All Faiths Cemetery in Queens.

There were published rumors (though not confirmed through Olcott's writings) that he wanted to display de Palm's cremated remains at the Centennial Exposition that was going to be held in Philadelphia.[52] What better way to flaunt cremation than the first World's Fair held on American soil? But securing the crematory proved a more arduous process than anticipated.

When it became clear that de Palm might be around for some time as work continued in Little Washington, Olcott enlisted Buckhorst to re-embalm the baron. This is an interesting proposition as a body prepared with arsenious acid should remain in an excellent state of preservation. Part of the need for re-embalming might speak to the embalmer's skill. In 1876, one didn't even need to attend an embalming demonstration to proclaim themselves technically proficient. It's unknown what, if any, training Buckhorst had in the embalming arts.

Lack of technical skill didn't slow Buckhorst down. He got creative in his endeavor to further preserve the baron, eviscerating the abdominal-thoracic cavity and packing it with a mixture of potter's clay and crystallized carbolic acid.[53] Carbolic acid, a phenol, would've been in ample supply at Roosevelt Hospital as it was used as an early antiseptic. Phenols are still commonly used as embalming chemicals but only for cavity injection;* if used on the skin, as Buckhorst did, it causes severe discolorations.

Later, before de Palm was shipped to Little Washington, Buckhorst, who was billed as the "Theosophical Society's undertaker," proudly displayed his handiwork to the press. De Palm's remains were described as "in perfect preservation. The limbs are flexible, and the skin is tough and elastic like rubber."[54] Buckhorst told the reporters before they left that he wanted some of the "dust" from de Palm after the cremation, that "he had spent a great deal of time with it and he ought to have some compensation."[55]

Once LeMoyne gave the green light to use his newly completed crematorium, Olcott promptly set upon securing the proper authorizations. On December 5, well over six months after de Palm's death, the baron arrived at the train depot in Little Washington and was transported to Gallows Hill.

---

* There are some instances (i.e., difficult cases) where phenols are used as topical bleaching agents.

On December 6, James Wolf, the fireman who'd been stoking the retort with coke since 2:00 a.m., explained to the assembled onlookers and reporters—the event attracted international press from as far as Australia—that it must be "brought to white heat before the incineration of the body could begin."[56] By the time de Palm would be loaded in the retort, Wolf would've fired the furnace for over six hours to bring it to temperature.

De Palm's casket was opened for a final inspection. Buckhorst's efforts had reduced de Palm to a mere ninety-two pounds; his skin, as a result of the harsh carbolic acid, was described by a reporter for the Boston *Evening Journal* as a "chocolate color."[57]

Olcott cleared the room and had de Palm removed from the coffin and wrapped in a winding sheet saturated with alum to prevent premature combustion. Then the remains were placed in a concave "basket" of iron latticework. The purpose of the basket was to allow heat 360-degree access to the body, as this was a reverberating furnace relying on the combustion of the charge from heat, not direct flame.

In addition to the press and local lookie-loos, about twenty-five physicians from city medical boards witnessed the spectacle as Olcott anointed the shrouded body with myrrh, frankincense, and cinnamon, almost as if he didn't fully believe his own propaganda about this new scientific method being odorless.[58]

Olcott and LeMoyne then bickered about whether to place the body in feet first or head first—Olcott wanting to adhere to the tradition of the body "[going] into the sepulchre feet first."[59] But LeMoyne knew best how to operate his machine.

At 8:30 a.m. de Palm was slid in head first.[60]

Two hours and twenty minutes later, at roughly 10:50 a.m., after the remains collapsed through the iron basket, Olcott pronounced the incineration complete.[61] Despite the bafflement of the general public and mixed reviews from the press—the *Wheeling Daily Register* glibly reported on "To-day's Corpse Roasting"—an American tradition was birthed.

The following day after the retort had cooled, Olcott collected the cremated remains and placed them in a "Hindoo" urn as well as little glass vials, which he distributed to the physicians in attendance.[62] It is unknown, though probable, that Buckhorst received some of the "dust" he so desired, although de Palm's cremains wouldn't have looked like cremains coming from a modern crematory.

Cremated remains come out of the retort as desiccated bone fragments and must be pulverized to achieve the fluffy, ash-like consistency the public now expects. National standards have ping-ponged over time. In an effort to keep the public from scattering the ash-like ground cremains, the 1941 Cremation Association of America (CAA)* *Manual of Standard Crematory-Columbarium Practice* recommended, "We have no right to crush, grind or pulverize human bone fragments. They should be placed in the temporary container or urn, just as they were removed from the cremation vault. . . . To do otherwise encourages desecration, gives an impression of valueless ash, and will eventually destroy the memorial idea."[63] Instead, cemeteries (where many crematories were located) wanted the public to purchase columbarium niches and ground plots to permanently memorialize the decedent.

The first public crematory wouldn't open for another eight years, in 1884. LeMoyne's machine would sit idle for well over a year, but not for lack of requests. LeMoyne fielded over sixty requests from de Palm's cremation until the publication of his booklet "Cremation: An Argument to Prove That Cremation Is Preferable to Inhumation of Dead Bodies" two years later in 1878 and he turned down each and every one "for the reason that it was not intended to be followed as a business."[64]

The second cremation wouldn't take place in Washington, Pennsylvania, but in Salt Lake City, Utah, seven months after de Palm. A Boston-born physician named Charles Winslow had a crematory erected for himself as stipulated in his will, though unlike LeMoyne's retort that was reverberating, or relied on heat alone to complete the cremation process, Winslow's was a variation of direct flame more akin to modern machines.[65]

Winslow bears the honor of being the first person cremated solely for sanitary reasons. De Palm† (like Henry Laurens) chose cremation partly due to concern of live burial. Winslow, a physician, had seen exhumed corpses and wholeheartedly subscribed to the rhetoric of Sir

---

* CAA is the predecessor to CANA, the Cremation Association of North America.
† Olcott's argument to de Palm advocating cremation was based on sanitary reasons, so it can't be stated that de Palm chose cremation solely due to concern for live burial, though de Palm did claim to know someone who was buried alive.

Henry Thompson and other sanitary reformers such as Persifor Frazer, Jr., and Rev. O. B. Frothingham. Winslow actually preferred to have an "ancient" cremation, as his will stated: "I should be satisfied if the method of my cremation as practiced by the ancient Romans was adopted." Cremation advocates at the time were shrewd enough to realize an open-air pyre would do nothing to further their cause; in fact, the potential negative press might set the movement back. So they wisely opted to use the concession Winslow built: "But if this is not convenient or practicable, my body may be burned in a retort, as is now practiced in such cases in Germany."[66]

An estimated one thousand people, including a voracious press eager to report more on this unusual disposition practice, gathered to witness Winslow's conflagration.[67] As was one of the major stumbling blocks in the early days of the cremation movement, the event was a secular occasion. As the Washington *Evening Star* reported, "No prayer was said, nor were any religious words uttered."[68] One of the reasons the cremation rate was still under 1 percent at the turn of the twentieth century is because cremationists aligned themselves with secularism or alternate religions (such as de Palm and Theosophy) and that not only didn't fit into the Christian death rite but it also tacitly billed cremation as almost *anti*-Christian—a very threatening prospect to Christians.

The *Evening Star*, perhaps eager to offer salacious details of the event, wasn't generous in describing the process, adding, "The first appearance, as seen through the mica aperture, was that of roasting . . . the fumes from the furnace were unpleasantly perceptible at a distance from the scene."[69] The *Eureka Daily Sentinel* was a bit more generous in reporting on the outcome: "[The ashes were] perfectly white, clear and odorless. They were placed in a half-gallon glass vessel, with a ground stopper and prepared for their destination in Massachusetts."[70]

Winslow's cremated remains weren't the only thing destined for Massachusetts. Prior to cremation, Winslow left instructions that his heart be removed and embalmed and sent to Nantucket to be buried in his mother and father's grave. Winslow's cremains were destined for Mount Auburn Cemetery where they were to be "placed in the same grave upon the same coffin which contains the precious remains of my great dear and venerated wife."[71] In a final ironic twist, Winslow, who stipulated no services be held at his cremation, ended the final disposition provision in his will by quoting Ecclesiastes: "Then shall the dust return to the earth as it was, and the spirit shall return to the God who gave it."[72]

The *Eureka Daily Sentinel* put the total cost of cremating Winslow's body at $1,500 "because of the delay and necessary expenditures of money attending it."[73]

Oddly, the retort used on Winslow was never used again for a human. It was turned into a garbage incinerator.[74]

The third modern cremation to take place in America was the first woman cremated. Jane Bragg Pitman died of stomach cancer in Cincinnati on February 11, 1878, and four days later was shipped to Little Washington to be cremated on Gallows Hill. After fourteen months of cold hearth, LeMoyne had found reason to stoke the fires again.

CANA historian Jason Engler suspects Mrs. Pitman was bestowed the honor of using Dr. LeMoyne's machine because he deemed her "worthy."[75] Benjamin "Benn" Pitman, Jane's husband, had been the court stenographer during the Lincoln assassination trials. LeMoyne was an ardent abolitionist, and Benn Pitman's connection with the Great Emancipator made him just the kind of fine, upstanding citizen who met LeMoyne's exacting standards. Benn Pitman had corresponded with LeMoyne when his wife took ill and arranged with LeMoyne that he could use his crematory when the time came.

Mrs. Pitman was Swedenborgian and didn't believe in funerary extravagance. Her husband even bucked the mourning custom, refusing to allow a crepe swag to be attached to his door, asserting theirs had "always been a cheerful house."[76] The funeral service was a simple, austere event held in the parlor of their Cincinnati home where Mrs. Pitman lay in repose in a closed casket.[77] The cremation, much to the dismay of the press, was strictly private.

Mr. Pitman traveled alone, save a Cincinnati reporter, with his wife's remains to "The House of Burnt Bones," as one newspaper patly described LeMoyne's estate. There, along with LeMoyne, three of his children, the lone reporter, and the fireman (James Wolf had been sacked), according to the St. Paul *Anti-Monopolist*, "shoved the body in like an oyster knife going into a clam," without "a prayer, or a tear, or even a sigh."[78]

Mr. Pitman watched the proceedings on his wife of almost thirty years, and later described the cremation as a "beautiful sight."[79] Afterward, he arranged to have LeMoyne ship him the cremated remains once they cooled and were recovered. Pitman scattered them around his wife's favorite rosebush.

LeMoyne's crematory and the nation's cremation rate stagnated for the next twenty months. Then on October 16, 1879, the fires in Little Washington were stoked again. This time for the good doctor himself.

LeMoyne's cremation was the polar opposite of de Palm's. Not only was it a religious affair (in the traditional Christian sense) but also completely private. The family insisted on secrecy because they were displeased with the media circus Olcott and LeMoyne drummed up for de Palm's cremation.[80] LeMoyne's service was so private that the newspapers speculated if it had actually happened, and townsfolk hid in the woods behind the crematorium, convinced the doctor's body would be buried under the cover of darkness.

Services began at the house at 9:00 a.m. with relatives* and a few close friends. Some sources state a large number of people were present, and while that's true, four policemen kept the onlookers out on the road.[81] The funeral was conducted by the Reverends Drs. James Brownson and George Hays. It included scripture readings followed by a prayer offered by Rev. Dr. Hays, then the pallbearers loaded the rosewood casket in the hearse for the mile ride to Gallows Hill.

John Dye, the builder of the crematory, fittingly acted as the fireman for LeMoyne's cremation. This was most certainly because with LeMoyne dead, Dye now knew the most about the retort's operation.

As the casket was carried into the crematorium, Rev. Dr. Hays proclaimed to the onlookers, "We have now brought the dead to his place of choice."[82] In the privacy of the crematorium, Hays said the benediction and at 10:30 a.m. LeMoyne was loaded into the machine—the one built for this specific event.

LeMoyne's cremated remains were buried outside of his crematorium, and a small obelisk erected over them. It reads: *A fearless advocate of the right.*

A total of forty-two cremations were handled at the crematorium, with LeMoyne's son Frank LeMoyne taking up the mantle until

---

* One of LeMoyne's sons didn't show. One theory is he didn't show because he opposed cremation, but Engler believes the real reason is he opposed the fanfare—despite it being private—surrounding the event.

closing it in June of 1901. LeMoyne's daughter, Charlotte, moved to Los Angeles, California, and carried on her father's work for cremation and equal rights. Charlotte LeMoyne Wills was one of the founders of Rosedale Cemetery, the first racially integrated cemetery in Los Angeles and one of the first in the country, and she was instrumental in forming the Cremation Society of Southern California, the first on the West Coast.[83]

The crematorium in Little Washington still stands today.

The first public crematorium, Lancaster Crematorium, opened at Greenwood Cemetery in Lancaster, Pennsylvania, in the late fall of 1884, just over five years after the death of LeMoyne. A cremation cost twenty-five dollars, with fifteen dollars going to supply the ton of soft coal and steamboat coke mixture required to fire the retort.[84] By now, a number of cremation societies had been organized in major cities with the same general purpose as seen in the bylaws of the New York Cremation Society: "To disseminate sound and enlightened views respecting the incineration of the dead; to advocate and promote, in every proper and legitimate way, the substitution of this method for burial."[85] While cremation seemed to certainly be a topic of interest, by the close of 1884 only forty-one cremations had been performed since de Palm's in 1876.[86]

Despite its association with alternate religions (such as de Palm and Theosophy) and secularism, the growing number of societies and literature—the first cremation journal, *The Modern Cremation*, was published in 1886—made the Catholic Church nervous. Pope Leo XIII denounced it by issuing Canon Law 1203 in 1886, which read, "The bodies of the faithfully deceased must be buried, and cremation is reprobated."[87] And while some Protestant sects embraced cremation, such as LeMoyne being buried by Rev. Dr. Brownson, the long-time pastor at First Presbyterian in Little Washington, Americans also began to embrace cremation for the same reason they embraced metal caskets: modernity. Cremation was billed by cremationists as sanitary, sensible, and *modern*. And thus began a cultural shift toward cremation that moved the needle on theology. As the theology gradually shifted, so did ritualization of how Americans bury their dead.

This change didn't happen overnight. At the turn of the twentieth century there were twenty-four crematories operating in fifteen states, but the percentage of Americans choosing cremation as a form of disposition hadn't yet reached 1 percent.[88] During the early twentieth century, the sanitary reform argument lost steam and ceased, as evidenced by *The Columbarium*, the last cremation propaganda periodical ceasing publication in 1896, and cremation slowly gained popularity as cemeteries pushed to associate beauty through memorialization in rural cemeteries such as West Laurel Hill just outside of Philadelphia and Ferncliff in New York. Crematoriums of this era were grand and ornate, boasting large chapels where services were held and the body was casketed as the rule, not the exception. Many crematoriums, such as Missouri Crematory and Philadelphia Crematory, both built in 1888, didn't even have a casket entrance into the lower level where the retort was. The body arrived there by an elevator from the chapel above.[89] This proves that cremation at this time wasn't seen as merely a method of disposal as it can be used in contemporary America but rather a *choice* of disposition.

In 1963, the national cremation rate was 3.7 percent when two events happened, one seismic and one subtle.[90] The Holy Office published *Piam et constantem*, a vague document reaffirming the long-standing tradition of Catholics burying their dead *but* adding cremation was not "opposed per se to the Christian religion."[91] Despite the document sort of giving Catholics permission for cremation, centuries of burial inertia—coupled with its association with paganism and use as a means of punishment—meant it would be years before cremation gained traction. The event that shook the bedrock of the funeral profession was Jessica Mitford's scathing exposé *The American Way of Death*. In it, Mitford bashes the profession for the cost of dying; arguing funeral directors prey upon grieving families. The book whipped the public into a frenzy that resulted in congressional hearings. Surely, Mitford argued, there's a simpler (i.e., cheaper) way. Direct disposition via cremation fit the bill. CANA historian Engler views this shift in the 1960s to using cremation as a means of direct disposal not only on Mitford's book but also the resulting proliferation of cremation societies that advocated people didn't need a funeral—they could "just" cremate.[92]

There are a lot of complex psychological and sociological reasons as to why more and more Americans are choosing cremation over burial.

The cremation rate passed the 50 percent mark in 2016, and it continues to climb at a national rate of 1.6 percent per year.[93] The National Funeral Directors Association suggests, "The main reasons for the continued rise in cremation rates are its lower cost, the perceived environmental impact, an increasingly transient population, weakening of traditional religious prohibitions, and changing consumer preferences."[94] The bottom line is cremation has become a social movement. Consumers choose it for a number of reasons, the two major ones being simplicity and the range of options it affords them in the funeralization process.

From humble origins as one man's sanitary quest in middle-of-nowhere-Pennsylvania about 150 years ago, flame burial is now *the* form of disposition. Eight out of ten Americans will choose cremation within the next two decades. Which begs the question: What if you don't want the flame or the field? American consumers have come to expect choices, and entrepreneurs are busy creating new, exciting ways for them to decompose.

CHAPTER 13

Mushroom Suits and the Future (of Funeral Service)

T he future. Who knows—besides soothsayers and the readers of tea leaves—what funerals of the future will look like? The one thing that's certain is they won't look like the funerals of today. As technology advances and societal norms change, the death rite of tomorrow will morph into something unlike the funeral of yesterday. But that's natural. If one looks at "snapshots" of the funeral experience of 1700, 1800, 1900, and 2000 America, they're different ritual sets, though the core of the rite has remained: gathering to bury (or burn) the dead. As the culture changes, it keeps those elements of the funeral experience that make sense and casts off those that don't. Simply, a funeral is the product of its time and place. And the American funereal experience continues to evolve.

In 2019 actor Luke Perry died at age fifty-two. The only headlines that overshadowed his untimely death were those of his final disposition: burial in a mushroom suit. Like the pilot engine leading the Lincoln Special signaling to the waiting crowds what was coming, Perry's burial could very well signal a shift, a mainstream embracing, of a more natural form of disposition.

The Infinity Burial Suit by Coeio is the latest iteration of the mushroom suit by founder Jae Rhim "JR" Lee, initially inspired by visiting a green cemetery. The completely biodegradable suit is made of organic cotton impregnated with a bio-mix designed to, according to Coeio's website, "aid in decomposition, work to neutralize toxins found in the body, and transfer nutrients to plant life."[1]

During natural decomposition, aided by bacteria and fungi from the body's own microflora, the body produces toxic metabolites such as hydrogen sulfide, cadaverine, and putrescine.* Fungi, specifically saprotrophic (flesh-eating) molds, are particularly well suited to break down nitrogenous compounds, starches, and sugars, the products of decomposition. Fungi do this by extending branching tubes called hyphae, almost like English ivy growing across a brick wall. The hyphae secrete enzymes that break down the body's chemicals into compounds the environment can readily use.[2] The mushroom suit speeds up the process of decomposition by the simple function of making fungi more readily available in a greater concentration. The suit (or shroud if one prefers, much like medieval European burials) is placed on the decedent, and they are buried in a simple grave without a casket at a recommended depth of four feet.[3]

Coeio's burial suit is indicative of a larger movement: green burial. The green burial experience is more natural, moving away from embalming chemicals, the fuel used in cremation, the treated woods and metal caskets placed in the earth, and the metal and concrete burial vaults. Really, it's a movement that hearkens back to early American burial practices by using renewable, sustainable products—such as wicker, reed, and bamboo—for the casket (if there is a burial receptacle). Often the remains are buried shrouded. The green burial movement is more than just responsibly sourced products. The goals of the movement encompass broader ideas such as land conservation, fair trade, worker safety, carbon emissions reduction, and habitat conservation.[4] Green burial seeks a sustainable long-term disposition model.

The Green Burial Council is a nonprofit organization that establishes "green" standards and certifies cemeteries—and funeral homes—that meet certain criteria. Many funeral service providers offer green options because, contrary to popular opinion, green burial doesn't negate the "traditional" American funeral. Rather, green works in

---

* Cadaverine and putrescine, like their names denote, are metabolites partially responsible for the awful smell of decomposition.

tandem with the existing traditions. People can still choose embalming to satisfy state regulations for a public viewing, be laid out in a casket, and have a service followed by burial. The embalming—or ecobalming—fluids that meet current green standards comprise mostly plant-based essential oils. Not that these are new fluids; in fact, they've been around much longer than formaldehyde and formaldehyde's heavy-metal predecessors. The ecobalming fluids are a lot like the Egyptian's cedar oil and the European anatomist's turpentine oil.*

The first contemporary natural burial ground, Ramsey Creek, opened in 1998 in South Carolina, and only about forty more opened over the following decade.[5] Now Americans have more choices than ever when it comes to natural burial; they no longer have to drive several states for a green burial site. In the past decade alone, the number of cemeteries offering green burial has grown by fivefold.[6] This explosive growth not only reflects the demand for this type of disposition but also the contribution of the "hybrid" model cemetery. The "new" natural burial cemeteries aren't necessarily brand-new cemeteries but rather existing cemeteries pivoting to meet consumer tastes. Hybrids are traditional (rural or lawn) cemeteries that have a section devoted to natural burials.

"Natural" and "conservation" burial grounds, which are 100 percent natural, don't look like cemeteries at all. They look like their natural surroundings. Author Ann Hoffner has meticulously compiled the nation's green cemeteries in *The Natural Burial Cemetery Guide*.† She describes her book as "state-by-state where, how, and why to choose green burial."[7]

There are many different shades of green when it comes to green burial. By opening sections for eco-friendly burial, established traditional cemeteries have created greater access for people who live hundreds of miles from the closest natural or conservation burying ground. Hoffner says many older, neglected cemeteries have been revitalized by offering natural burial in the remaining land, and it's more cost effective for the cemeterian than starting a new cemetery. Congressional Cemetery in Washington, DC—where Frank Sands, the undertaker for President

---

* Turpentine oil is derived from pine resin.
† There are seventy-nine cemeteries nationwide certified by the Green Burial Council. A cemetery doesn't have to have the certification to offer natural burial, as such there are many more "green" cemeteries than that.

Lincoln, and Henry Cattell, Lincoln's embalmer, are buried—has been revitalized as a hybrid cemetery.[8]

Hoffner's parents both chose green burial after she became immersed in the subject in 2012 while doing research for an article on plastic recycling. Her father died in 2016, and her mother in 2020. Despite the green burial movement being so closely associated with the home funeral movement, Hoffner chose to deal with a local funeral home both times—a choice she doesn't regret. "From my perspective it would've been difficult to do everything without a funeral home," she explained. "I wanted to concentrate on the aspects I wanted to." She went on to say, "The rituals and ceremonies [of the traditional funeral] are still there. We're translating it into an ecologically friendly way."[9]

Green cemetery graves are marked differently than the polished granite and marble dies found in traditional cemeteries. Sometimes they're marked with nothing more than a GPS location, though often they're marked with a natural feature such as a sapling, shrub, or stone cairn. There's a happy medium for permanent memorialization while maintaining the ecological integrity of the natural burial ground. For her parents, Hoffner selected from a bin of large stones unearthed from digging graves and had a stonecutter engrave them.[10]

Burial in a green cemetery isn't the only option for the eco-conscious. One can be naturally buried at home—if one chooses natural organic reduction in Washington State.*

Washington legalized human composting, or "natural organic reduction," in May of 2020. The idea for the new type of disposition (burial, cremation, and body donation being the other typical forms) was championed by Katrina Spade, founder and CEO of Recompose, a company located south of Seattle, as a more eco-friendly way of disposition. Recompose's process uses a fraction of the energy—only one-eighth—compared to burial or cremation.[11] Herland Forest Natural Burial Cemetery, the first facility to be granted a natural organic reduction (NOR) license, has developed a methodology that has almost no carbon footprint.[12] Herland Forest is an offshoot of a sustainability project began in 1986 on the southern slope of Mount

---

* As of the writing of this book, NOR is also legal in Oregon and Colorado, and there is pending legislation for several other states.

Adams as way to feed, fuel, and clothe people using woody biomass as an energy source—a concept similar to the society in the utopian novel *Herland* by Charlotte Perkins Gilman for which the forest is named. Herland saw the potential to expand the scope of their project by returning humans to the biomass and began the process of becoming licensed as a cemetery in 2010. They began their first burials five years later.[13]

Herland's NOR process is simple, mimicking Mother Nature. The decedent is laid in an insulated, sealed cradle and encased in two hundred gallons of wood chips. Anyone who's made compost is familiar with the need to rotate the compost pile. The cradle is on a rail system so it can be rotated by hand to keep the mixture oxygenated. When rotation alone isn't enough to maintain 155°F, oxygen is injected into the cradle; when the reaction gets to the point where rotation and additional oxygen aren't enough to maintain temperature, heating elements powered by photovoltaic cells maintain temperature. At the end of the process, the soil is screened, any metal is removed, and remaining bone fragments are pulverized. Whereas Recompose's process takes thirty days, Walt Patrick, the president and trustee of Windward Foundation, the organization that manages Herland Forest, says their process timeline is based on the time of year.[14] In summer, the process will be a little quicker, and in winter a little slower.

Each body is transformed into about one cubic yard of soil that can be returned to the family members. Herland Forest invites the family to take as much soil as they want, and the family can spread it much like cremains or use it to plant a tree or flowers in their backyard to create a living memorial. If there's soil remaining, Herland Forest will use it to enhance the diversity of their permaculture forest since Herland is more than "just" a green burial space—their goal is a more complete integration and natural disposition experience.

The idea of returning humans to the biomass, or literally turning someone into a tree, is part of the Logos of the green burial movement, but Patrick and his team go beyond other green burial cemeteries to ensure the survival of the trees. They bury two hundred gallons of wood chips with the remains to transform the grave into a water battery. Graves are shallower than the traditional six feet to keep things closer to the biosphere, and drainage pipes are installed to promote the production of carbon dioxide, something the forest trees can use, rather than methane. Herland Forest also offers a forty-acre campground next to the cemetery, and picnic tables throughout the cemetery, so families can camp and commune with their dead—a throwback to the Victorian-era sentiment of visiting the dead.[15]

NOR is similar to green burial—albeit an accelerated methodology—in the respect that it's a form of disposition that seeks to reduce one's carbon footprint. The big difference is in the memorialization. Families choosing natural burial memorialize the decedent in a similar fashion as the traditional burial because there's a stationary gravesite, whereas families choosing NOR have variable memorialization options similar to cremation. Though instead of five pounds of cremated remains, a cubic yard of organic soil weighs about a half ton.

Promession is another eco-friendly form of disposition that's theoretical at this point, but it has the potential to be a mainstream choice of disposition in the future. The idea of freeze-drying the body was postulated by the Swedish biologist Susanne Wiigh-Mäsak. Her idea was to "combine biological knowledge with a dignified and ethically correct way of being remembered."[16] The process, which Wiigh-Mäsak's company Promessa calls "green cremation," entails removing the remains from the coffin, then spraying the remains with liquid nitrogen at a temperature of -196°C to crystallize the body cells. After which the remains are vibrated to disintegrate and then the particles are freeze-dried in a chamber in which any remaining water is removed through sublimation. The particles are then filtered from metals before being placed in a bio-friendly container. The interesting thing about Wiigh-Mäsak's procedure is that, except for the removal of water, nothing is done to alter the remains—the decedent is there in their "entirety." The container given to survivors is 30 percent of the decedent's original weight; and when buried shallowly, it will yield soil within a year.[17] The procedure is reminiscent of the 1966 Adam West *Batman* movie where the villains have a dehydrating weapon that turns people into dust. The backpack of the weapon fills with water as each person is zapped. Holy green cremation, Batman!

Alkaline hydrolysis is another "new" method* of disposition gaining traction in the public's consciousness. Sometimes called "flameless cremation" or "bio-cremation," alkaline hydrolysis is similar to flame cremation in that the end product is pulverized carbon bone fragments that look like ash, but different in the respect that chemicals rather than flame create the cremated remains. Alkaline hydrolysis was first patented in 1888 in America—a mere twelve years after flame cremation sparked to life—by the British chemist Amos Herbert Hobson as an agricultural process to treat the "bones and animal waste . . . for fertilizing purposes, and for obtaining gelatine, glue, and size"—size being a type of adhesive.[18] It remained an agricultural process for over a century before it was looked at as a form of human disposition because of the environmental benefits, and is now a legal form of disposition in twenty-one states.

The average flame cremation retort uses about twelve to fourteen hundred cubic feet (twelve to fourteen ccf) of natural gas per case. Converting that to electricity means roughly 350 to 410 kilowatts—about the amount of electricity the average home uses in two weeks.[19] Alkaline hydrolysis uses only about a quarter of the energy. The biggest benefit touted by proponents lies in the complete lack of emissions. Modern retorts are very efficient machines, emitting only miniscule amounts of particulate matter and volatile organic compounds, but they're still pumping something into the atmosphere. There are zero atmospheric pollutants with alkaline hydrolysis. The sterile liquid remaining at the conclusion of the process, or effluent, is simply flushed into the municipal sewer system.

The process is simple, if not a bit sci-fi sounding. The decedent is placed in a metal sling and placed into a giant cylinder that looks like a stainless-steel hot water heater. Water and an alkaline chemical such as potassium hydroxide or sodium hydroxide are mixed; then the liquid is heated and agitated and/or pressurized so that all soft tissues are completely dissolved down to their most basic molecular building blocks. The process take can up to sixteen hours (or as little as three, depending on the equipment used), but the result, after the effluent is flushed away, is bone. The bones are then pulverized similarly to how the bones left in flame cremation are processed. The cremated remains from alkaline

---

* Oregon was the first state to legalize it, in 2009, as a form of disposition, although it wasn't put into use until 2011 . . . in Florida and Ohio.

hydrolysis typically yield 20 to 30 percent more volume as the bones haven't been subjected to the extreme desiccation of flame cremation, and they are more crystalline and powdery, similar to white beach sand.

The method of disposition isn't the only thing changing on the funerary landscape. Through education, the way we treat our dying, our newly dead, and the funeral service itself is changing along with the American attitude toward death. Death educator and thanatologist Gail Rubin says, "Death is really a consumer issue. Like a wedding, a funeral can be pretty darn expensive, and it's the party nobody wants to plan."[20] Rubin, the author of *A Good Goodbye: Funeral Planning for Those Who Don't Plan to Die*, is an advocate for having *the* conversation (about death) and changing the narrative on a subject that has been so long taboo to something that can be discussed openly and honestly. According to Rubin, the conversation began in 1999 when Stephanie West Allen, the author of *Creating Your Own Funeral or Memorial Service: A Workbook*, registered October 30 as the holiday "Create a Great Funeral Day," after watching her husband struggle with planning his mother's funeral. Rubin followed in 2010 with *A Good Goodbye*, a book that aims to not only help people plan a memorable service but also potentially save money by weighing their options ahead of time; it also includes practical tips, such as how to write an obituary. In addition to her book, Rubin organized a "Before I Die Festival" (BIDF) in New Mexico in 2017. BIDFs, which originated in the United Kingdom in 2013, are now held in different American cities and feature panel discussions on funeral-related topics such as grief, estate planning, and pet loss. They also have traditional festival elements such as art shows, theater performances, parades, vendor malls, and tours (of funeral homes and cemeteries, of course).

The BIDF isn't the only way Americans are getting together and actively talking about death. Death café events—another English transplant—have sprung up in many cities so people can get together and talk . . . about death. Though there is a facilitator, participants lead death cafés. Any topic about death and dying, whether it's related to physical, emotional, or financial issues, is fair game. Rubin hosts a death café in Albuquerque to further promote dialogue on her favorite subject—death. As she likes to say, "Talking about sex won't make you pregnant, and talking about funerals won't make you dead."[21]

It's not just the topic of death and dying that's changing tack. There's a decided shift in where Americans are dying. For the first time in a century, Americans are deinstitutionalizing their dying and dead in a retroactive movement. According to the Centers for Disease Control and Prevention, from 2000 to 2014, hospital and long-term care facility deaths fell and in-home deaths rose by almost 30 percent.[22] A new non-medical practitioner has emerged to help people die at home in a state of preparedness: the death doula. Sometimes called end-of-life doula, the death doula is a specialized caregiver who offers the dying and their families spiritual and emotional guidance during the last stage, as well as fulfills more practical tasks such as sitting vigil so exhausted family members can rest. Additionally, doulas educate families on what to expect during the dying process. It sounds intuitive that our species would innately *know* how to care for our dying, but that's not the case. As we turned dying over to the professionals—doctors and nurses—the culture lost touch with the sights, sounds, and smells, and the doula is there to prepare, guide, and help families reconnect with the process.

The doula movement is an offshoot of hospice, one that Lee Webster, a hospice volunteer since 1985 and cofounder of the National End-of-Life Doula Alliance, calls an "intentional death," meaning the dying are choosing the terms on which they leave the earth.[23] The doula helps the dying and their families achieve this through predeath planning, which can include completing advance care directives, getting their financial affairs in order, attending to legal matters, conducting meaning and legacy work, and developing a vigil plan.[24] Legacy work is helping the dying communicate a narrative to pass on, such as through writing a memoir or scrapbooking. The vigil plan is who is going to be present during the final days.

Kris Kington-Barker, an instructor and board member with the International End of Life Doula Association, says, "[Doulas] can add an additional layer of support to the medical team . . . [and] assist in bring-ing non-medical approaches to aiding in physical comfort with guided imagery, music, [and] repositioning."[25] But their work doesn't end once the person dies. In the period immediately after death, the doula works with family members to process the story of their loss and begin the grieving process, and to offer referrals. The doula relationship is typically ended with a gratitude ceremony that can be as simple as a handwritten note from the doula to the family members.[26]

Kington-Barker says she's seen an increase in families seeking funeral directors' support to assist families with home funerals. She attributes the rise of home funerals and the popularity of the death doula movement to baby boomers: "As more boomers . . . come to terms with aging, decreasing health, and the inevitable reality of their eventual death they are also more open to exploring ways to die differently and be remembered and honored than they observed for earlier generations."[27] Not only are more Americans choosing to die at home but also increasing numbers of Americans are choosing a home funeral. In that sense, the American funeral experience has come full circle.

In 2009 the National Home Funeral Alliance was formed to educate and help families facilitate home funerals. Lee Webster, who is the author of *Essentials for Practicing Home Funeral Guides* and the executive director for New Hampshire Funeral Resources, Education & Advocacy, says the impetus behind the home funeral is to "bring back the connection to death. Really," she continues, "there's a social justice aspect to it. People's response typically is, 'I didn't know you could do this.' Followed by, 'This is right for my family.'"[28] The book educates families about what their rights are and what they may choose to seek help with. Despite focusing on being family directed, orchestrated and coordinated, some families choose to involve a funeral director to varying degrees in the process, based on their comfort level. These services that are codirected by the family and funeral director are called "blended services." Ten states have laws involving a restrictive step (or steps) that prevent the family from doing everything themselves, and in those states the family must enlist the services of a funeral director. In the remaining forty states, a family can act as their own funeral director and do everything from bedside to graveside. Echoing Hoffner's sentiment, Webster said that most people planning a home funeral "are thinking about peaceful hospice deaths. There are many other situations where the family is going to need the expertise of a funeral director."[29]

Like the layers-out of the dead of the late eighteenth and early nineteenth centuries, who were called to wash and dress the dead, the family doesn't call the local funeral home. They perform the tasks themselves—or a layperson familiar with such tasks instructs the family on how to perform them. And like the colonial and antebellum Americans who took the tradesman undertaker—the local carpenter—a knotted string to craft a coffin, families can hire a local carpenter to make a custom casket, make their own with plans downloaded off the internet, or buy one at Costco. Chuck Lakin is a modern-day artisanal coffin maker, making coffins* out of his Maine woodshop. A reference librarian by profession, Lakin is a self-taught craftsman who turns out ten to twelve coffins a year out of his shop. Lakin describes his coffins, whether preordered or made-to-order, as "simple, graceful and functional."[30] He has conducted build-your-own-coffin workshops, and he offers one-on-one tutorials. His website, Last Things: Alternatives at the End of Life, features free blueprints for six build-your-own coffins. All of the coffins are Lakin's designs, and two of the units can function as furniture† until the time of need. The coffins are completely free of metal (except the six-sided "toe pincher" that can have the screws backed out and replaced with wood dowels once the glue dries), which makes them perfect for eco-friendly burial.[31]

Depending on state laws, the family may have several days to hold a wake—and knock together one of Lakin's creations—before burial . . . or cremation. According to Webster, there's an interesting phenomenon called "cremation conversion" associated with green burial. Of families choosing green burial, 75 to 85 percent said they would've selected cremation had there not been a convenient green cemetery.[32] The current cremation rate—about 57.5 percent in 2021—may not truly reflect cremation demand, if one accounts for an untapped demand for green burial based on supply. Regardless, the price tag, or lack thereof, isn't driving the home funeral movement. "Affordability is the last thing people look at," says Webster, meaning that people choosing home funerals are doing so because it fits their belief system, not to save a buck.[33] Surprisingly, despite their high price tag, funerals are seldom purchased based on price but rather on value received. And there's a big piece of the funeral where consumer value is shifting: the funeral service itself.

---

* Lakin makes both four- and six-sided vessels, but he prefers to call every burial vessel he makes a "coffin."
† One functions as a vertical bookcase or a horizontal entertainment center, and another as a storage chest.

The shift in the way funeral services are performed (and valued by funeral-goers) is due mainly to the rise of the "unchurched." In the past, the funeral service was predetermined. If the dead was Protestant, they had the funeral service of that denomination; if they were Catholic, they had a Mass of Christian Burial; if they were Jewish, the Mourner's *Kaddish* (a prayer) is recited at the gravesite; and so on for all the religious denominations. A recent Pew study found that 17 percent of Americans in 2019 defined their religion as "nothing in particular," up from 12 percent in 2009—atheists and agnostics are *in addition* to the nothing-in-particulars.[34] And of course, there are those who officially identify with a religion but don't go to church. So it begs the question: What kind of funeral service do you have for the unchurched that will provide meaning?

Baptist minister and counselor Doug Manning came up with the solution: funeral celebrants. Manning could see from the pulpit that the traditional religious funeral service simply wasn't cutting it anymore for a portion of the population, a portion that he saw growing every year. In 1905, an unnamed but "well-known" lawyer died in New York. *The Casket* reported that it was his wish that no minister officiate. Instead, a friend delivered the address, who said in part, "In my last talk with him he told me to say upon this occasion, among other things, that he had no knowledge of the hereafter but that he was willing to stake his future on the honor and uprightness of his life. He lived a brave and honest life and died a fearless death."[35] That, in a nutshell, is Manning's philosophy almost a century before he brainstormed the concept of the funeral celebrant. The well-known lawyer was also very prescient, as his method of funeralization was poised to become one of the major methods of funeralization in the twenty-first century: the humanist-based service.

Everything clicked into place for Manning with a tour of Australia in 1993 conducting grief-work seminars. Manning discovered "civil celebrants" that had been around since the 1970s. Only about 10 percent of Australia is religious, and the government established civil celebrants so Aussies could get married. Funerals became a natural role they filled. In 1995—the same year Glenda Stansbury joined Manning's publishing company, InSight Books—Manning was more intentional about seeking out civil celebrants on a tour of New Zealand. Manning and Stansbury formulated the idea for funeral celebrants after that trip, but to their dismay, they found there was zero interest. In an article for *Dodge Magazine*, Manning wrote, "Turning the Titanic might be easier than changing funeral service."[36] Despite the fact that funeral directors were struggling to provide funeral services that people wanted, the idea of funeral celebrant services was met with complete indifference.

The idea languished for four years until Manning and Stansbury talked (the now defunct) Mount Ida College into allowing them to host a three-day course for their funeral celebrant training. Fifty people showed up. "People were energized about truly personalized services," Stansbury says, "giving grieving people what they really need."[37]

Stansbury says what sets their program apart from the traditional religious services is they ground their training in grief work. "It's not anti-religious," Stansbury says. She's quick to point out that Manning is a Baptist minister and she's a church musician. She estimates about 90 percent of the people she serves choose to have a religious element in the service. "We've raised the expectation of what funerals need to do for the family."[38]

There are no templates or cookie-cutter services in Manning and Stansbury's celebrant services. The celebrants are trained to start every service with a blank slate. Stansbury, still a practicing celebrant despite her busy schedule as a trainer and adjunct mortuary school professor, shows every family she sits down with her blank notebook and tells them, "I'm starting from scratch."[39] Stansbury says the essence of their services is "healing begins when the story is told."[40]

Despite the initial suspicion from funeral service providers (as well as state and national leadership), they gradually gained the support of state associations—New Jersey was the first in 2002. The first national organization to adopt funeral celebrancy was when ICCFA* University began to offer it as the College of the 21st Century Services. Stansbury says her goal is that before she dies, "celebrants are part of the accepted conversation like in New Zealand and Australia."[41]

About forty-five hundred people have been through celebrant training, and InSight is beginning to train internationally. Aside from

---

* International Cemetery, Cremation and Funeral Association.

the obvious 60 percent of trainees being funeral staff, about 15 percent are clergy, and the rest are an interesting mixture of hospice and medical personnel, teachers, and event planners. Clearly Manning and Stansbury have tapped into a demand issue. Not only are they fast becoming part of the conversation but their model has potential to be *the* conversation.[42]

The "well-known" lawyer's funeral oration in 1905 included, in part, this (rather dark) oration, delivered by the celebrant:

> O death, how bitter is the thought of thee! how speedy thy
> approach! how stealthy thy step! how universal thy sway! the
> powerful cannot escape thee; the strong have no strength to
> oppose thee; there is no rich for thee, since none can buy life
> with treasures. All things have their waxing and waning, but thou
> remainest! ever the same. Thou art a sword that is never blunt—a
> net into which all fall—a prison into which all must enter—a sea
> on which all must venture—a penalty which all must suffer—and
> a tribute which all must pay. [43]

The funeralization traditions the settlers brought with them to Jamestown are a far cry from what Americans practice today, but the roots are clearly visible. One thing is certain: the "traditional" American funeral isn't static. It's in a constant state of flux. No matter what happens fifty, one hundred, or two hundred years from now, two things remain certain: people will still die and need a funeral, and the American funeral rite will continue to morph to meet the demands of the culture.

Memento mori.

Acknowledgments

Every book needs a champion, otherwise it's just a file sitting on an author's hard drive. *Last Rites* has three: Kemi Faderin, who saw the need for this history—the men and women who have plied the dark arts—to be told and sold the book; Haven Iverson, my editor at Sounds True, who whipped this piece into readable shape; and finally, Amy Bishop, my wonderful agent, who kept her hand on the tiller and helped sail this project into port. And I'd be remiss not to offer my profuse thanks to Caren Johnson, a longtime friend throughout my writing career. Caren was instrumental in bending my initial ideas for this book into saleable shape—her publishing industry knowledge got this whole ball rolling.

In a letter to Robert Hooke in 1675, Isaac Newton penned the famous line, "If I have seen further it is by standing on the shoulders of giants." Many professionals—giants—lent me their time and expertise to make this happen, and for that I'm forever grateful: Todd W. Van Beck, a prolific author of all things funereal, who shared not only his knowledge but also his published pieces and unpublished research; Mike Squires at *Southern Calls*, who let me browse his extensive collection (what I affectionately call the Squires National Archives) of *Casket*, *Sunnyside*, and *Shroud* issues and ephemera; Jason Engler, CANA historian, who shared his extensive cremation and funeral knowledge and gave me a personal tour of the National Funeral History Museum; Tom Randall at the Dodge Company, who let me borrow forty-five-years' worth of back issues of *Dodge Magazine*; Dr. Brent Tharp, an expert on the evolution of the American coffin/casket; forensic anthropologist Scott Warnasch; Dave Salmon of Warfield-Rohr Casket Co., who lent me his copies of *The Casket*, as well as Thomas Parmalee and Chris McGuire at Kates-Boyleston (publishers of *American Funeral Director* among others), who helped track down some old articles and allowed me use of them; the man behind the veil of Funetorium for some hearse knowledge; Civil War reenactor embalming surgeon, author, and funeral director James

Lowry, who sent me his book on embalming surgeons and a treasure trove of material; the NFDA leadership and Dodge Company, who generously allowed me use of their published material; Iconografix Books, Reference Point Press, Geoffrey Sumi and Johns Hopkins Press for "Impersonating the Dead: Mimes at Roman Funerals" from the *American Journal of Philology*; Jessie Dobson and Oxford University Press for "Some Eighteenth Century Experiments in Embalming" from the *Journal of the History of Medicine and Allied Sciences*; J. M. C. Toynbee and Johns Hopkins University Press and Thames & Hudson Ltd., London, for *Death and Burial in the Roman World*; and Dr. Julian Litten, author of *The English Way of Death: The Common Funeral Since 1450*. Please note that any historical gaffes you may come upon are not those of the experts: they may be laid squarely at my feet.

Also, profuse thanks to the folks out there championing eco-burial who shared their stories and knowledge with me. I'm forever grateful. They include author Ann Hoffner, former president of the Green Burial Council Lee Webster, death educator Gail Rubin, president of the Windward Foundation (Herland Forest) Walt Patrick, coffin maker Chuck Lakin, death doula Kris Kington-Barker, and pioneering funeral celebrant Glenda Stansbury; also, biology/forensic anthropology graduate student Arden Mower for the mycological expertise, and the folks who taught me the trade: Rick, Nicky, Nick, Bill, Pete, Ron, Mike, Phil, and Kathy.

I wrote the bulk of this during the COVID-19 pandemic—everything was closed—and Lois Stoehr, curator of education at Winterthur Museum, and the staff of the Winterthur Library were lifesavers (as well as before the pandemic), as was Terry Reimer, director of research at the National Museum of Civil War Medicine, and Sue Isaac, information services manager at the Royal College of Surgeons, England.

A big thank you to the scribblers of the Wilmington-Chadds Ford Writer's Group who offered critique on various pieces, specifically Peter Muller; production editor Jade Lascelles and the rest of the amazing team at Sounds True; and the talented Beth Sims, for the author photo.

I'd be remiss not to mention Brian Fallon—I wore out two needles listening (almost exclusively) to *Local Honey* while wrestling this bear into the cage.

Lastly, to you, the reader: I sincerely appreciate your interest in funeral service.

Notes

THE DARK ARTS: AN INTRODUCTION

1. *Rochester (NY) Herald*, as quoted by *The Casket* 3, no. 5 (May 1876): 6.

CHAPTER 1: A SEISMIC SHIFT

1. John K. Lattimer, *Kennedy and Lincoln: Medical & Ballistic Comparisons of Their Assassinations* (New York: Harcourt Brace Jovanovich, 1980), 38–39, 47–48.
2. "Terrible News," *Chicago Tribune*, April 15, 1865.
3. Owen Edwards, "The Death of Colonel Ellsworth," *Smithsonian Magazine*, April 2011, smithsonianmag.com/history/the-death-of-colonel-ellsworth-878695/.
4. Todd W. Van Beck, Bob Inman, and Mac McCormick, "The History of Civil War Embalming" (unpublished manuscript in author's possession, April 29, 2020), PDF file.
5. Van Beck, Inman, and McCormick, "History of Civil War Embalming."
6. Kimberly Largent-Christopher, "Embalming Comes in Vogue During Civil War," *Washington Times*, April 2, 2009.
7. Edward C. Johnson, "Cattell's Skill with Lincoln's Remains Publicized Embalming," *Casket and Sunnyside* 105, no. 2 (September 1975): 16. There is debate on how Cattell is related to Brown. Johnson offers the evidence that Catherine Cattell, Henry's mother, remarried in 1860 a man with the last name Brown, believed to be Charles Brown.
8. "The Funeral of Willie Lincoln," *Evening Star* (Washington, DC), February 24, 1862.
9. "Funeral of Willie Lincoln."
10. "Funeral of Willie Lincoln."
11. Lindsay Fitzharris, "Embalming and the Civil War," *National Museum of Civil War Medicine* (blog), February 20, 2016, civilwarmed.org/embalming1/.
12. "President Abraham Lincoln's Autopsy," *Abraham Lincoln's Assassination*, Roger J. Norton (website), accessed October 11, 2018, rogerjnorton.com/Lincoln60.html.
13. C. Keith Wilbur, *Civil War Medicine* (Philadelphia: Chelsea House Publishers, 1995), 98.
14. "President Abraham Lincoln's Autopsy."
15. Lattimer, *Kennedy and Lincoln*, 34.
16. "The Claim Disputed," *Evening Star* (Washington, DC), October 8, 1901.
17. Dorothy Meserve Kunhardt, *Twenty Days: A Narrative in Text and Pictures of the Assassination of Abraham Lincoln* (New York: Harper & Row, 1965), 95.
18. "Zinc Chloride," Centers for Disease Control and Prevention, The National Institute for Occupational Safety and Health, accessed October 15, 2018, cdc.gov/niosh/ipcsneng/neng1064.html.

19. Kunhardt, *Twenty Days, 95.*

20. "The Obsequies," *New York Times*, April 25, 1865.

21. "Embalming General Grant," *Cincinnati Enquirer* (Cincinnati, OH), August 3, 1885.

22. "Obsequies of the Murdered President," *Cleveland Morning Leader* (Cleveland, OH), April 22, 1865.

23. Kunhardt, *Twenty Days*, 95.

24. E. D. Daniels, *A Twentieth Century History and Biographic Record of LaPorte County Indiana* (New York: Lewis, 1904), 377.

25. "The Claim Disputed."

26. Teresa Boeckel, "Abraham Lincoln's Coffin, plus 4 Things to Know about His Death," *York Daily Record* (York, PA), April 14, 2015.

27. George Alfred Townsend, *The Life, Crime, and Capture of John Wilkes Booth and the Pursuit, Trial, and Execution of His Accomplices* (New York: Dick and Fitzgerald, 1865), 14.

28. Robert M. Reed, *Lincoln's Funeral Train: The Epic Journey from Washington to Springfield* (Atglen, PA: Schiffer, 2014), 18.

29. "The Funeral Obsequies in Washington & New York," *Cincinnati Enquirer* (Cincinnati, OH), April 20, 1865.

30. Steve Palmer, "In Appreciation and with Respect," *Dodge Magazine* 111, no. 3 (Summer 2019): 31.

31. Reed, *Lincoln's Funeral Train*, 24–25.

32. Reed, 132.

33. "The Obsequies," *New York Times*.

34. Reed, *Lincoln's Funeral Train*, 27.

35. Reed, 27.

36. Wendy Sotos, "1,700 Miles of Mourners," *Civil War Times* 57, no. 5 (October 2018): 43.

37. "In Memoriam!" *Philadelphia Inquirer*, April 22, 1865.

38. Sotos, "1,700 Miles of Mourners," 44.

39. W. Lee Fergus, "The Lincoln Funeral Train," *Stamps Magazine* (August 25, 1956), reprinted in *Mekeel's & Stamps Magazine* (November 10, 2006): 22.

40. *Journal of the Select Council of the City of Philadelphia from January 1 to July 1, 1865* (Philadelphia: E. C. Markley & Son, Printers, 1865), 662, books.google.com /books?id=BPVEAQAAMAAJ&pg.

41. "President Lincoln's Remains," *Baltimore Sun*, April 24, 1865.

42. "The Close at City Hall," *New York Herald*, April 26, 1865.

43. "Death of Peter Relyea, The Undertaker," *New-York Tribune*, January 23, 1896.

44. "Death of Peter Relyea, The Undertaker."

45. "The Funeral," *Philadelphia Inquirer*, April 26, 1865.

46. "The Funeral," *Philadelphia Inquirer*.

47. "The Close at City Hall."

48. "Our Tribute: Obsequies to Abraham Lincoln," *New York Herald*, April 26, 1865.
49. "Last Night's Dispatches," *Buffalo Commercial* (Buffalo, NY), April 26, 1865.
50. "The Funeral," *Philadelphia Inquirer*.
51. "The Journey of the Dead," *Buffalo Morning Express* (Buffalo, NY), April 28, 1865.
52. "The Funeral Train," *New York Herald*, April 28, 1865.
53. "The Remains in New York," *New York Times*, April 25, 1865.
54. Chris Woodyard, *The Victorian Book of the Dead* (Dayton, OH: Kestrel 2014), 166.
55. Reed, *Lincoln's Funeral Train*, 29.
56. Fergus, "Lincoln Funeral Train," 23.
57. "The Funeral Pageant," *Cleveland Morning Leader*, April 29, 1865.
58. "Ohio's Capital in Mourning," *Cincinnati Enquirer* (Cincinnati, OH), May 1, 1865.
59. "Obsequies of President Lincoln in Columbus," *Daily Ohio Statesman* (Columbus, OH), May 1, 1865.
60. Reed, *Lincoln's Funeral Train*, 86.
61. "The Funeral Train," *Cleveland Morning Leader* (Cleveland, OH), May 2, 1865.
62. Sotos, "1,700 Miles of Mourners," 50.
63. "The Funeral Train," *New York Herald*, May 2, 1865.
64. "The President's Funeral," *Chicago Tribune*, May 2, 1865; "The President's Funeral," *Chicago Tribune*, May 3, 1865.
65. "The President's Funeral," *Chicago Tribune*, May 2, 1865.
66. "The President's Funeral," *Chicago Tribune*.
67. "The President's Funeral," *Chicago Tribune*.
68. "Local News," *Daily Missouri Republican*, September 4, 1865.
69. "The Hearse That Carried Lincoln," *Sunbury Weekly News* (Sunbury, PA), September 30, 1881.
70. "The Hearse That Carried Lincoln"; "The Procession," *Courier-Journal* (Louisville, KY), May 8, 1865.
71. "Funeral Obsequies at Springfield," *Daily Missouri Republican* (St. Louis, MO), May 6, 1865.
72. "The Last of Earth," *Chicago Tribune*, May 5, 1865.

CHAPTER 2: THE BOOK OF THE DEAD

1. Herodotus, *Herodotus*, ed. E. Capps, T. E. Page, and W. H. D. House, trans. A. D. Godley, vol. 1, bk. 2 (New York: G. P. Putnam, 1921), 365.
2. Herodotus, *Herodotus*, 327.
3. E. A. Wallis Budge, *The Book of the Dead* (1895; Global Grey, 2020), 51. Citations refer to Global Grey edition.
4. James Teackle Dennis, *The Burden of Isis* (London: John Murray, 1910; Global Grey, 2020), 2–3.
5. Dennis, *Burden of Isis*, 3.

6. Susan V. Lawrence, "Unraveling the Mysteries of the Mummies," *Science News* 118 (December 1980): 362–64.

7. Herodotus, *Herodotus*, 369.

8. William W. Lace, *Mummification and Death Rituals of Ancient Egypt* (San Diego: Reference Point Press, 2013), 27.

9. Herodotus, *Herodotus*, 373.

10. Lorna Oakes and Lucia Gahlin, *Ancient Egypt* (London: Annes Publishing, 2007), 396.

11. Lace, *Mummification and Death Rituals of Ancient Egypt*, 27.

12. Dan Vergano, "Grisly Mummy Mysteries from Ancient Egypt Are Unraveled," *USA Today*, October 4, 2013.

13. Lace, *Mummification and Death Rituals of Ancient Egypt*, 28.

14. Robert W. Habenstein and William M. Lamers, *The History of American Funeral Directing*, 8th ed. (Brookfield, WI: National Funeral Directors Association, 2014), 13.

15. Egyptian display, National Museum of Funeral History, Houston, TX, author notes, October 21, 2020.

16. Herodotus, *Herodotus*, 371.

17. Alfred Wiedemann, *The Ancient Egyptian Doctrine of the Immortality of the Soul* (London: H. Grevel, 1895), 27–29.

18. Wiedemann, *Ancient Egyptian Doctrine of the Immortality of the Soul*, 27–28.

19. Wiedemann, 29–30.

20. Jason Urbanus, "Did the 'Father of History' Get It Wrong?" *Archaeology* (July/August 2013): 14.

21. Eliab Myers, *The Champion Text-Book on Embalming*, 5th ed. (Springfield, OH: Champion Chemical Company, 1918), 225.

22. Herodotus, *Herodotus*, 373.

23. Vergano, "Grisly Mummy Mysteries from Ancient Egypt Are Unraveled."

24. A. H. Sayce, *Egypt of the Hebrews and Herodotos* [*sic*] (New York: Macmillan, 1895), 177.

25. Herodotus, *Herodotus*, 373.

26. Adolf Erman, *Life in Ancient Egypt*, trans. H. M. Tirard, (London: Macmillan, 1894), 319.

27. Erman, *Life in Ancient Egypt*, 325.

28. Lace, *Mummification and Death Rituals of Ancient Egypt*, 17.

29. Donovan Webster, "Valley of the Mummies," *National Geographic* 196, no. 4 (October 1999): 86–87.

30. Wiedemann, *Ancient Egyptian Doctrine of the Immortality of the Soul*, 9.

31. Erman, *Life in Ancient Egypt*, 307.

32. Lace, *Mummification and Death Rituals of Ancient Egypt*, 14–15.

33. Lace, 54.

34. Joshua J. Mark. "Egyptian Book of the Dead," World History Encyclopedia, March 24, 2016, ancient.eu/Egyptian_Book_Of_The_Dead/.

35. Lace, *Mummification and Death Rituals of Ancient Egypt*, 30.

36. Lace, 30.

37. Thomas T. Lewis, "Pharaonic Egypt," *Salem Press Encyclopedia*, 2014. Topic Overviews Public Libraries database, search.ebscohost.com/login.aspx?direct=true&db=tol&AN=96411564.

38. T. Scott Gilligan and Thomas F. H. Stueve, *Mortuary Law*, rev. 10th ed. (Cincinnati, OH: Cincinnati Foundation for Mortuary Education, 2005), 36.

39. "Doctor Salary in Accra, Ghana," Average Salary Survey, accessed January 17, 2021, averagesalary.com/doctor/accra-ghana#; Munachim Amah and Ized Uanikhehi, "Celebrating Death in Style: Ghana's Fantasy Coffins," CNN, last modified November 27, 2018, cnn.com/2017/12/29/africa/ghana-fantasy-coffin/index.html.

40. Zahi Hawass, as told to Margaret Zackowitz, "The Mummy Hunter and Mr. X," *National Geographic World*, no. 318 (March 2002): 22–26. MasterFile Premier database, search.ebscohost.com/login.aspx?direct=true&dbf5h&AN=6314070&site=ehost-live.

41. Webster, "Valley of the Mummies," 80–84.

CHAPTER 3: LETHAL COMBAT AND OTHER ROMAN OBSEQUIES

1. Tom Muller, "Secrets of the Colosseum," *Smithsonian Magazine*, January 2011, smithsonianmag.com/history/secrets-of-the-colosseum-75827047/.

2. Suetonius, as quoted by Donald R. Dudley, *Urbs Roma: A Source Book of Classical Texts on the City and Its Monuments* (London: Phaidon Press, 1967), 142.

3. Strabo, *Geographica* 6.2.6, perseus.tufts.edu/hopper/text?doc=Perseus%3Atext%3A1999.01.0198%3Abook%3D6%3Achapter%3D2%3Asection%3D6.

4. Jérôme Carcopino, *Daily Life in Ancient Rome: The People and the City at the Height of the Empire*, ed. Henry T. Rowell, trans. E. O. Lorimer (New Haven, CT: Yale University Press, 1940), 242.

5. "Gladiator History," Tribunes and Triumphs, accessed January 28, 2021, tribunesandtriumphs.org/gladiators/gladiator-history.htm; Titus Livius, *The History of Rome* (Cambridge: Harvard University Press, 1936), bk. 16, chap. 6.

6. W. Warde Fowler, *Social Life at Rome: In the Age of Cicero* (New York: Macmillan, 1909), 303–4.

7. Livius, *History of Rome*, bk. 31, chap. 50.

8. Livius, *History of Rome*, bk. 39, chap. 46.

9. Fowler, *Social Life at Rome*, 302.

10. Carcopino, *Daily Life in Ancient Rome*, 231.

11. Muller, "Secrets of the Colosseum."

12. Arthur Darby Nock, "Cremation and Burial in the Roman Empire," *Harvard Theological Review* 25, no. 4 (October 1932): 321–60, jstor.org/stable/1508378.

13. Nock, "Cremation and Burial in the Roman Empire."

14. Robert W. Habenstein and William M. Lamers, *The History of American Funeral Directing*, 8th ed. (Brookfield, WI: National Funeral Directors Association, 2014), 26.

15. John Lanktree, *A Synopsis of Roman Antiquities: Being a Description of the Religion, Laws, Military System, and Domestic Life of the Roman People*, rev. ed. H. W. Duncan (London: Ward and Lock, 1857), 208.

16. Bertram S. Puckle, *Funeral Customs: Their Origin and Development* (London: T. W. Laurie, 1926; Global Grey, 2019), 51. Citations refer to Global Grey edition.

17. Lanktree, *Synopsis of Roman Antiquities*, 211.

18. Lanktree, 212.

19. Lanktree, 211.

20. Lanktree, 211.

21. "Ancient Roman Funerals," *Shadyside* 1, no. 3 (November 1891): 3.

22. "Ancient Roman Funerals," 3.

23. Habenstein and Lamers, *History of American Funeral Directing*, 27.

24. Habenstein and Lamers, 27.

25. "Pompeii Fetes," *St. Louis Globe-Democrat*, April 12, 1891.

26. Fowler, *Social Life at Rome*, 318.

27. Geoffrey S. Sumi, "Impersonating the Dead: Mimes at Roman Funerals," *American Journal of Philology* 123, no. 4 (Winter 2002): 578.

28. Edgar Jackson, "Grief and Ceremonial Acting Out," *Dodge Magazine* 69, no. 2 (March 1977): 14, 28.

29. Sumi, "Impersonating the Dead," 573.

30. Sumi, 573.

31. Diodorus, as quoted by Sumi, "Impersonating the Dead," 560.

32. A. C. Rush, *Death and Burial in Christian Antiquity* (Washington, DC: Catholic University of America Press, 1941), 193, as cited by Sumi, "Impersonating the Dead," 576.

33. Polybius, *The Histories*, trans. Robin Waterfield (New York: Oxford University Press, 2010), 460.

34. Harold W. Johnston, *The Private Life of the Romans* (Chicago: Scott, Foresman, 1903), 328.

35. Hugo Erichsen, *The Cremation of the Dead: Considered from an Aesthetic, Sanitary, Religious, Historical, Medico-Legal, and Economical Standpoint* (Detroit: D. O. Haynes, 1887), 17.

36. Lanktree, *Synopsis of Roman Antiquities*, 213.

37. Lanktree, 52.

38. Lanktree, 53.

39. Lanktree, 53.

40. Lanktree, 53.

41. Cyril E. Robinson, *A History of the Roman Republic* (New York: Barnes & Noble, 1932), 50.

42. J. M. C. Toynbee, *Death and Burial in the Roman World* (Baltimore: Johns Hopkins University Press, 1971), 55.

43. Lanktree, *Synopsis of Roman Antiquities*, 53.

44. Toynbee, *Death and Burial in the Roman World*, 97, 99.

45. Lanktree, *Synopsis of Roman Antiquities*, 213.

46. Tacitus, *Annals* 16.6.

47. Erichsen, *Cremation of the Dead*, 17.

48. Erichsen, 17.

49. Erichsen, 17.

50. Toynbee, *Death and Burial in the Roman World*, 49.

51. Toynbee, 50.

52. Habenstein and Lamers, *History of American Funeral Directing*, 66.

53. Toynbee, *Death and Burial in the Roman World*, 51, 136.

54. Toynbee, 37.

55. Toynbee, 96.

56. Toynbee, 63–64.

57. Puckle, *Funeral Customs*, 180.

58. Lanktree, *Synopsis of Roman Antiquities*, 213–14.

59. Lanktree, 214.

60. Lanktree, 214.

61. Lanktree, 214.

62. Lanktree, 214.

63. Lanktree, 215.

64. Toynbee, *Death and Burial in the Roman World*, 45.

65. "Hart Island, the Largest Public Burial Ground in U.S., May Soon Be Controlled By NYC Parks Department," CBS New York, May 30, 2019, newyork.cbslocal.com/2019/05/30/hart-island-burial-ground-nyc-department-of-correction-nyc-department-of-parks/.

66. Carcopino, *Daily Life in Ancient Rome*, 240–41.

67. Puckle, *Funeral Customs*, 21.

68. Robert Fulton, "AIDS, a Sociological Perspective," *Dodge Magazine* 83, no. 5 (November/December 1991): 6.

CHAPTER 4: THE BLOODY BARBER-SURGEONS

1. "Life and Character of the Celebrated Mr. Martin Van Butchell, Surgeon Dentist and Fistula Curer, of Mount-Street, Berkeley-Square" (London: T. Keating, 1803), 196, 198, Medical Heritage Library, Royal College of Surgeons of England.

2. "Life and Character of the Celebrated Mr. Martin Van Butchell," 193.

3. "Life and Character of the Celebrated Mr. Martin Van Butchell," 209.

4. "Memoirs of the Noted Martin Van Butchell, Surgeon, Dentist, and Professor in the Art of Cutting Fistulas, &c. &c.," *Portraits and Lives of Remarkable and Eccentric Characters* (Westminster: J. Arnett, 1819), 87, Medical Heritage Library, Royal College of Surgeons of England.

5. Jessie Dobson, "Some Eighteenth-Century Experiments in Embalming," *Journal of the History of Medicine and Allied Sciences* 8, no. 4 (1953): 435, jstor.org/stable /24619780.

6. Robert G. Mayer, *Embalming: History, Theory, and Practice*, 4th ed. (New York: McGraw-Hill, 2006), 470.

7. Dobson, "Some Eighteenth-Century Experiments in Embalming," 435.

8. Notes of Lectures Given by William Hunter, Royal College of Surgeons of England Archives, MS0204/1.

9. Dobson, "Some Eighteenth-Century Experiments in Embalming," 435.

10. Notes of Lectures Given by William Hunter.

11. Dobson, "Some Eighteenth-Century Experiments in Embalming," 436.

12. "Life and Character of the Celebrated Mr. Martin Van Butchell," 194; Dobson, "Some Eighteenth-Century Experiments in Embalming," 440.

13. Harold T. McKone, "Embalming: A 'Living' Rite," *Today's Chemist at Work* (December 2002): 33.

14. Julian Litten, *The English Way of Death: The Common Funeral Since 1450* (London: Robert Hale, 1991), 37.

15. Robert W. Habenstein and William M. Lamers, *The History of American Funeral Directing*, 8th ed. (Brookfield, WI: National Funeral Directors Association, 2014), 66.

16. Charles A. Bradford, *Heart Burial* (London: George Allen & Unwin, 1933), 23.

17. Bradford, *Heart Burial*, 23.

18. "King Edward," *The Casket* 3, no. 5 (May 1878): 2.

19. Habenstein and Lamers, *History of American Funeral Directing*, 67.

20. Sidney Young, *The Annals of the Barber-Surgeons of London* (London: Blades, East, & Blades, 1890), 22.

21. Young, *Annals of the Barber-Surgeons of London*, 23.

22. Young, 22, 23.

23. Young, 21.

24. Young, 23.

25. Young, 79.

26. Young, 78.

27. Young, 80.

28. Young, 236.

29. Young, 120.

30. Young, 112.

31. Young, 112.

32. Notes of Lectures Given by William Hunter.

33. George L. Carrick, "On Dr. Vivodtsef's Method of Embalming the Dead," *Edinburgh Medical Journal* 16, no. 6 (December 1870): 503–11.

34. Bradford, *Heart Burial*, 27–28.

35. Mayer, *Embalming*, 468.

36. Habenstein and Lamers, *History of American Funeral Directing*, 84.

37. Paul Salopek, "Honey, I'm Dead," *Out of Eden Walk* (blog), *National Geographic*, May 13, 2015, nationalgeographic.org/projects/out-of-eden-walk/articles/2015-05 -honey-im-dead/.

38. "Pakenham Preserved in Rum," *The Topeka (KS) Capital*, January 31, 1888.

39. Mayer, *Embalming*, 467.

40. Habenstein and Lamers, *History of American Funeral Directing*, 85.

41. Litten, *English Way of Death*, 37.

42. Litten, 37.

43. Habenstein and Lamers, *History of American Funeral Directing*, 67.

44. Habenstein and Lamers, 60.

45. Bernardino Ramazzini, *De morbis artificum*, as quoted by Habenstein and Lamers, *History of American Funeral Directing*, 61.

46. Habenstein and Lamers, *History of American Funeral Directing*, 149.

47. Litten, *English Way of Death*, 17.

48. Peter C. Jupp and Glennys Howarth, *The Changing Face of Death: Historical Accounts of Death and Disposal* (London: Macmillan, 1997), 57–58.

49. Susan Isaac, "Martin Van Butchell: The Eccentric Dentist Who Embalmed His Wife," *Royal College of Surgeons* (blog), March 1, 2019, rcseng.ac.uk/library-and -publications/library/blog/martin-van-butchell/.

50. Dobson, "Some Eighteenth-Century Experiments in Embalming," 440.

CHAPTER 5: MOURNING GLOVES AND LIQUOR

1. *Collections of the New York Historical Society*, 2nd ser., vol. 2, pt. 1 (New York: Bartlett & Welford, 1848), 110.

2. "A Glimpse of an Old Dutch Town," *Harpers New Monthly Magazine* 62 (December 1880–May 1881): 529.

3. Bertram S. Puckle, *Funeral Customs: Their Origin and Development* (London: T. W. Laurie, 1926; Global Grey, 2019), 43. Citations refer to Global Grey edition.

4. "A Glimpse of an Old Dutch Town," 529.

5. Stephen J. Kunitz, "Mortality Change in America, 1620–1920," *Human Biology* 56, no. 3 (1984): 559–82, jstor.org/stable/41463598.

6. David E. Stannard, "Death of the Puritan Child," *Death in America*, ed. David E. Stannard (Philadelphia: University of Pennsylvania Press, 1975), 17.

7. Stannard, "Death of the Puritan Child," 18.

8. *Westminster Directory: A Directory of the Public Worship of God*, Car. I, Parl. 3, sess. 5, Kingdom of Scotland, approved February 6, 1645. Kindle.

9. Todd W. Van Beck, "Early American Burial Practices," *Dodge Magazine* 100, no. 4 (Fall 2008): 27.

10. Margaret Coffin, *Death in Early America: The History and Folklore of Customs and Superstitions of Early Medicine, Funerals, Burials, and Mourning* (New York: Nelson, 1976), 80.

11. "Funerals Fifty Years Ago," *Sunnyside* 26, no. 10 (October 1896): 7.

12. Julian Litten, *The English Way of Death: The Common Funeral Since 1450* (London: Robert Hale, 1991), 100.

13. "Happy Days Gone," *Sunnyside* 4, no. 37 (August 1888).

14. Bella Landauer, "Some American Funeral Ephemera," *New York Historical Society Quarterly* 36, no. 2 (April 1952): 222.

15. Landauer, "Some American Funeral Ephemera," 223–24.

16. Coffin, *Death in Early America*, 71.

17. Alice Morse Earle, *Customs and Fashions in Old New England* (New York: Charles Scribner's Sons, 1894), 374.

18. Puckle, *Funeral Customs*, 73.

19. Coffin, *Death in Early America*, 208.

20. Earle, *Customs and Fashions in Old New England*, 368.

21. Puckle, *Funeral Customs*, 79.

22. Earle, *Customs and Fashions in Old New England*, 368.

23. Van Beck, "Early American Burial Practices," 27.

24. *Boston News-Letter*, as quoted by William L. Chaffin, "The Religious History of Easton, Mass.," ed. George Batchelor, *Christian Register* 84, no. 30 (July 27, 1905): 833.

25. Van Beck, "Early American Burial Practices," 27.

26. Robert W. Habenstein and William M. Lamers, *The History of American Funeral Directing*, 8th ed. (Brookfield, WI: National Funeral Directors Association, 2014), 122.

27. Van Beck, "Early American Burial Practices," 28.

28. Habenstein and Lamers, *History of American Funeral Directing*, 124.

29. Puckle, *Funeral Customs*, 58.

30. Puckle, 58.

31. Habenstein and Lamers, *History of American Funeral Directing*, 124.

32. Robert Blair St. George, *Conversing by Signs: Poetics of Implication in Colonial New England Culture* (Chapel Hill: University of North Carolina Press, 2000), 438.

33. Habenstein and Lamers, *History of American Funeral Directing*, 125.

34. Caleb Smith, postscript in Aaron Burr, *A Servant of God: Jonathan Belcher, Governor of His Majesty's Province of New Jersey* (New York: Hugh Gaine, Printer, 1757), accessed January 8, 2020, belcherfoundation.org/first.htm.

35. Jonathan M. Beagle, "Remembering Peter Faneuil: Yankees, Huguenots, and Ethnicity in Boston, 1743–1900," *New England Quarterly* 75, no. 3 (2002): 388–414, doi.org/10.2307/1559785.

36. *Boston News-Letter*, as quoted by Beagle, "Remembering Peter Faneuil."

37. Habenstein and Lamers, *History of American Funeral Directing*, 125.

38. *Boston News-Letter*, as quoted by Chaffin, "The Religious History of Easton, Mass.," 833.

39. *Boston News-Letter*, 833.

40. *Boston News-Letter*, 833.

41. Lois Stoehr, associate curator of education at Winterthur Museum, personal interview with author, May 8, 2019.

42. Stoehr, personal interview with the author, May 8, 2019.

43. Van Beck, "Early American Burial Practices," 28.

44. Samuel Sewall, *Collections of the Massachusetts Historical Society*, 5th ser., vol. 7 (Boston: University Press: John Wilson and Son, 1882), 127.

45. Habenstein and Lamers, *History of American Funeral Directing*, 124.

46. Nathaniel Hawthorne, *The House of Seven Gables and the Snow Image and Other Twice-Told Tales* (New York: Houghton Mifflin, 1897), 471–72.

47. Coffin, *Death in Early America*, 73.

48. Nathaniel Goodwin, *Thomas Olcott, One of the First Settlers of Hartford, Connecticut* (Hartford, CT: Tiffany and Burnham, 1845), vii.

49. Earle, *Customs and Fashions in Old New England*, 370.

50. Earle, 370.

51. Earle, 379.

52. Earle, 372.

53. Charles Pelham Greenough, "March Meeting, 1921. Gifts to the Society; Caleb Davis and His Funeral Dinner; The 'Character' and the Historian; Samuel Abbott Green," *Proceedings of the Massachusetts Historical Society* 54 (1920): 212–42, jstor .org/stable/25080116.

54. Greenough, "March Meeting, 1921."

55. Description of menu from Greenough, "March Meeting, 1921."

56. Greenough, "March Meeting, 1921."

57. Greenough, "March Meeting, 1921."

58. Puckle, *Funeral Customs*, 72.

59. Puckle, 72–73.

60. Philip A. Bruce, *Social Life of Virginia in the Seventeenth Century* (Richmond, VA: Whittet amd Shepperson, 1907), 220–21.

61. Walter S. Griggs, *Genealogy of the Griggs Family* (Pompton Lakes, NJ: Biblio Company, 1926), 65.

62. Hugo Erichsen, *The Cremation of the Dead: Considered from an Aesthetic, Sanitary, Religious, Historical, Medico-Legal, and Economical Standpoint* (Detroit: D. O. Haynes, 1887), 12; Habenstein and Lamers, *History of American Funeral Directing*, 27.

63. Puckle, *Funeral Customs*, 62.

64. Habenstein and Lamers, *History of American Funeral Directing*, 76–77.

65. "The Death of George Washington," George Washington's Mount Vernon, accessed February 17, 2020, mountvernon.org/library/digitalhistory/digital -encyclopedia/article/the-death-of-george-washington/.

66. James Thomas Flexner, *Washington: The Indispensable Man* (Boston: Little, Brown, 1974), 400.

67. John F. Schroeder and Benson J. Lossing, *Life and Times of Washington*, revised ed., vol. 4 (Albany, NY: M. M. Belcher Publishing, 1903), 1997.

68. Todd W. Van Beck, "George Washington: First in War, First in Peace, First in the Hearts of His Countrymen," American Funeral Director, July 2, 2018, kates -boylston.com/george-washington/.

69. Richard Klingenmaier, "The Burial of General George Washington: The Lesser Known Participants," *Alexandria Chronicle* (Spring 2012): 1.

70. Klingenmaier, "Burial of General George Washington," 3.

71. Van Beck, "George Washington: First in War."

72. Klingenmaier, "Burial of General George Washington," 3.

73. Washington Irving, *Life of George Washington*, ed. Jess Stein (Tarrytown, NY: Sleepy Hollow Restorations, 1975), 684.

74. Van Beck, "George Washington: First in War."

75. Van Beck, "George Washington: First in War."

76. Klingenmaier, "Burial of General George Washington," 3–4.

77. Klingenmaier, 3–4.

78. Bill from Henry and Joseph Ingle, "Presidential Funerals Display," National Museum of Funeral History, Houston, TX, author notes October 21, 2020.

79. Business Ledger of Moyers & Rich, cabinetmakers, Wythe County, VA, 1834–1840, Winterthur Digital Collection, winterthur.org/explore-wintercat/.

80. Klingenmaier, "Burial of General George Washington," 3.

81. Klingenmaier, 3–4.

82. Schroeder and Lossing, *Life and Times of Washington*, 2003.

83. Meredith Eliassen, "Mourning George Washington," George Washington's Mount Vernon, Center for Digital History at the Washington Library, accessed February 27, 2020, mountvernon.org/library/digitalhistory/digital-encyclopedia/article /mourning-george-washington/.

84. Edward G. Lengel, ed., *A Companion to George Washington* (Oxford: Wiley-Blackwell, 2012), 582.

85. Eliassen, "Mourning George Washington."

86. Frank Freidel and Lonnelle Aikman, *Washington: Man and Monument* (Washington, DC: Washington National Monument Association, 1965), 30.

87. Anita Schorsch, *Mourning Becomes America: Mourning Art in the New Nation* (New Jersey: Main Street Press, 1976).

88. Schorsch, *Mourning Becomes America*.

89. Albert Gendebien, foreword in Schorsch, *Mourning Becomes America*.

90. Schorsch, *Mourning Becomes America*.

91. Stoehr, personal interview with author, May 8, 2019.

CHAPTER 6: EMBALMING SURGEONS

1. Westchester County Archives Veterans Works Progress Administration Cemetery Records, accessed February 17, 2021, collections.westchestergov.com/digital/collection/vetcards/id/2330/rec/936.

2. Thomas M. O'Brien and Oliver Diefendorf, *General Orders of the War Department Embracing the Years 1861, 1862 & 1863*, vol. 1 (New York: Derby & Miller, 1864), 248.

3. O'Brien and Diefendorf, *General Orders of the War Department*, 248.

4. Robert Stiles, *Four Years Under Marse Robert* (Washington, DC: Neale Publishing, 1903; University of North Carolina, 1999), chap. 16, docsouth.unc.edu/fpn/stiles/stiles.html.

5. "The Kanawha Rout," *York Enquirer* (York, SC), September 19, 1861.

6. "Burying the Dead," *New York Herald*, April 17, 1862.

7. Ulysses S. Grant, *Personal Memoirs of U.S. Grant* (New York: C. L. Webster, 1885; New York, Bartleby.com, 2000), chap. 25, bartleby.com/1011/25.html.

8. Drew Gilpin Faust, *This Republic of Suffering: Death and the American Civil War* (New York: Vintage Books, 2008), 67.

9. Burr to Brig. General M. Patrick, Nov. 21, 1864, RG94, Entry 2.1, "Letters Received," National Archives and Records Administration.

10. Burr to Brig. General M. Patrick.

11. Burr to Brig. General M. Patrick.

12. Bunnell to Burr, July 22, 1862, RG94, Entry 2.1, "Letters Received," National Archives and Records Administration.

13. Brevet General M. Patrick, City Point, November 23, 1864, RG94, Entry 2.1, "Letters Received," National Archives and Records Administration.

14. Todd W. Van Beck, "U.S. President's Funerals," chap. 6, "John Q. Adams" (unpublished manuscript in author's possession, April 24, 2020), PDF file.

15. *House of Representatives, During the Second Session of the Thirtieth Congress, Begun and Held at the City of Washington, December 4, 1849* (Washington, DC: Tippin & Streeper, 1848), 215, babel.hathitrust.org/cgi/pt?id=hvd.hnwwln&view=1up&seq=7.

16. Howard A. Kelly and Walter L. Burrage, *A Cyclopedia of American Medical Biography, Comprising the Lives of Eminent Deceased Physicians and Surgeons from 1610 to 1910* (Baltimore: Norman Remington, 1920), 492.

17. Todd W. Van Beck, Bob Inman, and Mac McCormick, "The History of Civil War Embalming," (unpublished manuscript in author's possession, April 29, 2020), PDF file.

18. *The Lancet*, as quoted by J. B. Biddle et al. (ed.), "Preservation of Bodies for Dissection," *Medical Examiner* 2 (1839): 196, babel.hathitrust.org/cgi/pt?id=mdp .39015070469526&view=1up&seq=173.

19. Edward C. Johnson, "Jean Nicolas Gannal, the Chemist Embalmer Who 'Patented' the Carotid Artery," *American Funeral Director* 123, no. 8 (August 2000): 24–25.

20. "The Anti-Embalming Bill Killed," *Sunnyside* 4, no. 35 (June 1888).

21. Auguste Renouard, "Arsenical Poisoning," *The Casket* 31, no. 1 (January 1906): 10.

22. Edward C. Johnson, "Cattell's Skill with Lincoln's Remains Publicized Embalming," *Casket and Sunnyside* 105 (September 1975): 18; Van Beck, Inman, and McCormick, "History of Civil War Embalming."

23. John Anthony Gaussardia. Method of preserving dead bodies. US Patent 15,972, October 28, 1856.

24. Edward C. Johnson and Melissa Johnson Williams, "William Jackson Bunnell: Civil War Embalming Surgeon," *American Funeral Director* 123, no. 1 (January 2000): 67.

25. C. L. Oliphant and C. P. Dean, eds., *The Supplement to the United States Naval Medical Bulletin: Published for the Information of the Hospital Corps of the Navy* 11, no. 4 (Washington, DC: Government Printing Office, 1927), 290.

26. "Poisoned by a Dead Body," *Evening Post* (New York, NY), January 18, 1849.

27. "The Testimony," *New York Herald*, February 5, 1850; "The Late Murder in Leonard Street," *New York Daily Tribune*, October 15, 1850.

28. "Embalming the Dead—Wonderful Discovery," *Western Democrat* (Charlotte, NC), March 10, 1857.

29. Thomas Holmes, as quoted by Van Beck, Inman, McCormick, "History of Civil War Embalming."

30. "The Late Col. Baker," *Brooklyn (NY) Times Union*, October 31, 1861.

31. "Corporation Affairs," *Evening Star* (Washington, DC), November 1, 1864.

32. Todd W. Van Beck, "Arsenic in Embalming: The Myths, the Stories, and the Facts" (unpublished article in author's possession, May 18, 2020), PDF file.

33. Todd W. Van Beck, Bob Inman, and Mac McCormick, "The Life and Times of Dr. Daniel H. Prunk" (unpublished manuscript in author's possession, April 29, 2020), PDF file.

34. Prunk to Buckesto in an 1872 letter, as quoted by Van Beck, Inman, and McCormick, "Life and Times of Dr. Daniel H. Prunk."

35. "Answers to Progressive by Prof. A. Renouard," *The Casket* 22, no. 6 (June 1897): 6.

36. "Gossip at the Capital," *New-York Tribune*, February 26, 1888.

37. J. David Book, "Death Is Every Where Present," *Vermont History* 79, no. 1 (Winter/Spring 2011): 30.

38. Willard Thayer to Esther Thayer, October 17, 1862, in Jeffrey D. Marshall, ed., *A War of the People: Vermont Civil War Letters* (Hanover, NH: University Press of New England, 1999), 115–16.

39. Johnson and Williams, "William Jackson Bunnell," 68.

40. *The Sunnyside*, as quoted by Van Beck, Inman, McCormick, "History of Civil War Embalming."

41. Lieutenant Chester K. Leach to Ann Leach, January 23, 1862, in *Dear Wife: The Civil War Letters of Chester K. Leach*, ed. Edward J. Feidner (Burlington, VT: Center for Research on Vermont, 2002), 42.

42. "Corporal William Leach," Find a Grave, accessed June 15, 2020, findagrave.com /memorial/13533352/william-h-leach.

43. Lieutenant Leach to Ann Leach, March 26, 1864 in *Dear Wife*, 192.

44. H. W. Rivers, "Embalming the Dead—a Process Practicable to All," *New York Times*, December 26, 1862.

45. Book, "Death Is Every Where Present," 46.

46. Rivers, "Embalming the Dead—a Process Practicable to All."

47. Andrew Boyd, ed., *Boyd's Washington and Georgetown Directory* (Washington, DC: Hudson Taylor, 1864), 329.

48. "An Embalming Operation," *Evening Star* (Washington, DC), April 21, 1863.

49. Faust, *This Republic of Suffering*, 107.

50. "An Embalming Operation."

51. "Burying Soldiers—Embalming the Dead," *Cadiz Sentinel* (Cadiz, OH), December 24, 1862; "How Bodies Are Embalmed," *Times-Democrat* (New Orleans, LA), November 28, 1864.

52. Steven Lee Carson, "The Civil War Mortician," *American Funeral Director* 92, no. 4 (April 1970): 30.

53. Carson, "Civil War Mortician," 30.

54. "An Embalming Operation."

55. Carson, "Civil War Mortician," 30.

56. "An Embalming Operation"; Carson, "Civil War Mortician," 30–31.

57. Lieutenant Gen. Grant order January 9, 1865, RG94, Entry 2.1, "Letters Received," National Archives and Records Administration; *The Miscellaneous Documents of the House of Representatives for the Second Session of the Fifty-Third Congress 1893–'94* (Washington, DC: Government Printing Office, 1895), 76, books.google.com/books?id=OiQ2AQAAIAAJ.

58. *Miscellaneous Documents of the House of Representatives*, 76.

59. War Department, General Order 39, March 15, 1865, courtesy of the National Museum of Civil War Medicine.

60. "To Petrify Human Bodies," *Brooklyn (NY) Daily Eagle*, July 9, 1895; "Tried to Kill His Wife," *Brooklyn (NY) Daily Eagle*, May 12, 1896.

61. "Tried to Kill His Wife."

62. Christina R. Tyler and Andrea M. Allan, "The Effects of Arsenic Exposure on Neurological and Cognitive Dysfunction in Human and Rodent Studies: A Review," *Current Environmental Health Report* 1 (2014): 132–47, ncbi.nlm.nih.gov /pmc/articles/PMC4026128.

63. "Tried to Kill His Wife."

64. "Tried to Kill His Wife."

65. Matthew S. Lautzenheiser, *Legendary Locals of Dover* (Charleston, SC: Arcadia Publishing, 2013), 23.

66. "W. R. Cornelius Passes Away," *The Tennessean*, February 20, 1910.

67. *The Casket*, July 1892, as quoted by Robert W. Habenstein and William M. Lamers, *The History of American Funeral Directing*, 8th ed. (Brookfield, WI: National Funeral Directors Association, 2014), 210.

68. "W. R. Cornelius, Government Undertaker," *Nashville Daily Union*, January 24, 1864.

69. *The Casket*, July 1892, as quoted by Habenstein and Lamers, *History of American Funeral Directing*, 211.

70. *The Casket*, July 1892, as quoted by Habenstein and Lamers, *History of American Funeral Directing*, 211.

71. Edward C. and Gail R. Johnson, "Prince Greer, America's First Negro Embalmer," *Liaison Bulletin*, International Federation of Thanatopractic Associations (April 1973), as quoted by Habenstein and Lamers, *History of American Funeral Directing*, 211.

72. Van Beck, Inman, and McCormick, "History of Civil War Embalming."

73. "W. R. Cornelius Passes Away."

74. Van Beck, Inman, and McCormick, "History of Civil War Embalming."

75. "Dead Embalmer Wants No Embalming," *New-York Tribune*, January 1, 1900.

CHAPTER 7: GONE TO THEIR SLEEP

1. "Stories by the Titanic's Survivors," *Newport (TN) Plain Talk*, April 25, 1912.

2. "Summer Mourning, Comfortable, yet Correct," *Evening Star* (Washington, DC), May 26, 1912.

3. Emily Post, *Etiquette in Society, in Business, in Politics and at Home* (New York: Funk & Wagnalls, 1922; New York: Bartleby.com, 1999).

4. "Mourning Colors," *The Casket* 22, no. 6 (June 1897): 23.

5. Bertram S. Puckle, *Funeral Customs: Their Origin and Development* (London: T. W. Laurie, 1926; Global Grey, 2019), 63. Citations refer to Global Grey edition.

6. "Astor's Widow Will Wear White," *Washington Herald* (Washington, DC), May 22, 1912.

7. Puckle, *Funeral Customs*, 63; Post, *Etiquette in Society, in Business, in Politics and at Home*.

8. Puckle, *Funeral Customs*, 63.

9. "Mrs. Astor to Wear White 'Mourning,'" *Evening Journal* (Wilmington, DE), May 24, 1912.

10. "Mrs. Astor to Wear White 'Mourning.'"

11. "Mrs. Astor to Wear White 'Mourning.'"

12. Irene Clepper, "Gone but Not Forgotten: Designing for Death: Dr. Timothy Blade's Display at the University of Minnesota," *Dodge Magazine* 75, no. 4 (September 1983): 4.

13. Clepper, "Gone but Not Forgotten," 4.

14. "The Etiquette of Crape," *The Sunnyside* 4, no. 36 (July 1888).

15. Carl Lewis Barnes, *The Art and Science of Embalming* (Chicago: Trade Periodical, 1896), 365.

16. Alter Ego Manufacturing Company advertisement, *The Casket* 19, no. 2, (February 1894).

17. Barnes, *Art and Science of Embalming*, 365.

18. Frederick & Trump. Corpse cooler. US Patent 4,504, May 9, 1846.

19. Jason Engler, Facebook direct message to author, April 4, 2020.

20. "Public Opinion," *The Casket* 19, no. 2 (February 1894): 9.

21. "History of the Cemetery," Grove Street Cemetery, accessed March 15, 2020, grovestreetcemetery.org/history-cemetery.

22. Stanley French, "The Cemetery as Cultural Institution: The Establishment of Mount Auburn and the 'Rural Cemetery' Movement," in *Death in America*, ed. David E. Stannard (Philadelphia: University of Pennsylvania Press, 1975), 75.

23. French, "The Cemetery as Cultural Institution," 75.

24. French, "The Cemetery as Cultural Institution," 75.

25. "Mount Auburn Cemetery, a 19th Century Tourist Attraction," New England Historical Society, accessed March 26, 2020, newenglandhistoricalsociety.com /mount-auburn-cemetery-19th-century-tourist-attraction/.

26. Emmeline Stuart-Wortley, *Travels in the United States, Etc., During 1849 and 1850* (New York: Harper & Brothers, 1851), 47.

27. Stuart-Wortley, *Travels in the United States*, 47.

28. Stuart-Wortley, 47.

29. Stuart-Wortley, 48.

30. Martin Duberman, *James Russell Lowell* (Boston: Beacon Press, 1966), 192.

31. Nathaniel Dearborn, *A Concise History of, and Guide Through Mount Auburn* (Boston: Nathaniel Dearborn, 1843), 18.

32. James Farrell, *Inventing the American Way of Death* (Philadelphia: Temple University Press, 1980), 112.

33. "Green-Wood Carriage Service," *The Casket* 2, no. 6 (June 1877): 4.

34. Charles Cist, comp., *The Cincinnati Miscellany of Antiquities of the West: And Pioneer History and General and Local Statistics*, vol. 2 (Cincinnati, OH: Robinson & Jones, 1846), 85.

35. Farrell, *Inventing the American Way of Death*, 101.

36. Dearborn, *Concise History of, and Guide Through Mount Auburn*, 3; "Mount Auburn Consecrated," Mount Auburn Cemetery (website), accessed March 21, 2020, mountauburn.org/consecration/.

37. "Mount Auburn Consecrated," accessed March 21, 2020, mountauburn.org /consecration/.

38. Joseph Story, *An Address Delivered on the Dedication at the Cemetery at Mount Auburn, September 24, 1831* (Boston: Joseph T. & Edwin Buckingham, 1831), 6–7.

39. John A. Warder, "Landscape Gardening for the Cemetery," *The Casket* 6, no. 5, (May 1881): 3.

40. Farrell, *Inventing the American Way of Death*, 110.

41. Farrell, 113.

42. Puckle, *Funeral Customs*, 123.

43. Puckle, 123.

44. Todd W. Van Beck, "The History of Funeral Flowers," *Dodge Magazine* 99, no. 1 (Winter 2007): 27.

45. "Many Mourn George," *Waterbury (CT) Democrat*, November 1, 1897.

46. "Many Mourn George."

47. "Many Mourn George."

48. "Tributes of Flowers," *Boston Globe*, March 10, 1896.

49. "Tributes of Flowers."

50. "Beautiful Floral Tributes," *Evening Star* (Washington, DC), December 31, 1886.

51. "Funeral of Mrs. Edward Cooper," *New-York Tribune*, March 23, 1894.

52. Jessie Boies Obituary, *Morning Democrat* (Davenport, IA), January 3, 1894; "Obsequies of Miss Jessie Boies," *Courier* (Waterloo, IA), January 5, 1894.

53. "The Funeral," *New-York Tribune*, January 5, 1877.

54. "Floral Vulgarity," *San Francisco Chronicle*, November 22, 1891.

55. "Floral Vulgarity."

56. "At the House and Church," *New-York Tribune*, January 8, 1877.

57. Puckle, *Funeral Customs*, 121.

58. Todd W. Van Beck, "The Value and Benefit of Funeral Flowers," *Dodge Magazine* 99, no. 2 (Spring 2007): 30.

59. "The First Photographs of US Presidents," PetaPixel, accessed April 13, 2020, petapixel.com/2012/06/05/the-first-photographs-of-us-presidents/.

60. Arthur David Hosterman, *Life and Times of James Abram Garfield* (Springfield, OH: Farm and Fireside, 1882), 187.

61. Hosterman, *Life and Times of James Abram Garfield*, 187.

62. Aristotle, as quoted by Joe Smoke, "The Soul & Its Substitutes," in *Beyond the Dark Veil: Post-Mortem & Mourning Photography from the Thanatos Archive*, 3rd ed. (Fullerton: California State University, 2015), 24.

63. Smoke, "The Soul & Its Substitutes," 27.

64. Nancy West, "Pictures of Death, *The Atlantic*, July 19, 2017, theatlantic.com /technology/archive/2017/07/pictures-of-death/534060/.

65. Melissa DeVelvis, "Death, Immortalized: Victorian Post-Mortem Photography," Clara Barton Missing Soldiers Museum, accessed February 19, 2019, clarabartonmuseum.org/post-mortem-photography/.

66. *Photographic Times and American Photographer*, vol. 12, as quoted in Chris Woodyard, *The Victorian Book of the Dead* (Dayton, OH: Kestrel 2014), 162–63.

67. *Cincinnati (OH) Post*, January 20, 1910, as quoted by Woodyard, *Victorian Book of the Dead*, 156.

68. Unknown undertaker addressing the sixth annual Northwest Funeral Directors Association Meeting, *Sunnyside* 23, no. 12 (December 1893): 6.

CHAPTER 8: RESURRECTIONISTS

1. Howard Wilcox Haggard, *Devils, Drugs, and Doctors: The Story of the Science of Healing from Medicine Men to Doctor* (London: William Heinemann, 1913), 130–31.

2. Sidney Young, *The Annals of the Barber-Surgeons of London* (London: Blades, East, & Blades, 1890), 301.

3. Haggard, *Devils, Drugs, and Doctors*, 152.

4. Haggard, 151.

5. Haggard, 153.

6. *Pennsylvania Gazette* (Philadelphia, PA), October 24, 1765.

7. *Pennsylvania Gazette* (Philadelphia, PA), October 24, 1765.

8. Bess Lovejoy, "The Gory New York City Riot That Shaped American Medicine," *Smithsonian Magazine*, June 17, 2014, smithsonianmag.com/history/gory-new -york-city-riot-shaped-american-medicine-180951766/.

9. Haggard, *Devils, Drugs, and Doctors*, 153.

10. "New-York, April 15," *Pennsylvania Packet* (Philadelphia, PA), April 18, 1788.

11. "New-York, April 15."

12. "New-York, April 15."

13. "Philadelphia, April 19," *Pennsylvania Packet* (Philadelphia, PA), April 19, 1788.

14. "Great Excitement at Cleveland," *Charleston Courier* (Charleston, SC), February 21, 1852.

15. "Cleveland, Feb. 19," *Buffalo (NY) Morning Express and Illustrated Buffalo (NY) Express*, February 20, 1852; "Great Excitement at Cleveland," *Charleston Courier* (Charleston, SC), February 21, 1852.

16. "Great Excitement at Cleveland."

17. "Mob in Cleveland—College Partially Destroyed," *Detroit Free Press*, February 18, 1852.

18. D. H. Beckwith, *History of the Cleveland Homeopathic College 1850 to 1880* (Cleveland, OH: s.n., 1880), 12, babel.hathitrust.org/cgi/pt?id=osu .32435012562633&view=1up&seq=14.

19. *Laws of the State of New York: Passed at the Sessions of the Legislature Held in the Years 1777–1801, Being the First Twenty-Four Sessions*, vol. 3 (Albany: Weed, Parsons and Company, 1887), 5, books.google.com?id=RuATAAAAYAAJ&pg.

20. Todd W. Van Beck, "The Grave Robbers," *Dodge Magazine* 101, no. 1 (Winter 2009): 27.

21. "Intriguing Stories of Body-Snatching," *Gazette* (Montreal, Quebec, Canada), August 1, 1935; "Edinburgh Murders. Life of Burke the Murderer," *Lancaster (UK) Gazette*, February 7, 1829.

22. "A Son Finds His Father's Body on a Dissecting Table," *Brooklyn (NY) Daily Eagle*, May 31, 1878.

23. "Human Hyenas," *Cincinnati (OH) Enquirer*, May 31, 1878.

24. "An Outrageous Affair in Ohio," *Sunbury Gazette* (Sunbury, PA), June 7, 1878.

25. Todd W. Van Beck, "The Harrison Horror, Grave Robbing and the Invention of the Burial Vault," provided to author via email April 28, 2020. Previously published in *Canadian Funeral News* (October and November 2013) and as an INFDA document.

26. "Human Hyenas."

27. "Human Hyenas."

28. "Human Hyenas."

29. "An Outrageous Affair in Ohio"; "Human Hyenas."

30. "Human Hyenas."

31. "Human Hyenas."

32. "The Body-Snatchers," *Boston Post*, June 1, 1878.

33. "The Horrible Act of Body Snatching," *Boston Post*, June 1, 1878.

34. Some sources say Benjamin Harrison hired the watchman for a month. A week would have been sufficient time for resurrectionists' interest in Scott Harrison to wane as stated in "Human Ghouls," *Star Tribune* (Minneapolis, MN), June 1, 1878.

35. Van Beck, "Harrison Horror."

36. "A Ghastly Horror," *Wheeling (WV) Daily Register*, June 15, 1878.

37. "The Grave Robbers," *Detroit Free Press*, June 15, 1878.

38. "A Ghastly Horror."

39. "Body Snatching," *Detroit Free Press*, June 16, 1878.

40. Van Beck, "Harrison Horror."

41. Van Beck, "Harrison Horror."

42. Alembert W. Brayton, ed., "Restrictions to Medical Education in Indianapolis," *Indiana Medical Journal* 21, no. 5 (Nov. 1902), as quoted in *Indiana Medical Journal I–XIX,* 212, google.com/books/edition/Indiana_Medical_Journal/jpBXAAAAMAAJ?hl.

43. Philip K. Clover. Improvement in coffin-torpedoes. US Patent 208,672, filed June 29, 1878, and issued October 8, 1878.

44. Thomas N. Howell. Grave-torpedo. US Patent 251,231, filed October 24, 1881, and issued December 20, 1881.

45. "The Torpedo of the Grave," *Norfolk Virginian*, December 6, 1878.

46. Howell, Grave-torpedo.

47. "Torpedo Coffin," *The Casket* 6, no. 5 (May 1881): 6.

48. "A Grave Story," *Philadelphia Inquirer*, January 20, 1881; "Grave Robber Killed," *Jackson County Banner* (Brownstown, IN), January 27, 1881.

49. Advertisement for Boyd's Burglar-Proof Grave Vault in Columbus Coffin Company's illustrated catalog, 1882.

50. "Burglar Proof Grave," *Sunnyside* 26, no. 10 (October 1896): 7.

51. Todd W. Van Beck, "Ulysses S. Grant" (unpublished manuscript in author's possession, June 1, 2020), PDF file.

52. "History," Wilbert (website), accessed August 17, 2020, wilbert.com/about/history/.

53. "Pullman's Will Read," *Sun* (Wilmington, DE), October 26, 1897.

54. "Farmers Burned the Men in Effigy," *Indianapolis News*, April 23, 1903; "Ghoul Is Guilty," *Pittsburgh Press*, April 24, 1903.

55. "Ghoul Is Guilty," *Pittsburgh Press*, April 24, 1903.

56. "Fate of Alexander," *Indianapolis Journal*, February 12, 1903.

57. Even the paper called Cantrell's explanation of turning state's evidence "wonderfully weird." "Grave Robber's Story," *Passaic Daily News* (Passaic, NJ), February 4, 1903.

58. "Graves of 1,200 Are Robbed by Ghouls for Pay," *Bureau County Tribune* (Princeton, IL), February 13, 1903.

59. "Ghouls Are Indicted," *Indianapolis Journal*, October 26, 1902.

60. "Juror White's Illness," *Indianapolis Journal*, February 14, 1903.

61. "Cantrell's Busy Day," *Indianapolis Journal*, February 6, 1903.

62. "Hunting for Bodies," *Indianapolis Journal*, October 3, 1902.

63. "Graves of 1,200 Are Robbed by Ghouls for Pay."

64. Dr. S. L. Foote's name is misspelled as I. N. Foote, as it is in several other publications. "Wills His Body to Science," *Sunnyside* 26, no. 10 (October 1896): 20.

65. "Wills His Body to Science," 20.

66. "Dr. S. L. N. Foote," *Argentine Republic* (Argentine, KS), August 21, 1902. The *Kansas City Medical Index-Lancet* 23, no. 9, in their September 1902 (p. 333) issue, confirms Foote's death in Argentine, Kansas, on August 20.

67. National Conference of Commissioners on Uniform State Laws, "Revised Anatomical Gift Act (2006)," 115th Annual Conference, Hilton Head, SC, 3.

CHAPTER 9: VESSELS OF THE DEAD

1. "Only a Sleep," *Boston Globe*, December 22, 1889; "Ready for His Casket," *Boston Globe*, November 8, 1888.

2. "Ready for His Casket."

3. "Ready for His Casket." The description of Hiller's casket is culled from this article, though the article goes into much greater depth describing the minutiae of Hiller's casket.

4. "Only a Sleep"; "Dr. Hiller at Rest," *Boston Globe*, November 12, 1888.

5. "Only a Sleep."

6. "Only a Sleep."

7. "Only a Sleep."

8. "Only a Sleep."

9. This version gives the entire story of the Hiller saga: Ann Berghaus, Carolyn Harris, ed., "Hiller Family Story," Wilmington Memorial Library, accessed June 3, 2020, wilmlibrary.org/hiller/.

10. "Death's Pomp," *Boston Globe*, December 9, 1889.

11. Egypt exhibit, National Museum of Funeral History, Houston, TX, author notes October 21, 2020.

12. "Ancient Roman Funerals," *Shadyside* 1, no. 3 (November 1891): 3.

13. William Andrews, *Old Church Lore* (London: William Andrews, 1891), 218–19, books.google.com/books/about/Old_Church_Lore.html?id=RTw9AAAAYAAJ. There is debate on whether King Arthur was an actual historical figure. Regardless if his existence was mythologized, burial in hollowed-out logs during that time period wasn't uncommon, according to Robert W. Habenstein and William M. Lamers, *The History of American Funeral Directing*, 8th ed. (Brookfield, WI: National Funeral Directors Association, 2014), 72.

14. Bertram S. Puckle, *Funeral Customs: Their Origin and Development* (London: T. W. Laurie, 1926; Global Grey, 2019), 27. Citations refer to Global Grey edition.

15. Genesis 50:26 (King James Version).

16. Julian Litten, *The English Way of Death: The Common Funeral Since 1450* (London: Robert Hale, 1991), 86.

17. Habenstein and Lamers, *History of American Funeral Directing*, 71

18. Brent W. Tharp, "'Preserving Their Form and Features': The Role of Coffins in the American Understanding of Death, 1607–1870" (PhD diss., William & Mary, 1996), 54.

19. Tharp, "Preserving Their Form and Features," 157.

20. Almond D. Fisk. Improvement in coffins. US Patent 5,920, issued November 14, 1848.

21. Fisk. Improvement in coffins.

22. "Crane & Breed," Coachbuilt website, accessed July 13, 2020, coachbuilt.com/bui /c/crane_breed/crane_breed.htm; "Important Discovery," *Jeffersonian* (Stroudsburg, PA), March 22, 1849.

23. Willie P. Mangum et al. to Fisk and Raymond, Washington, April 5, 1850, printed in *New Orleans Crescent*, June 7, 1850.

24. Average wood prices are a comparison of John L. Beard's and T. J. Atkins's average prices in 1850 from appendix D and E in Tharp, "Preserving Their Form and Features," 239–40; the Fisk price is from the *New York Daily Tribune*, October 30, 1850.

25. Scott Warnasch, email message to the author, July 17, 2020.

26. Warnasch, email message to the author, July 17, 2020.

27. *Boyertown Cast Iron Catalog* (ca. 1928), National Museum of Funeral History, Houston, TX.

28. Warnasch, email message to the author, July 17, 2020.

29. Warnasch, email message to the author, July 17, 2020.

30. Tharp, "Preserving Their Form and Features," 204.

31. Tharp, 205

32. A.C. Barstow. Burial case. US Patent 23,652, issued April 19, 1859.

33. Crane, Breed & Co. catalog, as quoted by Tharp, "Preserving Their Form and Features," 199.

34. Habenstein and Lamers, *History of American Funeral Directing*, 170.

35. Nathaniel Hawthorne, *Our Old Home*, vol. 1 (London: Smith, Elder, 1863), 138, books.google.com/books?id=QwMzAAAYAAJ&printsec.

36. William Tebb and Edward Perry Vollum, *Premature Burial and How It May Be Prevented*, 2nd ed. by Walter R. Hadwen (London: Swan Sonnenschein, 1905), 45.

37. Death Notices, *Charleston (SC) Courier*, May 4, 1852.

38. On Edisto Beach's website, the legend of Julia Legare isn't presented as anything more than a fun tourist legend, though this version is a good representation of the myth. "The Legend of Julia Legare," Edisto Beach (website), accessed July 10, 2020, edistobeach.com/the-legend-of-julia-legare/.

39. Tebb and Vollum, *Premature Burial*, 18.

40. Jan Bondeson, *Buried Alive: The Terrifying History of Our Most Primal Fear* (New York: W. W. Norton, 2001), 188.

41. Tebb and Vollum, *Premature Burial*, 35.

42. Tebb and Vollum, 41, 59.

43. *St. Louis Globe-Democrat*, as quoted in "Preparing to Bury a Living Man," *Shroud* 2, no. 12 (August 1882): 5.

44. Bondeson, *Buried Alive*, 144–45.

45. "Peculiar Burial Customs," *The Casket* 28, no. 9 (September 1903): 9.

46. Tebb and Vollum, *Premature Burial*, 263.

47. Dr. Icard in *La Presse Medicale*, August 17, 1904, as quoted by Tebb and Vollum, *Premature Burial*, 338.

48. Jackie Wullschlager, *Hans Christian Andersen: The Life of a Storyteller* (New York: Alfred A. Knopf, 2001), 199.

49. Wullschlager, *Hans Christian Andersen*, 440.

50. "Dr. Heuser's Strange Wish," *Philadelphia Inquirer*, January 24, 1891.

51. "Burial Alive," *Cincinnati (OH) Enquirer*, June 6, 1929.

52. Robert G. Mayer, *Embalming: History, Theory, and Practice*, 4th ed. (New York, McGraw-Hill, 2006), 116.

53. Mayer, *Embalming*, 116–17.

54. J. Deniker, "J. V. Laborde (1830–1903)," *Nature* 68 (June 4, 1903): 105–6, doi.org/10.1038/068105b0.

55. "Premature Burial Bill," *The Casket* 31, no. 5 (May 1906): 18.

56. Carl Lewis Barnes, *The Art and Science of Embalming* (Chicago: Trade Periodical, 1896), 6.

57. "Notable Case of Embalming," *The Casket* 30, no. 2 (February 1905): 12.

58. "The Art of Embalming: How the Dead Are Made to Look Lifelike by Fluids," *New York World*, February 26, 1888, as quoted by *American Funeral Director* 123, no. 1 (January 2000): 70.

59. Thomas Holmes to Hudson Samson, March 1, 1877, in Edward C. and Gail R. Johnson and Melissa Johnson-Williams, "Dr. Holmes's Method of Preserving Remains," *American Funeral Director* 112, no. 2 (February 1989): 48.

60. Christian H. Eisenbrandt. Coffin to be used in cases of doubtful burial. US Patent 3,335, issued November 15, 1843.

61. Christian H. Eisenbrandt. Coffin to be used in cases of doubtful burial.

62. Franz Vester. Improved burial-case. US Patent 81,437, filed July 9, 1868, and issued August 25, 1868.

63. "A Safety Coffin," *Sunnyside* 26, no. 10 (October 1896): 13.

64. Hubert Deveau. Grave-signal. US Patent 522,110, filed January 2, 1894, and issued June 26, 1894.

65. Tebb and Vollum, *Premature Burial*, 320.

66. Tebb and Vollum, 322.

67. "Premature Interment," *Bucyrus (OH) Evening Telegraph*, October 14, 1897.

68. "Signals from the Grave," *Evening Star* (Washington, DC), December 20, 1899; Clark Bell, ed., *Medico-Legal Journal* 17, no.1 (1899): 294–99.

69. Tebb and Vollum, *Premature Burial*, 322.

70. *Natural History of Pliny*, trans. John Bostock and H. T. Riley (London: Henry G. Bohn, 1855), 210.

CHAPTER 10: THE TEMPLE OF HONOR

1. "Cold in Death: Carter Harrison Shot by a Lunatic," *Morning Call* (San Francisco, CA), October 29, 1893.

2. "Chicago's Death Chief," *St. Paul (MN) Daily Globe*, October 30, 1893.

3. "Chicago's Death Chief."

4. "Chicago's Death Chief."

5. "Chicago's Death Chief."

6. "Chicago's Death Chief."

7. "Close of the Fair," *Indianapolis (IN) Journal* , October 31, 1893.

8. "Chicago's Death Chief."

9. "Chicago's Death Chief."

10. "To His Long Rest," *Iron County (MO) Register*, November 9, 1893.

11. "Will Be the Expensive Funeral Hearse," *Daily Public Ledger* (Maysville, KY), November 1, 1893, 3; Robert W. Habenstein and William M. Lamers, *The History of American Funeral Directing*, 8th ed. (Brookfield, WI: National Funeral Directors Association, 2014), 241–44.

12. "Chicago's Murdered Mayor," *Sunnyside* 23, no. 12 (December 1893): 20.

13. Josiah Seymour Currey and Juergen Beck, *Chicago: Its History and Its Builders,* vol. 5 (Altenmunster, Ger.: Jazzybee, 2015), 147–49.

14. "Will Be the Expensive Funeral Hearse."

15. Fifty thousand is based on sixty to eighty people passing the casket per minute. "The Honored Dead," *Iron County (MO) Register*, November 9, 1893.

16. "The Murdered Mayor," *Wilmington (DE) Daily Republican*, November 1, 1893.

17. "Chicago's Murdered Mayor," 20.

18. Habenstein and Lamers, *History of American Funeral Directing*, 241.

19. "To His Long Rest," *Iron County (MO) Register*, November 9, 1893.

20. "Our Tribute," *New York Herald*, April 26, 1865.

21. "Funeral Obsequies of Mr. Adams," *Weekly National Intelligencer* (Washington, DC), March 4, 1848.

22. "Pressing for a Look," *St. Louis (MO) Globe-Democrat*, August 7, 1885.

23. "Pressing for a Look."

24. "Borne from the Mountain," *Buffalo (NY) Weekly Express* (Buffalo, NY), August 6, 1885; "Bringing the Hero Home," *New York Times*, August 6, 1885.

25. "Bringing the Hero Home."

26. "The Last March," *Inter Ocean* (Chicago, IL), August 9, 1885.

27. Habenstein and Lamers, *History of American Funeral Directing*, 43.

28. Todd W. Van Beck, "The Grave Robbers," *Dodge Magazine* 101, no. 1 (Winter 2009): 29.

29. *Pennsylvania Gazette*, April 5, 1753, as quoted by Brent W. Tharp, "'Preserving Their Form and Features': The Role of Coffins in the American Understanding of Death, 1607–1870" (PhD diss., William & Mary, 1996), 88.

30. Walter McCall, *American Funeral Vehicles 1883–2003* (Hudson, WI: Iconografix, 2003), 9.

31. McCall, *American Funeral Vehicles*, 9–10.

32. McCall, 10.

33. McCall, 12.

34. McCall cites Thomas McPherson, funeral transportation historian, as identifying the first automobile cortege in McCall, *American Funeral Vehicles*, 15.

35. "Auto Funeral for Cabby Pruyn: Procession Will Whiz to Grave," *Inter Ocean* (Chicago, IL), January 14, 1909.

36. "Auto Hearse Quickly Made," *Chicago Tribune*, January 15, 1909.

37. "Beautiful Automobile Hearse May Soon Grace Los Angeles Funerals," *Los Angeles Evening Express*, February 13, 1909.

38. "Auto Funeral for Cabby Pruyn: Procession Will Whiz to Grave."

39. "A Splendid Pageant," *Baltimore Sun*, August 10, 1885.

40. "A Splendid Pageant."

41. Todd W. Van Beck, "Ulysses S. Grant" (unpublished manuscript in author's possession, June 1, 2020), PDF file.

42. McCall, *American Funeral Vehicles*, 6.

43. "A Funeral Car," *San Francisco Chronicle*, December 24, 1897; "A Useful Car," *Chicago Chronicle*, December 19, 1897.

44. "A Useful Car."

45. "A Useful Car."

46. McCall, *American Funeral Vehicles*, 18; Fred Hulberg. Combined hearse and passenger vehicle. US Patent 919,868, filed October 16, 1908, and issued April 27, 1909.

47. Todd W. Van Beck, *The Genius of Frank E. Campbell: The Story of How One Man Changed Funeral Service and Unwittingly Set the Stage for Movie Stars* (self-pub., CreateSpace, 2018), 36.

48. Todd Harra, "Waterman's Cortege," *Southern Calls* 24 (June 2019): 54.

CHAPTER 11: MOURNING THE GREAT WAR

1. "Principal Wars in Which the United States Participated—U.S. Military Personnel Serving and Casualties," Defense Casualty Analysis System, accessed October 7, 2020, dcas.dmdc.osd.mil/dcas/pages/report_principal_wars.xhtml.

2. "Mourning Jewelry," *Chattanooga (TN) Daily Times*, January 17, 1918.

3. "Our Military Strength," *Chattanooga (TN) Daily Times*, May 19, 1918.

4. "Mourning Jewelry."

5. "Woman's Committee, Council of National Defense," *Journal and Tribune* (Knoxville, TN), September 8, 1918.

6. "Mourning Ring Comes Back in Popular Favor," *Times* (Shreveport, LA), August 21, 1919.

7. "Mourning Ring Comes Back in Popular Favor."

8. "Mourning Jewelry."

9. John M. Barry, *The Great Influenza* (New York: Penguin, 2018), prologue, Kindle.

10. *The Embalmer's Monthly*, January 1919, as quoted by Bill Werner, "A History of the 1918–1919 Flu Epidemic from a Funeral Service Perspective—Part II," *Dodge Magazine* 112, no. 4 (Fall 2020): 22–25.

11. "Camden Needs More Doctors and Nurses," *Philadelphia Inquirer*, October 15, 1918.

12. "Student Grave Diggers," *Lancaster (PA) Examiner*, October 12, 1918.

13. "Grave Diggers Are Greatly Overworked," *Reading (PA) Times*, October 18, 1918.

14. Thomas M. O'Brien and Oliver Diefendorf, *General Orders of the War Department Embracing the Years 1861, 1862 & 1863*, vol. 1 (New York: Derby & Miller, 1864), 248.

15. 37th Cong., 2nd Sess. 199, 200, *An Act to Define the Pay and Emoluments of Certain Officers of the Army, and for Other Purposes*, Sec. 18, Library of Congress.

16. O'Brien and Diefendorf, *General Orders of the War Department*, 158.

17. "Engineer on Gen. Kelley's Staff," *Wheeling (WV) Daily Intelligencer*, August 5, 1863.

18. "Interesting to the Military," *Daily True Delta* (New Orleans, LA), October 26, 1864.

19. "Evening Dispatches," *Courier Journal*, October 11, 1864; "Interesting to the Military."

20. "John Rodgers Meigs, First Lieutenant, United States Army," Arlington National Cemetery Website, accessed October 19, 2020, arlingtoncemetery.net/jrmeigs.htm.

21. "Care for the Graves of Soldiers," *Baltimore (MD) Sun*, December 28, 1865.

22. *Report of the United States Army to the Secretary of War for the Year Ending June 30, 1865* (Washington, DC: Government Printing Office, 1865), 177; "Principal Wars," Defense Casualty Analysis System.

23. Edward Steere, *The Graves Registration Service in World War II*, QMC Historical Studies, no. 21 (Washington, DC: Government Printing Office, 1951), 9. Courtesy of Hathi Trust.

24. Steere, *Graves Registration Service in World War II*, 9. Steere wrote that 26,125 Union soldiers weren't accounted for by 1870, but that was based on an 1866 number of 342,000 estimated deaths. The current Defense Casualty Analysis System puts that number over 360,000, meaning closer to 44,000 soldiers weren't accounted for, and likely pushes the percentage of unidentified higher.

25. Steere, *Graves Registration Service in World War II*, 10.

26. Steere, 10.

27. "Purple Cross Will Send Home Soldiers Who Fall in Europe," *Daily Advocate* (Victoria, TX), August 1, 1917.

28. "Purple Cross Body Formed," *Daily Times* (Davenport, IA), August 27, 1917.

29. "Purple Cross Will Send Home Soldiers Who Fall in Europe."

30. *Lindsborg (KS) News*, August 17, 1917; *Muscatine (IA) Journal*, November 22, 1917.

31. "Purple Cross Is Working to Insure [*sic*] That Bodies of Fallen Heroes Come Home," *Montgomery (AL) Advertiser*, July 29, 1917.

32. Steere, *Graves Registration Service in World War II*, 13.

33. "Pershing Against Removal of Dead," *Washington Post*, August 24, 1919.

34. This interview was widely published. C. E. Rodgers, "First Gold Star War Mother Hopes and Prays for Return of His Body," *Brisbee (AZ) Daily Review*, May 30, 1919.

35. "Plans Outlined to Obtain Bodies of Dead Soldiers," *Pittsburgh Post-Gazette*, November 8, 1919.

36. Blanche K. Wheeler, "The Soldier Dead," *New-York Tribune*, February 13, 1920.

37. "Colonel Glad to Give Son to Nation," *Boston Post*, July 18, 1918.

38. "Was a Visit of Thrills, *Sun* (Pittsburg, KS), September 19, 1918.

39. "Life of Theodore Roosevelt in Brief: President at 42; Got Record Vote," *Chicago Tribune*, January 7, 1919.

40. Carolyn Vance Bell, *Missoulian* (Missoula, MT), June 20, 1920.

41. "Plans Outlined to Obtain Bodies of Dead Soldiers."

42. "War Mothers Talk of Returning Dead," *Town Talk* (Alexandria, LA), October 3, 1919.

43. "To Bring Yank Heroes Home," *Akron (OH) Beacon Journal*, January 14, 1920.

44. Rodgers, "First Gold Star War Mother Hopes and Prays for Return of His Body."

45. "Gold Stars," *Cincinnati (OH) Enquirer*, July 11, 1921.

46. Gary Laderman, *Rest in Peace: A Cultural History of Death and the Funeral Home in Twentieth-Century America* (New York: Oxford University Press, 2003), 53.

47. Thomas J. Bonniwell, *We Have to Die* (New York: Worthington Press, 1940), 19.

48. Steere, *Graves Registration Service in World War II*, 13.

49. "The Unknown Soldier of World War I State Funeral: 23 October-11 November 1921," Arlington National Cemetery (website), accessed November 9, 2020, arlingtoncemetery.net/unk-wwi.htm. The figure of 1.1 percent is a percentage of total WWI deaths. As a percentage of battle deaths (53,402), it's twice as much, 2.3 percent.

50. "The Unknown Soldier of World War I State Funeral."

51. "Alone with the Dead, Sergeant Selects U.S. 'Unknown Soldier,'" *Princeton (IN) Daily Clarion*, October 25, 1921.

52. "Alone with the Dead, Sergeant Selects U.S. 'Unknown Soldier.'"

53. "Alone with the Dead, Sergeant Selects U.S. 'Unknown Soldier.'"

54. "Unknown Hero Body Started on Way to U.S.," *New-York Tribune*, October 25, 1921; "Alone with the Dead, Sergeant Selects U.S. 'Unknown Soldier.'"

55. "Unknown Hero Body Started on Way to U.S."

56. "Mountains of Flowers Laid at Bier of Fallen Warrior," *Evening Star* (Washington, DC) November 11, 1921.

57. "Nation's Nameless Hero Now Rests in Arlington," *Standard Union* (Brooklyn, NY), November 11, 1921.

58. "Nation to Halt Two Minutes at Sound of Bugle," *Charlotte (NC) Observer*, November 5, 1921.

59. Todd W. Van Beck, *The Genius of Frank E. Campbell: The Story of How One Man Changed Funeral Service and Unwittingly Set the Stage for Movie Stars* (self-pub., CreateSpace, 2018), 5.

60. Van Beck, *Genius of Frank E. Campbell*, 12–13.

61. Van Beck, 17.

62. Berthold A. Baer, "Ask Fifty Thousand," *Evening World* (New York, NY), January 23, 1920.

63. *New-York Tribune*, December 11, 1920.

64. "J. William Lee's Undertaking Establishment," *Evening Times* (Washington, DC), April 20, 1896.

65. "The Latest News in Real Estate," *Philadelphia Inquirer*, January 3, 1907.

66. Berthold Baer, "The Doer," *New-York Tribune*, March 14, 1920.

67. Van Beck, *Genius of Frank E. Campbell*, 16.

68. Van Beck, 14.

69. "J. William Lee's Undertaking Establishment"; "The Latest News in Real Estate."

CHAPTER 12: FLAME BURIAL

1. Richard B. Morris, introduction to *A Letter from Henry Laurens to His Son John Laurens August 14, 1776*, foreword by Alfred C. Berol (New York: Columbia University Press, 1964), 14.

2. Morris, *Letter from Henry Laurens*, 14; "Henry Laurens," National Park Service, accessed October 6, 2019, nps.gov/chpi/learn/historyculture/henry-laurens.htm.

3. "Henry Laurens," National Park Service.

4. Sara Bertha Townsend, *An American Soldier: The Life of John Laurens* (Raleigh, NC: Edwards & Broughton, 1958), 10.

5. Townsend, *American Soldier*, 14.

6. Townsend, 14.

7. "Baron De Palm's Request, His Remains to Be Cremated on Wednesday," *New York Times*, December 4, 1876.

8. "Baron De Palm's Request, His Remains to Be Cremated on Wednesday."

9. Todd W. Van Beck, *The Story of Cremation* (self-pub., CreateSpace, 2016), 7.

10. Van Beck, *Story of Cremation*, 7.

11. Larry Whitaker, "Should We Install a Crematory?" *Dodge Magazine* 82, no. 5 (November/December 1990): 10–11.

12. Martin P. Nilsson, *The Minoan-Mycenaean Religion and Its Survival in Greek Religion*, as quoted by Robert W. Habenstein and William M. Lamers, *The History of American Funeral Directing*, 8th ed. (Brookfield, WI: National Funeral Directors Association, 2014), 18.

13. Bertram S. Puckle, *Funeral Customs: Their Origin and Development* (London: T. W. Laurie, 1926; Global Grey, 2019), 175. Citations refer to Global Grey edition.

14. Virgil, *Aeneid*, trans. Frederick Holland Dewey (New York: Translation Publishing Company, 1917), 271.

15. Virgil, *Aeneid*, 271.

16. Whitaker, "Should We Install a Crematory?" 10–11.

17. Van Beck, *Story of Cremation*, 16.

18. Tacitus, *The Annals of Imperial Rome*, trans. J. Jackson, vol. 5 (Cambridge: Harvard University Press, 1937), bk. 15, penelope.uchicago.edu/Thayer/E/Roman/Texts/Tacitus/Annals/15B*.html.

19. Van Beck, *Story of Cremation*, 17.

20. Paul Keresztes, "The Massacre at Lugdunum in 177 A.D.," *Historia: Zeitschrift Für Alte Geschichte* 16, no. 1 (1967): 75–86, jstor.org/stable/4434968.

21. Ed Hinson and Dan Mitchell, *The Popular Encyclopedia of Church History* (Eugene, OR: Harvest House, 2013), 358.

22. Van Beck, *Story of Cremation*, 20.

23. Colleen Murphy, ed., *Cremation Standards for Funeral Service Professionals* (Brookfield, WI: National Funeral Directors Association, 2015), 7.

24. Van Beck, *Story of Cremation*, 22.

25. Edward J. Trelawny, intro. by Edward Dowden, *Trelawny's Recollections of the Last Days of Shelley and Byron* (London: H. Frowde, 1906), 88. Courtesy of Hathi Trust.

26. Trelawny, *Recollections of the Last Days of Shelley and Byron*, 88–89.

27. Trelawny, 88.

28. Dale Bailey, "Cromwell's Head, Poe's Bones, and Other Grave Curiosities," *Dodge Magazine* 100, no. 4 (Fall 2008): 31.

29. Lodovico Brunetti, *Cremazione dei Cadaveri*, 1873. Cremation Association of North America Collection at John Crerar Library, University of Chicago.

30. Jason Engler, email correspondence with author, January 26, 2021.

31. Professor Brande, as quoted by Edwin Chadwick, *A Report of a Special Inquiry Into the Practice of Interment in Towns* (Philadelphia: C. Sherman, 1845), 30–31.

32. "Cremation," *Sunday Times* (Chicago, IL), February 1, 1874.

33. Engler, email correspondence with author, January 26, 2021.

34. "The LeMoyne Crematory," Washington County Historical Society (website), accessed April 14, 2021, wchspa.org/creamatory [*sic*].

35. "Report of the Proceedings of the Cremation Association of America, 1939; Cremation Association of North America," as quoted by Jason Engler, email correspondence with author, February 2, 2021.

36. "The Latest Cremation," *Philadelphia Inquirer*, February 15, 1878.

37. "The Baron Burned," *The Times* (Philadelphia, PA), December 7, 1876; "Baron de Palm's Body," *Rochester (NY) Democrat and Chronicle*, November 23, 1876.

38. "The Latest Cremation."

39. "A Theosophical Funeral: The Baron de Palm to Be Buried According to Egyptian Rites," *New York Herald*, May 27, 1876.

40. "A Theosophical Funeral."

41. "A Theosophical Funeral."

42. Henry Steel Olcott, old diary leaves, 1941, Theosophical Publishing House, as quoted by Jason Engler, email correspondence with author, April 27, 2021.

43. Engler, email correspondence with author, January 26, 2021.

44. "The Von [*sic*] Palm Cremation," *New York Herald*, May 20, 1876.

45. "To-day's Corpse Roasting," *Wheeling (WV) Daily Register*, December 6, 1876; "Baron Von [*sic*] Palm's Body, *New York Herald*, November 29, 1876.

46. "The Funeral of the Late Baron de Palm," *Boston Daily Advertiser*, May 29, 1876.

47. Puckle, *Funeral Customs*, 52.

48. "A Queer Funeral: Services Held Over the Remains of Baron de Palm Yesterday," *New York Herald*, May 29, 1876.

49. "The Funeral of the Late Baron de Palm," *Boston Daily Advertiser*, May 29, 1876.

50. "A Queer Funeral."

51. "The Funeral of the Late Baron de Palm."

52. "The Von [*sic*] Palm Cremation."

53. "Ashes to Ashes: Baron De Palm's Body Cremated," *Boston Evening Journal*, December 7, 1876.

54. "To-Day's Corpse Roasting."

55. "To-Day's Corpse Roasting."

56. "A Cremation Pilgrimage: Preparations for Burning the Remains of Baron de Palm," *New York Herald*, December 6, 1876.

57. "Ashes to Ashes: Baron De Palm's Body Cremated."

58. "Ashes to Ashes: Baron De Palm's Body Cremated."

59. "The Baron Burned," *The Times* (Philadelphia, PA), December 7, 1876.

60. "The Baron Burned."

61. "Ashes to Ashes: Baron De Palm's Body Cremated."

62. Jason Engler, personal interview with the author, December 19, 2019.

63. *Manual of Standard Crematory-Columbarium Practices*, as quoted by Jason Engler, "Cremated Remains: A History," *The Cremation Logs*, May 9, 2018, Cremation Association of North America, cremationassociation.org/blogpost/776820/301401/Cremated-Remains-A-History.

64. F. Julius LeMoyne, introduction to "Cremation: An Argument to Prove That Cremation Is Preferable to Inhumation of Dead Bodies" (Pittsburgh: EW Lightner, 1878).

65. Engler, personal interview with the author, December 19, 2019.

66. "Cremation," *Eureka (NV) Daily Sentinel*, August 5, 1877.

67. "The Cremation of the Late Dr. Winslow," *Rutland (VT) Daily Globe*, August 6, 1877.

68. "How Winslow Was Cremated," *Evening Star* (Washington, DC), August 7, 1877.

69. "How Winslow Was Cremated."

70. "Cremation," *Eureka Daily Sentinel*.

71. "The Third Cremation: The Body of Dr. C. F. Winslow Reduced to Ashes in Salt Lake City Yesterday," *Gold Hill (NV) Daily News*, August 1, 1877.

72. "The Third Cremation."

73. "Cremation," *Eureka Daily Sentinel*.

74. Engler, personal interview with the author, December 19, 2019.

75. Engler, personal interview with the author, December 19, 2019.

76. "The Next Cremation," *Wheeling (WV) Daily Register*, February 15, 1878.

77. "Pleasant Obsequies," *Cincinnati (OH) Enquirer*, February 15, 1878.

78. "Cremating Mrs. Pittman [*sic*]," *Anti-Monopolist* (St. Paul, MN), February 28, 1878.

79. "Cremating Mrs. Pittman [*sic*]."

80. "Dr. LeMoyne's Body," *Knoxville Daily Chronicle*, October 24, 1879.

81. "The Great Cremator Cremated," *Bossier Banner* (Bossier Parish, LA), November 6, 1879.

82. "Dr. LeMoyne's Body."

83. Jason Engler, email correspondence with author, January 26, 2021.

84. "The Cost of Cremation," *Semi-Weekly New Era* (Lancaster, PA), November 29, 1884.

85. Augustus Cobb, *Earth-Burial and Cremation: The History of Earth-Burial with Its Attendant Evils, and the Advantages Offered by Cremation* (New York: G. P. Putnam's Sons, 1892), 135.

86. Habenstein and Lamers, *History of American Funeral Directing*, 296.

87. Canon Law 1203, quoted by Fr. Benedict Hughes, "Cremation? Not for Catholics: History of Burial vs. Cremation," Congregatio Mariae Reginae Immaculatae (website), accessed April 20, 2021, cmri.org/articles-on-the-traditional-catholic -faith/cremation-not-for-catholics/.

88. Habenstein and Lamers, *History of American Funeral Directing*, 296.

89. Jason Engler, personal interview with author, October 21, 2020.

90. CANA statistic as cited by Jason Engler, email to author, February 2, 2021.

91. Holy Office, "*Piam et constantem*: Instruction on Cremation," Catholic Culture, accessed April 20, 2021, catholicculture.org/culture/library/view.cfm?recnum=11422.

92. Engler, personal interview with author, October 21, 2020.

93. National Funeral Directors Association, "2019 NFDA Cremation and Burial Report," July 2019.

94. National Funeral Directors Association, "2019 NFDA Cremation and Burial Report."

CHAPTER 13: MUSHROOM SUITS AND THE FUTURE (OF FUNERAL SERVICE)

1. "FAQS" and "Our Story," Coeio, accessed December 1, 2020, coeio.com/faqs/ and coeio.com/coeio-story/.

2. Fungi mechanisms detailed by Arden Mower, email message to author, December 7, 2020.

3. "FAQS" and "Our Story."

4. "Natural Burial FAQ," Green Burial Council, accessed December 3, 2020, greenburialcouncil.org/green_burial_defined.html.

5. About forty green cemeteries up to about 2010: Ann Hoffner, personal interview with author, December 10, 2020.

6. The actual number of green cemeteries can be a moving target, given that cemeteries open and close, and some aren't selling burial plots anymore, and there can be different definitions of "green." Ann Hoffner's *The Natural Burial Cemetery Guide* has 167 green cemeteries listed, but she knows of another (roughly) two dozen that don't want a listing in her book. The list compiled by the New Hampshire Funeral Resources, Education & Advocacy uses a different slightly (broader) criteria to define a green cemetery, and includes 270 American green cemeteries. Ann Hoffner, email message to author, December 12, 2020. Also, "Green Burial Cemeteries in the US and Canada," New Hampshire Funeral Resources, Education & Advocacy, accessed December 20, 2020, nhfuneral.org/green-burial-cemeteries-in-the-us-and-canada.html.

7. The Natural Burial Cemetery Guide website, accessed December 10, 2020, greenburialnaturally.org/.

8. Ann Hoffner, personal interview with author, December 10, 2020.

9. Hoffner, personal interview with author, December 10, 2020.

10. Hoffner, personal interview with author, December 10, 2020.

11. "Environmental Impact" and "The History," Recompose, accessed December 3, 2020, recompose.life/who-we-are/#history and recompose.life/our-model /#environmental-impact.

12. Walt Patrick, personal interview with author, December 22, 2020.

13. Patrick, personal interview with author, December 22, 2020.

14. "The Process," Recompose, accessed December 3, 2020, recompose.life/our-model /#the-process; NOR process detailed by Walt Patrick, personal interview with author, December 22, 2020.

15. Patrick, personal interview with author, December 22, 2020.

16. "About," Promessa, accessed December 6, 2020, promessa.se/about/#squelch-taas -accordion-shortcode-content-0.

17. "How It Works," Promessa, accessed December 22, 2020, promessa.se/about -life-death/.

18. Amos Herbert Hobson. Process of separating gelatine from bones. US Patent 394,982, filed April 5, 1888, and dated December 25, 1888.

19. "Average kWh Usage for a 2,000 sq. ft. Home," Home Professionals, accessed July 14, 2021, homeprofessionals.org/solar/average-kwh-usage-for-a-2000-sq-ft-home/. The average home is defined at two thousand square feet.

20. Gail Rubin, personal interview with author, December 21, 2020.

21. Rubin, personal interview with author, December 21, 2020. For more information visit agoodgoodbye.com.

22. *QuickStats:* Percentage Distribution of Deaths, by Place of Death – United States, 2000–2014. MMWR Morb Mortal Wkly Rep 2016;65:357, doi.org/10.15585 /mmwr.6513a6.

23. Lee Webster, personal interview with author, December 18, 2020.

24. Kris Kington-Barker, email to author, December 19, 2020.

25. Kington-Barker, email to author, December 19, 2020.

26. Kington-Barker, email to author, December 19, 2020.

27. Kington-Barker, email to author, December 19, 2020.

28. Webster, personal interview with author, December 18, 2020.

29. Webster, personal interview with author, December 18, 2020.

30. Chuck Lakin, personal interview with author, December 20, 2020.

31. Lakin, personal interview with author, December 20, 2020.

32. Webster, personal interview with author, December 18, 2020.

33. Webster, personal interview with author, December 18, 2020.

34. "In U.S., Decline of Christianity Continues at Rapid Pace," Pew Research Center, October 17, 2019, pewforum.org/2019/10/17/in-u-s-decline-of-christianity -continues-at-rapid-pace/.

35. "Fearless in Death," *The Casket* 30, no. 11 (November 1905): 20.

36. Doug Manning, "Come on In—the Water Is Safe," *Dodge Magazine* 98, no. 3 (June/July 2006): 12.

37. Glenda Stansbury, personal interview with author, December 24, 2020.

38. Stansbury, personal interview with author, December 24, 2020.

39. Stansbury, personal interview with author, December 24, 2020.

40. Stansbury, personal interview with author, December 24, 2020.

41. Stansbury, personal interview with author, December 24, 2020.

42. The information about funeral celebrants and InSight was collected from Glenda Stansbury, personal interview with author, December 24, 2020.

43. "Fearless in Death," *Casket* 30, no. 11 (November 1905): 20

Index

Adams, John Quincy, 89, 116, 174
Alexander, Joseph, 141–44
All Souls Day, 45–46
alternate forms of disposition
    alkaline hydrolysis (flameless cremation),
        229–30
    promession, 228
American funeral service practices and
    traditions, 2, 66–67
    cemeteries, 113–18
    Civil War era, 85–89, 92–105, 188–90, 195
    coffins, 67
    colonial customs, 66–82
    costs, 73–76
    embalming, introduction into the United
        States, 90–91
    layers-out, 66
    meals, post-funeral, 73–76
    photography, 43
    Victorian practices, 110–13, 125–26
Anubis, 26, 28–29, 33
The Art and Science of Embalming, 110–11
Arthur (King Arthur), 149, 260n13
Astor, John Jacob and Madeleine, 107–10, 184

Barstow, A.C., 154
Belcher, Jonathan and Mary, funerals of, 70–71
Bigelow, Jacob, 116
Book of the Dead, 31, 33–34
Boyd, George W., 139–40
Brown, Charles (undertaker), 14, 18
Brunetti, Lodovico, 209
burial
    grave alarms, 163–67
    green burial, 224–25, 233; alkaline
        hydrolysis (flameless cremation), 229–30;
        human composting, 226–28; mushroom
        suits, 223–24; natural burial grounds,
        225–26; promession, 228
    premature burial, 156–67, 203–4
    public health concerns, 210–11
    vaults and other security devices, 127, 145;
        Boyd's grave vault, 139–40; Cantrell and
        Alexander scandal, 141–44; "coffin-
        torpedo" and "grave-torpedo," 137–39;
        Grant, Ulysses S., 140; Haase's concrete
        vaults, 140; mortsafe, 139; Van Bibber's
        burial safe, 139
    See also cemeteries; coffins; cremation; funeral
        service practices and traditions

Burke, William, 132
Burr, Richard (embalmer), 85–88, 95

cadavers for medical use, 128–29, 137,
    140–41, 144–45
    See also resurrectionists
Campbell, Frank E. (undertaker), 199–201
Cantrell, Rufus, 141–44
cartonnages, 29–30, 43
The Casket (trade magazine), 3, 91, 96, 104,
    106, 111, 113, 162, 234
caskets, 147, 149, 155, 167
    casket, etymology of, 155
    custom and artisanal, 233
    grave alarms, 163–67
    shape, 155
    See also burial; coffins
catafalques, 11, 17, 19, 54, 120, 148, 173
Cattell, Henry Pratt (embalmer), 7–8, 239n7,
    10–11
cemeteries, 48, 69, 113–18
    Bonaventure, 116
    Civil War battlefield cemeteries, 189–90
    Congress Green, 133–34
    Fields of Honor, 192–93
    Green-Wood, 115
    Herland Forest Natural Burial Cemetery,
        226–7
    Laurel Hill, 115
    Magnolia, 116
    Mount Auburn, 114–18
    natural burial grounds, 225–27
    Oak Hill Cemetery, 189
    security, 134
    See also burial
cenotaph, 174
Civil War era, 85–89, 92–105, 188–90, 195
    Grant, Ulysses S., 87–88, 100–1, 140, 147,
        151, 174, 178
    See also Lincoln, Abraham
Clover, Philip, 137–38
coffins, 67, 126, 149, 156, 167
    coffin, etymology of, 150
    coffin furniture, 151
    "coffin-torpedo" and "grave-torpedo,"
        137–39
    Fisk, Almond D., 151–54
    grave alarms, 163–67
    Hiller, Henry, 147–49
    metal coffins, 151, 154

coffins (*continued*)
  ogee, 154
  origins of, 149–51
  shape, 154–56
  See also burial; caskets
Constantine, 39, 60, 207
Cornelius, W.R. (undertaker), 103–5
cremation, 39, 112, 203, 205
  banning of, 207
  books and academic literature, 207–8, 220
  Browne, Thomas, 207–8
  Christian and Jewish beliefs, 206–7
  conversion to green burial, 233
  Greek beliefs, 205
  Laurens, Henry, 203–4
  LeMoyne, F. Julius, 211–12, 214, 216,
    219–20
  modern cremations, notable: de Palm,
    Joseph Henry Louis, 212–16; Pitman,
    Jane Bragg, 218–19; Winslow, Charles,
    216–18
  Mungo Lady, 204
  popularity of, 220–222
  premature burial, 203
  public health concerns, 210–11
  as punishment, 206–7
  pyres, open-air, 208–9
  Roman practices, 44–45, 205–6
  Stone Age practices, 205
  technological advances, 209–10
Cruikshank, William (embalmer), 52–53
cypress, 40

Davis, Caleb (funeral of), 75
de Palm, Joseph Henry Louis, 212–16
death doulas, 231
death masks, 29–30, 43, 53–55, 124
death notices, 200
death, planning for, 230
Doctors' Riot of 1788, 130–31

Eckels, Howard S., 191
eco-burial. *See* green burial
Egyptian funeral service practices
  and traditions
  afterlife beliefs, 32–33, 35–36
  akh, 32
  ba, 32
  Book of the Dead, 31, 33–34
  cartonnages, 29–30, 43
  coffins, 149
  duat, 25, 32
  embalming, 25–30, 35
  ka, 32, 36
  mummification, 27–30, 35
  Osiris, 26

wabt wat, 27–28, 57
Ellsworth, Elmer E., 6–7, 94
embalming
  arsenic, 96, 102
  Civil War era, 85–89, 92–105
  Dwight, Albert S., 85–88
  ecobalming, 225
  Egyptian practices, 25–30, 35
  Ellsworth, Elmer E., 7
  embalmers: Burr, Richard, 85–88, 95;
    Cattell, Henry Pratt, 7–8, 239n7, 10–11;
    Cruikshank, William, 52–53; Gannal,
    Jean, 90–91; Gaussardia, J. Anthony,
    91–92; Harlan, Richard, 90–91; Holmes,
    Thomas, 7, 93–98, 101–3, 106, 163;
    Hunter, William, 52–53, 57; Paré,
    Ambrose, 58
  History of Embalming (Gannal/Harlan),
    90–91
  Henry I of England, 54
  Innominata, 7, 95–96, 98, 102–3
  life-like appearance, 162–63
  Lincoln, Abraham, 2, 6, 10–11
  pollinctores, 40
  preparation rooms in funeral homes, 201
  schools and academic texts, 105–6; *The
    Art and Science of Embalming*, 110–11;
    History of Embalming (Gannal/Harlan),
    90–91
  Van Butchell, Martin and Maria, 52–53,
    62–63
  Victorian practices, 110–12

Faneuil, Andrew, funeral of, 71
Fisk, Almond D., 151–54
flowers, 118–23
flu pandemic of 1918, 186–87
Frederick, Robert (undertaker), 111–12
funeral celebrants (civil), 234–36
funeral directors / undertakers
  death notices, 200
  funeral homes, 198–201
  furnishing undertakers, 171
  home funerals, 231–33
  libitinarius, 39–41, 48–49
  National Funeral Directors Association
    (NFDA), 14, 105–6, 126, 222
  undertaker and *funeral director*, distinction
    between terms, 14
  undertakers: Brown, Charles, 14, 18;
    Campbell, Frank E., 199–201; Cornelius,
    W.R., 103–5; Frederick, Robert, 111–12;
    Jordan, Collins H., 171–72; Lee, J.
    William, 201; Relyea, Peter, 16; Sands,
    Frank, 14, 18; Trump, Granville A.,
    111–12

undertakers, early English and American
origins, 62
Victorian practices, 110–13
funeral, etymology of, 39
funeral games, 38
funeral homes, 198–201
funeral service practices and traditions
American, 2, 66–67; cemeteries, 113–18;
Civil War era, 85–89, 92–105, 188–90,
195; coffins, 67; colonial customs,
66–82; costs, 73–76; embalming,
introduction into the United States, 90–
91; layers-out, 66; meals, post-funeral,
73–76; photography, 43; Victorian
practices, 110–13, 125–26
Egyptian: afterlife beliefs, 32–33, 35–36;
akh, 32; *ba*, 32; Book of the Dead, 31,
33–34; cartonnages, 29–30, 43; coffins,
149; *duat*, 25, 32; embalming, 25–30,
35; *ka*, 32, 36; mummification, 27–30,
35; Osiris, 26; *wabt wat*, 27–28, 57
English, 1, 54–55, 184; barber-surgeons,
55–57; 61–62; Victorian, 110
flowers, 118–23
funeral, etymology of, 39
home funerals, 231–33
medieval/pre-modern, 54–55; barber-
surgeons, 55–58, 61–62; bone burial,
59–60; burial inside of churches and on
church grounds, 60–61; sextons, 61
photography (postmortem), 124–25
restrictions/sumptuary laws, 77
Roman: *apotheosis*, 47; burial, 43–45;
burial for the poor, 48; coffins, 149;
cremation, 44–45, 205–6; cypress, 40;
designator, 40–41; effigies, 47; funeral
games, 38; funeral meals, 45–46; funeral
procession/cortege, 41–43; gladiators,
37–38; *imagines*, 43; imperial funerals,
47; *libitinarius* (funeral director), 39–41,
48–49; mimes, 42–43; Parentalia, 46;
pollinctores (embalmer), 40; *praeco*
(herald), 41; vestal virgins, 44
See also burial; caskets; coffins; cremation;
embalming; funeral directors /
undertakers; hearses; World War I
funerals, in private homes, 231–33

Galen, 128
Garfield, James A., 123
Gaussardia, J. Anthony (embalmer), 91–92
gladiators, 37–38
Grant, Ulysses S., 87–88, 100–1, 140, 147,
151, 174, 178
grave alarms, 163–67
grave robbing. *See* resurrectionists

The Great War. *See* World War I
green burial, 224–25, 233
human composting (NOR [natural organic
reduction]), 226–28
mushroom suits, 223–24
natural burial grounds, 225–26
Greenhill, Thomas, 28
Griggs, John (funeral of), 76

Hare, William, 132
Harlan, Richard, 90–91
Harrison, Carter H., 169–72
hearses, 172–75, 178–79, 181
Adams, John Quincy, 174
ambulances, 179
American use of, 175–81
automobile funeral, 177
catafalque, 173
Ghostbusters (movie), 179
Grant, Ulysses S., 174, 178
hearse, etymology of, 174
Lincoln, Abraham, 173
Mayor Carter E. Harrison funeral, 170–72
non-traditional hearse types, 179–81
Herodotus, 26–27, 30
Hiller, Henry, 147–50
Hillhouse, James, 113–14
History of Embalming (Gannal/Harlan), 90–91
Hoffner, Ann, 225–6
Holmes, Thomas (embalmer), 7, 93–98,
101–3, 106, 163
Hunter, William (embalmer), 52–53, 57

influenza pandemic of 1918, 186–87

Johnson, Andrew, 123
Jordan, Collins H. (undertaker), 171–72

Kauffman, Angelica, 82

Laurens, Henry and Martha, 203–4
layers-out, 66
Lee, J. William (undertaker), 201
leichenhäuser, 159–60
LeMoyne, F. Julius, 211–12, 214, 216, 219–20
Lincoln, Abraham, 1–2
assassination, 5–6
autopsy, 9
coffin, 11–12, 17
embalming, 2, 6, 10–11
funeral / funeral train, 11–23, 173
Lincoln, William Wallace, 7–8

mausoleums, 44–46, 148, 157–58
Meigs, Montgomery C., 188–90

memento mori, 124
mourning
  clothes, 41, 69–70, 108–10, 184–85
  colors, 108–9
  flowers, 118–23
  gifts, 69–71, 73
  jewelry, 71–72, 185–86
  paintings, 82
  period, 107–8
  praeficae, 41, 45
  professional mourners, 41
  rending of garments, 41
  restrictions/sumptuary laws, 77
  World War I, 184–86, 198
mourning jewelry, 71–72, 185–86
mummification, 27–30, 35
mushroom suits, 223–24

The National Burial Cemetery Guide (Hoffner), 225
National Funeral Directors Association (NFDA), 14, 105–6, 126, 222

pall, 68
pallbearers, 175
Paré, Ambrose, 58 (embalmer)
Perry, Luke, 223
photography (postmortem), 124–25
Porter, David (funeral of), 74
Post, Emily, 108
potter's fields, 48
Pruyn, Wilbur, 177
Puritan burial customs, 66, 69
  See also American funeral service practices and traditions

Relyea, Peter (undertaker), 16
Renouard, Auguste, 105–6
resurrectionists, 127–29, 141–42
  "Bone Bill" of 1854, 133
  Doctors' Riot of 1788, 130–32
  Harrison, John Scott, incident of body snatching, 133–37
  Massachusetts Anatomy Act of 1831, 132
  Pennsylvania Legislature anatomy act of 1883, 140–41
  Western Homeopathic College incident, 131–32
Roman funeral service practices and traditions
  apotheosis, 47
  burial, 43–45
  burial for the poor, 48
  coffins, 149
  cremation, 44–45, 205–6
  cypress, 40
  designator, 40–41

effigies, 47
funeral games, 38
funeral meals, 45–46
funeral procession/cortege, 41–43
gladiators, 37–38
imagines, 43
imperial funerals, 47
libitinarius (funeral director), 39–41, 48–49
mimes, 42–43
Parentalia, 46
pollinctores (embalmer), 40
praeco (herald), 41
vestal virgins, 44

Sands, Frank (undertaker), 14, 18
sextons, 61
Shelley, Percy Bysshe, 208–9
Spanish-American War, 190
stethoscopes, 159, 161
Story, Joseph, 117
sumptuary laws, 77

The *Titanic*, 107–8
Tomb of the Unknown Solider, 196–98
Trump, Granville A., 111–12

Undertakers. *See* funeral directors / undertakers
Uniform Anatomical Gift Act (UAGA), 144–45

Van Bibber, Andrew, 139
Van Butchell, Martin, 51–53, 62–63
Vanderbilt, Cornelius, 122
Vesalius, Andreas, 128
vestal virgins, 44

Washington, George (funeral of), 77–82
White, James, 3
World War I
  brassards (armbands), 185
  burial grounds, overseas, 192–93
  deaths, soldiers and civilians, 183
  Fields of Honor, 192–93
  identification of dead soldiers, 195, 265n24
  influenza pandemic of 1918, 186–87
  mourning clothes, 184–85
  mourning customs, effect on, 183–84
  mourning jewelry, 185–86
  Pershing, John, 192–93, 195–96
  recovering dead soldiers, 191–92, 194–95
  Tomb of the Unknown Solider, 196–98
Wycliffe, John, 207
Wyngaard, Lucas, 65–66

About the Author

T odd Harra, Certified Funeral Service Practitioner (CFSP), is the vice president at McCrery & Harra Funeral Homes and Crematory in Wilmington, Delaware. A funeral director and embalmer, he attended Elon University and the American Academy McAllister Institute of Funeral Service. At the Fountain National Academy of Professional Embalming Skills, Todd earned certification in advanced postmortem reconstruction. He is an NFDA certified crematory operator and a member of the Academy of Professional Funeral Service Practice and the National Funeral Directors Association, and the president of the Delaware State Funeral Directors Association. Todd is an associate editor for *Southern Calls: The Journal of the Funeral Profession.* This is his fifth book about funeral service.

toddharra.com

facebook.com/toddharraauthor

About Sounds True

Sounds True is a multimedia publisher whose mission is to inspire and support personal transformation and spiritual awakening. Founded in 1985 and located in Boulder, Colorado, we work with many of the leading spiritual teachers, thinkers, healers, and visionary artists of our time. We strive with every title to preserve the essential "living wisdom" of the author or artist. It is our goal to create products that not only provide information to a reader or listener but also embody the quality of a wisdom transmission.

For those seeking genuine transformation, Sounds True is your trusted partner. At SoundsTrue.com you will find a wealth of free resources to support your journey, including exclusive weekly audio interviews, free downloads, interactive learning tools, and other special savings on all our titles.

To learn more, please visit SoundsTrue.com/freegifts or call us toll-free at 800.333.9185.

sounds true

BOULDER, COLORADO